USING COMPUTERS

Series: MATHEMATICS & ITS APPLICATIONS

MATHEMATICS & ITS APPLICATIONS

Series Editor: Professor G. M. Bell
Chelsea College, University of London

Mathematics and its applications are now awe-inspiring in their scope, variety and depth. Not only is there rapid growth in pure mathematics and its applications to the traditional fields of the physical sciences, engineering and statistics, but new fields of application are emerging in biology, ecology and social organisation. The user of mathematics must assimilate subtle new techniques and also learn to handle the great power of the computer efficiently and economically.

The need of clear, concise and authoritative texts is thus greater than ever and our series will endeavour to supply this need. It aims to be comprehensive and yet flexible. Works surveying recent research will introduce new areas and up-to-date mathematical methods. Undergraduate texts on established topics will stimulate student interest by including applications relevant at the present day. The series will also include selected volumes of lecture notes which will enable certain important topics to be presented earlier than would otherwise be possible.

In all these ways it is hoped to render a valuable service to those who learn, teach, develop and use mathematics.

MODERN INTRODUCTION TO CLASSICAL MECHANICS AND CONTROL
David Burghes, Cranfield Institute of Technology and Angela Downs, University of Sheffield.

TEXTBOOK OF DYNAMICS
Frank Chorlton, University of Aston, Birmingham

VECTOR & TENSOR METHODS
Frank Chorlton, University of Aston, Birmingham

ADVANCED TOPICS IN OPERATIONAL RESEARCH
Brian Conolly, Chelsea College, University of London

LECTURE NOTES ON QUEOUING SYSTEMS
Brian Conolly, Chelsea College, University of London

MATHEMATICS FOR THE BIOSCIENCES
G. Eason, C. W. Coles, G. Gettinby, University of Strathclyde

HANDBOOK OF HYPERGEOMETRIC INTEGRALS: Theory, Applications, Tables, Computer Programs
Harold Exton, The Polytechnic, Preston

MULTIPLE HYPERGEOMETRIC FUNCTIONS
Harold Exton, The Polytechnic Preston

COMPUTATIONAL GEOMETRY FOR DESIGN & MANUFACTURE
I. D. Faux and M. J. Pratt, Cranfield Institute of Technology

APPLIED LINEAR ALGEBRA
Ray J. Goult, Cranfield Instute of Technology

MATRIX THEORY & APPLICATIONS FOR ENGINEERING & CONTROL
Alex Graham, The Open University, Milton Keynes

GENERALISED FUNCTIONS: Theory and Applications
Roy F. Hoskins, Cranfield Institute of Technology

MECHANICS OF CONTINUOUS MEDIA
S. C. Hunter, University of Sheffield

USING COMPUTERS
Brian Meek aan Simon Fairthorne, Queen Elizabeth College, University of London

ENVIRONMENTAL AERODYNAMICS
R. S. Scorer, Imperial College of Science and Technology, University of London

PHYSICS OF THE LIQUID STATE: A Survey for Scientists and Technologists
H. N. V. Temperley, University College of Swansea, University of Wales and
H. D. Trevena, University of Wales, Aberystwyth

MATHEMATICAL MODELS OF MORPHOGENES: Catastrophe Theory and its Applications
René Thom, Institut des Hautes Etudes Scientifiques, Bures-sur-Yvelte, France

Using Computers

BRIAN MEEK, M.Sc.

Director, Computer Unit,
Queen Elizabeth College, University of London

SIMON FAIRTHORNE, B.Sc.

Department of Mathematics
Queen Elizabeth College, University of London

ELLIS HORWOOD, LIMITED

Publishers · Chichester

Halsted Press, a division of
JOHN WILEY & SONS
New York · London · Brisbane · Toronto

The publisher's colophon is reproduced from James Gillison's drawing of the ancient Market Cross, Chichester

First published in 1977 by

ELLIS HORWOOD LTD

Market Cross House, 1 Cooper Street, Chichester, Sussex, England

Reprinted with corrections 1978

Distributors:

Australia, New Zealand, South-east Asia:
JOHN WILEY & SONS INC.,
G.P.O. Box 859, Brisbane, Queensland 4001, Australia.

Canada:
JOHN WILEY & SONS CANADA LIMITED
22 Worcester Road, Rexdale, Ontario, Canada.

Europe, Africa:
JOHN WILEY & SONS LIMITED
Baffins Lane, Chichester, Sussex, England.

North and South America and the rest of the world:
HALSTED PRESS, a division of
JOHN WILEY & SONS
605 Third Avenue, New York, N.Y. 10016, U.S.A.

© 1977 Brian Meek: Simon Fairthorne/Ellis Horwood

Library of Congress Cataloging in Publication Data
Meek, Brian L
    Using Computers
Bibliography: p.
Includes index
1. Computers. 2. Electronic data processing.
1. Fairthorne, Simon, joint author. II. Title.
QA76.M39   001.6'4   76-26871
ISBN 0-470-98932-7 (Halsted Press)
ISBN 85312-045-5: Library Edition (Ellis Horwood)
ISBN 85312-046-3: Paperback Edition (Ellis Horwood)

Printed in England by Cox & Wyman Ltd.
London, Fakenham and Reading

Table of Contents

Preface		7
Chapter 1	**The Computer as a Concept**	9
1.1	Digital and Analogue	10
1.2	Early History of Computers	11
1.3	Charles Babbage	13
1.4	Computers after Babbage	20
Chapter 2	**The Computer as a Machine**	30
2.1	Store	31
2.2	Binary Arithmetic	41
2.3	Processors and Instructions	47
2.4	Input and Output	54
Chapter 3	**The Computer as a Problem Solver**	58
3.1	A Simple Problem	59
3.2	Algorithms and Flow Diagrams	62
3.3	Assemblers	65
3.4	Concept of High-Level Languages	71
3.5	Brief Survey of High-Level Languages	74
Chapter 4	**The Computer as a Number-cruncher**	77
4.1	Iteration and Errors	77
4.2	Roots of Equations	81
4.3	Numerical Integration	86
4.4	Differential Equations	91
4.5	Simultaneous Equations	94
4.6	Avoiding Programming Pitfalls	98
Chapter 5	**The Computer as a Data Handler**	101
5.1	Company Payroll Example	103
5.2	Data Preparation	107
5.3	Filestore	110
5.4	Sorting and Searching	116
5.5	Operational Research	126

Chapter 6 **The Computer as a Watchdog**   132
6.1   Applications of Process Control   132
6.2   Operating Systems   140
6.3   Airline Reservation System   155

Chapter 7 **The Computer as an Entertainment**   159
7.1   Games and Artificial Intelligence   159
7.2   People and Manors   168
7.3   Computers and the Arts   176

Chapter 8 **The Computer as a Social Force**   183
8.1   A Cashless Society?   183
8.2   Central Databanks   185
8.3   Computer Aided Learning   188
8.4   Computers in Everyday Life   190
8.5   Conclusion   197

Reading List   199

Index   203

Authors' Preface

This book will, we believe, be of value to anyone in contact with computers, whether in management, commerce, industry, education or research. Although it is one of a series in *Mathematics and its Applications*, detailed mathematical knowledge is not assumed, and we believe that many others will find it of interest and value. As the title implies, the main emphasis is on how and for what purposes computers can be used. Some information on how computers work is included because some understanding of at least the principles is required to be able to use computers effectively, but most of the book is concerned with their use.

The initial concept of this book was that of Professor George Bell, the series editor. We are grateful to him both for suggesting to us that we write it and for his subsequent encouragement.

Numerous people have helped us directly or indirectly during the preparation of the text. There is insufficient space to list them all, but special thanks must go to Belinda Fairthorne, David Griffin of Cramer Electronics Ltd, Professor David G. Kendall of Cambridge University, Tony Kerr of Queen Elizabeth College, Mick Mears of Chelsea Football Club, Mike Moses of GEC Computers Ltd, Mandy Pritchett of Post Office Telecommunications and Dr Peter Zinovieff of Electronic Music Studios (London) Ltd. We should like to express our gratitude to all those individuals and organisations who provided or helped us to obtain illustrations, and to the art editor, James Gillison, for his excellent work on the line drawings which has so enhanced the appearance of the text. Finally we particularly thank Pam Thompson of the Computer Unit at Queen Elizabeth College, who typed almost the whole of the final manuscript and dealt with a great deal of correspondence on our behalf with skill and efficiency.

Brian Meek
Simon Fairthorne
July 1976

Chapter 1

The Computer as a Concept

In the developed world of the twentieth century, man lives surrounded by a bewildering variety of machines on which his way of life and even life itself depends. These machines can be simple or complex, minute or enormous. Some, like a sewing-machine, are for specific applications while others, like an electric drill, can be used for a variety of purposes. Some machines, though designed for a specific purpose, are components in many different machines; for instance the electric motor gives the electric drill its flexibility. This is because the purpose of the motor – to provide power – is fundamental in many applications.

Another fundamental aspect of twentieth-century life is the vast amount and variety of information that surrounds man from media such as the telephone and radio. This has transformed everyday life as much as engines and motors. There are many machines developed to handle the information, for example television cameras to record pictures, transmitters to send these pictures to television receivers in people's homes.

The ease of using machines also varies and is not always related to their complexity. For example, some, like a refrigerator, can work untended, and little skill or training is required to use a television set or a tin-opener; whereas considerable aptitude, instruction and practice is needed to fly an aeroplane or use a potter's wheel. The amount of skill and training required may depend on the circumstances of use – driving a motor car on a country road is a skill relatively easily acquired compared to driving a racing car on a grand prix circuit. Knowledge of the principles behind the operation of a machine may be useful. It is possible to drive a car without knowing anything about what happens under the bonnet, although one can probably drive better for knowing something about car mechanics.

This book is about computers and their use. Computers are machines which handle information, and we shall show that, although complex, they are based on relatively simple principles. Since knowledge of these principles helps one to understand computers and make better use of them, in this opening chapter we shall introduce the concept of computers and describe how they developed. Chapter 2 will show how this concept is implemented in actual machines.

1.1 Digital and Analogue

The word computer derives from a Latin word meaning 'to reckon or compute'. As we shall see, computers were originally developed for performing numerical calculations and today many computers are still used for this purpose. Nevertheless, although most forms of information can be translated into numbers, it is important to realise that computing today is no longer confined to numerical work. Written textual information can be encoded into numeric form; for example one method (not the best) is to encode the digits '0' to '9' as the equivalent numbers, the small roman letters 'a' to 'z' as the numbers 10 to 35, the capital roman letters 'A' to 'Z' as 36 to 61, and punctuation marks, mathematical and other symbols as further numbers. Information such as the readings from measuring dials can be expressed in numerical form, and diagrammatic and other geometric information by the methods of coordinate geometry. Visual information can be expressed numerically by dividing a picture into tiny pieces, and for each piece the position is identified by numerical coordinates, with further numerical codes indicating its intensity and (if necessary) its colour. This method is used both in printing and for relaying television pictures from interplanetary probes. Any information which can be encoded numerically is potentially open to computing techniques. Thus, despite its derivation, a modern definition of computer would be 'a machine capable of receiving, storing, manipulating and yielding up information'.

Because most information can be encoded numerically, we shall confine ourselves initially to numerical information and numerical calculations. One of the most important features of numerical work is that there are two kinds of numbers: those which are obtained by counting and hence are *exact*, and those obtained by measurement, which are only *approximations*. The difference is between 'discrete', 'whole number' or 'integer' arithmetic, and 'continuous' or 'real number' arithmetic. Whole number arithmetic can be extended to include the rational numbers, i.e. numbers which can be expressed *exactly* as the ratio of two whole numbers. When we read a number on a dial (e.g. a voltmeter) or take a linear measurement (e.g. temperature on an ordinary thermometer) the result is usually expressed in rational terms (240 volts or $28 \cdot 4 = 284/10$ degrees) but this is only an approximation, limited by the accuracy of the measuring instrument. If we count 'six' apples the number is exact, not an approximation to $5 \cdot 9$ or $6 \cdot 1$ apples; but 'one kilogram of apples' is not an exact quantity but is an approximation to some weight between, say, 995 and 1005 grams.

There are two aspects of this to be taken into account when considering numerical calculations. One is that the numbers in any calculation may either be exact (obtained from counting) or approximate (obtained by measurement). The other is that the *representation* of these numbers during the calculation may be rational or may be continuous. In both cases the representation and the original numbers may not be the same – for example when the representation is rational and the original was a measurement such as 28·4 degrees, or when the representation is continuous and the original was an integer. Two common aids to calculation are logarithmic tables, where the values are represented exactly (to four or six decimal places) but are only approximations to the actual values, and slide rules, where all numbers (including integers) are represented by distances along the rule and so are represented only approximately.

Computers which deal with numerical information can be divided into three classes: (1) **digital**, in which the representation of numbers and the calculations on them are performed by counting processes (e.g. by counting teeth on gear wheels or counting electrical impulses); (2) **analogue**, in which the representation of numbers and the calculations on them are performed by measuring processes (e.g. in electronic computers by measuring voltages); and (3) **hybrid**, in which both kinds of process are used. Nowadays the word computer, unless qualified, normally means 'electronic digital computer'; 'electronic' because in most computers electronic processes have replaced all others because of their speed, reliability and cheapness, 'digital' because the exactness of digital processes implies a greater potential for accuracy. In this book we shall be almost wholly concerned with the use of electronic digital computers. It can be seen that in our discussion of encoding different kinds of information, the representations were digital and not analogue. Textual information, inherently exact in form, was represented by whole number codes; graphical and visual information, inherently inexact, was encoded by numerical but rational approximations.

The importance of computing is partly due to the wide range of information which can be numerically encoded and therefore open to computation. In almost every human activity we receive and evaluate all kinds of information. If the process of evaluation could be analysed and expressed as a sequence of explicit steps then it should be possible for a computer to be made to carry out the same evaluation automatically and initiate any actions required as a result. Many machines which in the past needed human guidance or control can now be operated under computer control. Thus computer involvement in human activity has an extremely wide scope. In this book we shall be mainly concerned with problems which are expressed in numerical form. This is such a wide field that even by itself it would ensure the great importance of computers.

1.2 Early History of Computers

Since the processing of information is such a fundamental part of human activity it is not surprising that attempts at automatic computation stretch back to the beginning of recorded history, nor that the basic conceptual breakthrough in the design of computers occurred at least one hundred years before the necessary technological advances were made. There are a number of useful introductions to the historical background to computers and a selection appears in the reading list immediately after the last chapter; here we shall sketch the broad outlines.

Although measuring is less accurate than counting, man has needed to do both for a long time. For these he used aids, at first probably measuring by using parts of the body (e.g. one forearm = one cubit) and counting by using fingers (hence the word 'digital'), stones or marks in the sand. Later more permanent forms of recording were evolved; almost all the early alphabets that have been translated have included characters for numbers. Some Linear B tablets, for example, contain lists of land holders and the amounts of seed corn allocated to each of them.

Man has not only wanted to record information but to perform calculations with it. An early example of this is provided by several Babylonian cuneiform tablets, dating from around 1800–1600 B.C., which give rules for solving many types of algebraic equations. Since the Babylonians were limited by lack of algebraic notation these rules were usually given in the form of worked examples. Part of the history of mathematics is a search for aids to numerical computation and many of these are still in common use today, such as adding the digits of a decimal whole number to determine if it is divisible by 3 or 9, or the familiar method of calculating a square root:

	22 09	number divided into pairs of digits starting from right
4	16	$4^2 = 16$ is largest square less than 22
	6 09	subtract and bring down next pair
7	6 09	double 4 = 8 and find largest digit n such that $n \times 8n$ is not greater than 609, $n = 7$
	0	subtract, terminate when 0

giving square root of 2209 as 47.

These rules have the common feature that they can be applied automatically by anyone who knows them, and the user does not have to understand the reasons why the rules work. In some cases these reasons are not difficult to find (as in adding-the-digits) while in others they are more obscure (as in the illustrated square-root method). Numerical computation depends on finding automatic rules such as these.

Rules alone were not enough to make numerical computations simple to perform, because their use still involved the user in a large amount of arithmetic work. The need for tables was recognised at an early stage and we find that the Babylonians had multiplication tables and tables of reciprocals. Some tables are simply records of computations which were done once by the compiler of the table, and can then be referred to by others. A major advance was the invention of logarithms, based on the mathematical result

$$a^x . a^y = a^{x+y}.$$

Logarithmic tables were general purpose, reducing a calculation of a multiplication or division to a simpler one of addition or subtraction. Note that the slide rule, though analogue (whereas the table of logarithms is digital), is based on the same mathematical result. In recent centuries tables have become of increasing importance in many areas, for instance in ballistics and navigation, with several of the applications of military significance, either directly or indirectly. (This is the reason for the large amount of governmental and military support given for research and development of computers throughout the last few centuries.) The value of tables of logarithms for small calculations only began to be seriously threatened in the 1970s with the coming of cheap pocket electronic calculators. The early motivation for the development of computers as we know them mainly arose from the need for more tables, and greater accuracy in those already existing. It was only later that it became recognised that, instead of using the computer to produce tables which are then used by humans in other calculations, the computer could be used to produce the end result directly without producing tables as an intermediate step.

While mathematical advances were important to the development of modern computation, there were also attempts to make machines to help man perform computational tasks. We have already mentioned the slide rule. But the earliest machine was almost certainly the abacus, known to the early Chinese, Chaldean and Greek civilisations. The abacus is little more than an aid to memory, but it is important since it shows that calculating has long been an important human activity if such a device was explicitly designed to aid it, and because it is still in routine daily use thousands of years after its inception.

From the early seventeenth century onwards there have been various attempts to produce machines capable of automatic computation. The great mathematicians Pascal and Leibnitz both constructed calculators. These machines were the forerunners of the mechanical and electromechanical desk calculators of the nineteenth and twentieth centuries, and also of more special-purpose devices like cash registers.

The history of computers in the modern sense, however, begins with Charles Babbage.

1.3 Charles Babbage

It surprises many people, who are new to computers but are aware of their recent growth, to learn that Babbage was born in the eighteenth century, in 1791 either at Totnes in Devonshire, or in London. He was admitted to Trinity College, Cambridge in 1810 and in 1816 was elected a Fellow of the Royal Society. Besides his life interest in the development of automatic calculating machines he was a keen mathematician and published papers in many areas; for instance he outlined the method of determining past climate from examining tree rings. Babbage was a strange character and his life story is full of points of dispute, partly because he wrote his autobiography in his old age after he had become embittered. His biographer Mabeth Moseley aptly titled her book *Irascible Genius*. In this book we shall concentrate on Babbage's scientific ideas and avoid disputed details, interesting though they may be.

The exact date when Babbage conceived his first main idea for automatic computation is unclear, but it was probably while he was an undergraduate at Cambridge when he and his friend Herschel were involved in tedious checking of astronomical tables. Throughout a long life he continued to work on his ideas, but died in 1871 with very little having been brought to fruition. It was not until more than seventy years after his death that his concept of a general-purpose computing engine began to be realised in practice.

His initial idea, from around 1812, was to build a simple special-purpose machine to produce tables of functions. It was based on the observation that if a polynomial function is evaluated and tabulated at regular intervals and the differences between adjacent values are tabulated, and then the differences between those quantities are tabulated, and so on, repeating this differencing process as far as necessary, then eventually one arrives at a set of *identical* values.

The Table below shows this differencing process applied to the polynomial function $y = x^3 - x^2 + 1$ for integer values of x from 1 to 7:

x	y	*1st differences*	*2nd differences*	*3rd differences*
1	1			
2	5	$4 = 5 - 1$	$10 = 14 - 4$	
		14		$6 = 16 - 10$
3	19		16	
		30		6
4	49		22	
		52		6
5	101		28	
		80		6
6	181		34	
		114		
7	295			

Here the 'third differences', obtained after three applications of the differencing process, are equal. The same is true for all cubics for all constant intervals in x; for any polynomial of degree n the nth differences are always equal. (The reader may like to investigate the mathematics of this result.)

In Babbage's day tables were of immense importance as aids to calculation, particularly for applications such as navigation. They had to be compiled laboriously by hand and inevitably contained errors. One method of detecting errors in tables was to calculate differences; if the function is a polynomial then one of the columns of differences will be constant, and if the function is not a polynomial but is reasonably smooth then the columns of differences will show some regularity. In both cases an error in the function values will cause disturbances in the pattern, which can be easily detected. (This can be seen by extracting values from a set of logarithms, introducing a deliberate error, and then constructing a table of differences on the above lines.)

Babbage's idea was to exploit this feature in reverse, because by starting with initial values for the table (i.e. the first number in each column in the Table above), and assuming constant values in the last column, then it is possible to build up the whole table from the right hand column across to the left by a process of successive *addition* instead of subtraction, ending up with the column of function values. When the table has been completed errors can be easily detected by calculating the last term directly and comparing this with the tabulated value. Babbage proposed the concept of a **Difference Engine** capable of performing this process automatically. It was really a twin idea: that the evaluation of a complicated function for a succession of equally spaced argument values could be replaced by the repeated application of one simple operation (a central idea in computing), and that if this simple operation could be mechanised then the whole process could be mechanised. The same implications of the difference method seem to have been realised as early as 1786, by J. H. Muller, but the idea was not followed up in practice and very probably Babbage conceived the idea independently.

The Difference Engine was capable only of calculating exactly the values of polynomial functions. This did not diminish its practical value, since one can approximate to reasonably smooth non-polynomial functions (such as the logarithmic function) by one or more polynomial functions whose degrees are within the capacity of the machine. For readers who have met the mathematical concept of series expansions of functions, a simple example of such an approximation is the truncation of a series expansion after a given number of terms. Such approximations are usually adequate in practice and many computer applications still use the same principle.

Since we are concerned with the concepts we shall not give a detailed description of the design of the Difference Engine. It is sufficient to mention that it was purely mechanical, each digit being recorded by the position of a wheel capable of being set in one of ten positions, representing 0, 1, 2, ..., 9, and back to 0 again after a complete revolution. Additions, and the necessary carrying from one digit position to the next (units to tens, tens to hundreds, etc.) were performed by suitable gearing mechanisms. By 1822 Babbage had constructed a small version capable of calculating quadratic functions to eight figures, but his full concept was, typically, much more ambitious: the Difference Engine proper was to be able to calculate sixth-order polynomials to twenty figures. (It is worth noting that even today most computers normally work to no more than fifteen significant decimal figures.)

The importance of being able to produce mechanically sets of accurate tables can be measured by the substantial support that Babbage now received.

In 1823 he was awarded the first Gold Medal of the Royal Astronomical Society and, more importantly, he received over the next twelve years considerable financial support from the British Government for the actual construction of the Engine. Despite the government support, which was much rarer then than now, the Engine was still not built when he became Lucasian Professor of Mathematics at Cambridge University in 1828. After many disputes between Babbage and both the machine tool builder and the government, work stopped in 1833 and the project was cancelled in 1842 after a total investment of £17,000. (It is difficult to make monetary comparisons, but in 1860 meat cost 5 old pence, about 2p, per pound.) Although Babbage lost interest in the Engine, several working models were built later by others. For example, with backing from the Swedish Government, George and Edvard Scheutz constructed a more modest Difference Engine. With Babbage's help it was shown in London in 1854 and an exact copy was made for the British Government and used in the Registrar-General's Department to calculate life tables for actuarial purposes.

The reason that Babbage lost interest in the Difference Engine was that in 1832 he had his real conceptual breakthrough – his Analytical Engine, which was to have been the world's first general purpose computer. It is this Analytical Engine which is of most interest to us. It presaged the development of twentieth-century computers in two respects, one practical and (in more than one sense) peripheral, the other conceptual and fundamental. Either would have been sufficient to preserve Babbage's name in the history of computing. Both were suggested by the development during the eighteenth century of textile machines capable of automatically weaving complex patterns under the control of either cards or tapes in which holes were punched, and which were mechanically sensed by the machine to control the weaving. The most widely used automatic looms were those of Jacquard in the early 1800s. Babbage saw that the same principle of holes in cards could be used to encode other kinds of information, and adapted it in the design of his new Engine. The principle was eventually used (with cards or paper tape) in the computers of the mid-twentieth century and today is still a major means of communicating information to computers.

The fundamental point was the use which Babbage foresaw for the cards. Data was to be stored in the Analytical Engine on banks of wheels, as in the Difference Engine, but was to be manipulated in a far more flexible way. Whereas the Difference Engine was a special purpose machine, built just to construct tables of functions by repeated additions, the Analytical Engine was to be capable of all the basic arithmetic operations. These were to be performed in a separate part of the machine called the **mill**, to which data would be transferred as required. Which data was to be so transferred, and which operations were to be performed on them, were to be controlled by two sets of cards – the **cards of the variables**, identifying the location of data to be used, and the **operation cards**, specifying the operations to be performed. Once the

Fig. 1.1(a) The Scheutz Difference Engine. The five registers of fifteen decimal digits can be seen at the front. These enabled quartic polynomials to be tabulated. The results were printed directly: the mechanism for this is at the back on the left.

[*Photograph: Crown Copyright, Science Museum, London*]

Fig. 1.1(b) Close up of part of the Scheutz mechanism, showing storage wheels marked with decimal digits. These pictures are of the British copy of the machine (see main text) now in the Science Museum, London.

[*Photograph: Crown Copyright, Science Museum, London*]

operation cards for a particular calculation were prepared, the calculation could be repeated at will for any data. Babbage used the word 'library' to describe the collection of sets of cards – today we would call it a **program library.**

This concept of specifying a sequence of instructions to a machine capable of performing the elementary arithmetic operations on data kept in store is that behind the modern program-controlled computer. The Analytical Engine had all the main units of the modern computer: the store (or memory); the mill (or arithmetic unit); input devices; output devices; together with mechanism for controlling them. Modern input devices input data as well as instructions. (Babbage did envisage tables being read into the store from cards, but data in the store and mill was to be set up by hand.) Modern computers tend to merge the two sets of cards into a single set, each instruction containing a specification of the operation to be performed and the location of the data required. Apart from the idea of keeping instructions as well as data in the store, everything of importance was there. Once again the device was conceived on the grand scale – the store was to contain 1000 data items, trivial in today's terms but extremely ambitious at the time, and each was to be kept to an incredible *fifty* significant figures.

Though Babbage did write about his ideas for the Analytical Engine he did not produce a complete, detailed exposition, but in 1840 he visited Turin and lectured on the subject. The idea of the Engine so interested a young army officer there that he wrote and published a description of it. He was Menabrea, later to become one of Garibaldi's generals and Prime Minister of Italy. This description was translated into English in 1842 by Augusta Ada, Countess of Lovelace, a daughter of Lord Byron. She was a talented mathematician and, with Babbage's encouragement, added many notes of her own to Menabrea's account. Besides examining the Engine critically she described how it could be instructed to perform given tasks, and included examples of what today we would call computer programs. Lady Lovelace saw, perhaps more clearly than Babbage himself, the crucial role played by the specification of the instructions for the Engine, and laid down some of the basic principles of programming without having had the advantage of actual experience on a working machine, which, in the context of the time when it was done, must be regarded as an outstanding intellectual feat.

Babbage lived for nearly forty years after conceiving the idea of the Analytical Engine, but although he constructed various trial pieces it was never built. He became more and more bitter and at odds with the world as a result of his failure, and he is reported as saying late in his life, that there was now no point in continuing with the Engine, because he had thought of a quicker and better way rather than by completing the Analytical Engine from the point it had then reached.

This gives a key to his failure – whenever he had a new idea or design, he abandoned all previous projects and started on the new concept. The only machine that he ever completed was the prototype Difference Engine in 1822.

A limiting factor was that the technology of his day was not advanced enough and therefore the engineering was too crude and unreliable to provide any real hope that his proposed Analytical Engine could have been constructed.

It is difficult to assess Babbage's achievements. Lady Lovelace visualised the implications of his work to an extent that he himself did not. He had the basic ideas for a computer and tried to construct such machines but his work was not followed through by others. Ironically, and sadly, his work had virtually no effect on the subsequent history of computers. In the mid-twentieth century, when the technology was adequate and the needs of the time demanded it, the computer would probably still have been developed whether Babbage had lived or not.

1.4 Computers after Babbage

The next step in the history of computers was the development of the punched card as a medium for carrying encoded information. The motivation came from the need to eliminate the long delays which had occurred in manually tabulating the American National Census returns of 1870 and 1880. Herman Hollerith, a statistician in the Census Bureau, devised machines utilising the same Jacquard loom punched card principle that had inspired Babbage nearly fifty years before, except that the cards contained data instead of control instructions. The parallel with the development of the automatic looms is interesting in that Hollerith initially experimented with perforated tape before adopting cards. He laid down a standard for punched cards which is basically the same as today's, with eighty columns, each column capable of carrying one alphabetic, numeric or other character represented as a pattern of holes, the size of the card being that of the then current dollar bills. Computer punched cards are still sometimes called 'Hollerith cards'. Note the interest and involvement again of a government, this time of the United States, in this development.

The early decades of the twentieth century saw the steady development of electromechanical equipment for using punched cards, by numerous companies including Hollerith's own which was merged with others in 1914 to become IBM (International Business Machines). Up to the 1920s nothing was produced which came close to Babbage's Analytical Engine – the punched cards only carried data and even the most elaborate electromechanical calculators and accounting machines had to be 'instructed' by the painstaking wiring of control circuits using a plugboard and connectors.

At that time there was no major scientific application of punch card systems: all the work was for accounting, tabulating statistics and performing statistical calculations. In the late 1920s and the 1930s in particular, there was much activity among mathematicians and logicians over the theoretical problems of whether, and in what way, mathematically defined functions were automatically computable. Computing is unusual in that a lot of the theory was worked out long before it became possible in practice (except in trivial cases), first by Lady Lovelace and then by Church, Gödel, Turing and others. The peak of achievement in this area was the remarkable result of Gödel (1931), that perfectly respectable, well-defined functions can exist which cannot be computed by any conceivable automatic device. Fortunately for users and manufacturers of computers, these functions do not arise in practical applications.

While this theoretical work was going on there were attempts to solve the problem of building practical automatic computers. Two of the pioneers were Aiken in the U.S.A. and Zuse in Germany, both working independently on electromechanical devices. None of Zuse's work became known outside Germany until after the end of World War II and he has never received wide credit for his developments; indeed, some books on the history of computers do not even mention his name. We shall give more attention to Aiken's work, both because of its influence and because it did produce the first close approximation to Babbage's Analytical Engine.

Aiken's Automatic Sequence Controlled Computer (ASCC) began as a project at Harvard University in 1937 with the support of the IBM Corporation. The machine was very similar in structure to Babbage's Engine but was on a more realistic scale; there were seventy-two registers of twenty-three decimal digits to store data. The storage of digits in the ASCC was similar to that in Babbage's Engine. The digits were stored on wheels with ten positions, but the whole operation was electromechanical rather than mechanical. Addition or subtraction could be done in any register but a separate unit existed for multiplication and division. Numbers could be fed in from punched cards but the instructions were carried on paper tape, combining the two features of Babbage's sets of cards. One interesting point is that it seems that, although Aiken was conscious of the influence of Babbage, he did not know of the work of Lady Lovelace, and the ASCC in its original form did not enable the automatic repetition of a sequence of instructions if required. Lady Lovelace had seen the importance in automatic computation of being able to go back to an earlier point in the sequence of instructions and repeat them.

The ASCC was completed in 1944 but by then electromechanical devices were being made obsolete by the new technology of electronics, and the main stream of computer development had moved elsewhere, to the Moore School of Electrical Engineering at the University of Pennsylvania. Like so many technical advances, electronics were brought into computing in response to military needs, and once again it was the need for tables which was at the root of the project, in this case for ballistic tables to aid the accurate use of artillery.

The project produced the ENIAC (the first of many pronounceable acronyms which have prominently featured in computer development, and some would say plagued it), the letters standing for 'Electronic Numerical Integrator and Calculator'. The engineers principally responsible for its design were Eckert and Mauchly and the basis of their design was the **ring counter**, a circuit capable of possessing any one of ten possible states, and thus able to represent a decimal digit. The ENIAC had twenty registers each containing ten such ring counters plus another circuit to hold the sign of the ten-digit number so represented.

In many respects the ENIAC was inferior to the ASCC. Though both had data supplied by punched cards, the ENIAC had to have its instructions manually set by means of switches and plug-and-socket connections rather than supplied by paper tape, and hence was more a calculator than a 'computer'. Furthermore, whereas today we think of electronic devices being much more reliable in operation than electromechanical ones, in those days this was far from the case because of the dependence on thermionic valves. It was a considerable achievement to keep any such complex electronic device going for any length of time and the ENIAC had 18,000 valves. Stories are told about how all the lights in West Philadelphia would dim whenever it was switched on. Nevertheless, it was apparent as soon as the ENIAC was demonstrably workable that the future of computing lay with electronics. The difference was one of sheer speed; the multiplication time for the ENIAC was one five-hundredth of that of the ASCC, meaning that even if it could only be kept going for a few hours a week it could out-perform the electro-mechanical device. Completing the ENIAC as a functioning machine was the breakthrough needed to enable computers as we know them today to be developed. ENIAC went into regular service in 1946, though it had been doing useful work since the previous year, and remained in use until 1955. After World War II the military need declined, but computing had gained a momentum of its own and the story since then has been one of continuous advance.

In 1944 John von Neumann, a mathematician already of world stature, became associated with the ENIAC project, which was then at an advanced stage of development. It was von Neumann who made the conceptual advance which led to computers as we know them today. We have seen that ENIAC did not use the Babbage-Aiken technique of reading in instructions from outside, but had them wired in manually for any given problem. Though it was tedious and time-consuming to instruct the machine, there was also a disadvantage in reading instructions from cards or paper tape in that, while the instructions could be individually obeyed inside the machine at electronic speeds, the speed of the whole calculation would be limited by the (essentially mechanical) rate at which the instructions could be supplied. Von Neumann saw that the best of both worlds could be achieved by keeping instructions as well as data in the memory of the computer. Once read in, they could be repeatedly obeyed at electronic speeds. All that was needed was to design some coded representation for the instructions, like that used on Aiken's paper tape but suitable for internal storage, and the necessary electronic circuits to decode these instructions in the correct sequence and cause them to be obeyed. Before the ENIAC project was completed, plans were already in hand to produce the EDVAC (Electronic Discrete Variable Computer) embodying this principle.

After the war many scientists in different parts of the world set to work on computers, once their feasibility had been demonstrated. Ironically the first working stored-program computers were produced in Britain, at Cambridge and Manchester Universities. Britain had a slight lead because of another wartime project which involved a number of people subsequently prominent in the computing field. This has received even less attention than the work of Zuse as it was concerned with automatic aids to code-breaking and hence has been enshrouded in official secrecy.

In the years immediately after the war Britain had both a technical and a potential commercial lead. The first commercial sale of a computer was made in the early 1950s, of a machine based on the Manchester work. The world's first business applications computer was built by J. Lyons and Company, then simply a catering chain, and was completed in 1951. This was LEO (Lyons Electronic Office) and its design was based on EDSAC (Electronic Digital Sequential Automatic Computer), the original Cambridge stored-program machine. However, this lead was shortlived. In late 1946 Eckert and Mauchly, the ENIAC designers, left the Moore School team to set up their own firm and they produced the first UNIVAC machine for the 1950 U.S. Census. The firm was taken over in 1950 by Remington Rand (later Sperry Rand), and computers bearing the name UNIVAC are still produced. Despite its involvement with the ASCC, IBM was relatively slow in entering the field, but when it did it made sure, with its enormous resources, that the venture would be a success. Due to the weight of American economic and technological power and to lack of foresight on the part of British governments and business leaders, the American industry in general, and IBM in particular, came to achieve the dominant position in the computing world which it retains to this day.

From the early 1950s onwards, all computers have been of the stored-program type. It is worth stressing the importance of the stored-program technique. We have already mentioned its first enormous advantage, that by having its instructions in store the computer can execute them at electronic speeds instead of being limited by the mechanical rate of input. This advantage on its own is sufficient to make the stored-program technique worthwhile. There is a further advantage which is fundamental and even more important. Taken in isolation, the store-program concept might lead one to produce a computer with separate stores for instructions and for data. The problem with this approach is that some kinds of calculation involve many instructions working on very little data, whereas others involve relatively few distinct instructions being performed on a large amount of data. To make the computer as versatile and as efficient as possible in the use of a given storage capacity, it is clearly best to design a single store, any part of which can be used either for instructions or for data, depending on the requirements of the user.

Von Neumann's concept of a stored-program computer is still the basis of all modern computers, but there have been many advances since then. We shall mention a few of these below, concentrating on the basic ideas, and some will be discussed further in later chapters.

As the use of computers increased so did the amount of data handled by them. This required larger and cheaper storage and led to the concept of secondary store, where data could be held relatively cheaply and brought into the main store of the computer when required. Also more sophisticated input and output devices were developed to handle this increasing movement of data, e.g. lineprinters which print a line of characters at a time, at rates of 1000 or more lines per minute.

It was realised that while data was being transferred in and out of store, the arithmetic unit was idle. Time-sharing was developed, enabling one program to be running during this idle time, i.e. while others programs were waiting for data. Time-sharing (or multiprogramming) allowed several programs to be in the computer at the same time, and led to the need for programs running in the machine at the same time to be protected from one another. The first implementation of protection facilities allocated one specific area of store to each program. The program could refer to data in this area but not to any outside it. This created problems when a program wanted to extend its data area or when one program finished and its replacement required a different size of area.

The concept of paging was developed to overcome this. It was first introduced on the Atlas computer at Manchester University in 1958, and has had a profound influence on computer design ever since. In paging, the store is divided into several areas of equal size, called pages. Each program has a number of pages allocated to it but they need not be next to each other in store. A table is maintained for each program giving a list of which pages the program is using together with where these pages are located in store. When the program refers to an item of data, the table is consulted to find the actual location of the data. Some of the pages available to the program may be on secondary store as well as main store, but can be brought into main store when required. This gives the program the impression that more store is available to it than the main store itself contains.

In some applications computer users may require a fast response to enquiries, i.e. booking seats on aircraft, and in cases like this the user wants to be able to type in his requirements on a typewriter-like terminal. Multi-access facilities were developed to enable many users to have simultaneous access to the computer in this way and also to give each user protection similar to that in time-sharing. The person typing at a terminal often does not want to be physically close to the computer, e.g. there will be airline booking offices in different main cities. Facilities were therefore developed for users remote from the computer to communicate with it, normally by telephone links but later also via satellites, etc.

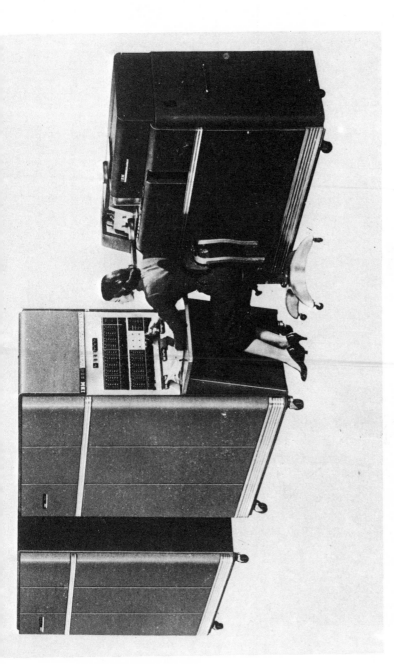

Fig. 1.2(a) **Mid-1950s.** The IBM 650, the first big-selling computer. The unit with the operator's console houses the processor and store (a 2000-word drum); the unit on the left houses the power supply and the smaller one on the operator's right the input-output (a card reader – electromechanical, not photoelectric – and card punch).

[Photograph courtesy of IBM United Kingdom Ltd.]

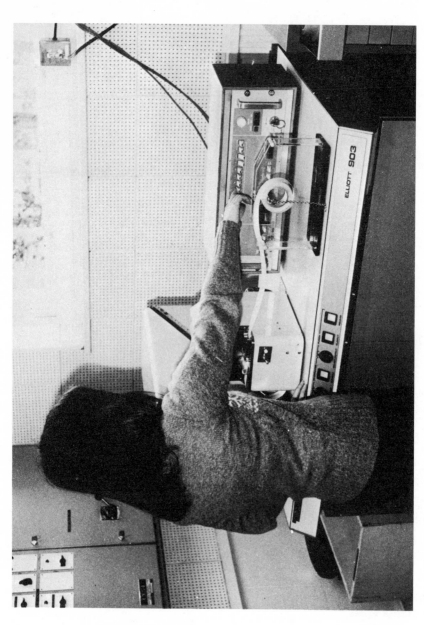

Fig. 1.2(b). **Mid-1960s.** By this time the invention of core store and the replacement of thermionic valves by transistors meant that a computer of greater speed and power than the 650 could be run off an ordinary 13-amp mains socket, and was physically much smaller. The machine shown is an Elliott 903 with 8192 (8K) word store installed in Queen Elizabeth College in 1967.

[Photograph by Tony Kerr, Queen Elizabeth College]

Fig. 1.2(c). **Late 1960s/early 1970s.** While the most powerful computers remained physically large, small computers became mini-computers. Transistors had made desk-sized computers possible: integrated circuits made them shelf-sized, and also cheaper. The best-selling mini-computers were the PDP–8 and PDP–11 ranges made by the Digital Equipment Corporation: in the picture are a PDP–8/M (on the floor) and a PDP–11/05, both of comparable power to the Elliott 903 in Fig. 1.2(b).

[Photograph courtesy of Digital Equipment Corporation]

While these and other facilities were being developed to satisfy the needs of users, the basic technology of the computer was also changing. These changes are often described in terms of 'generations'; first generation machines used valves, second generation used transistors, and third generation machines use integrated circuits. This has resulted in the physical size of computers being drastically reduced. ASCC was 51 feet long and 8 feet high, whereas a modern computer of far greater capacity and power can easily fit on to a desk-top.

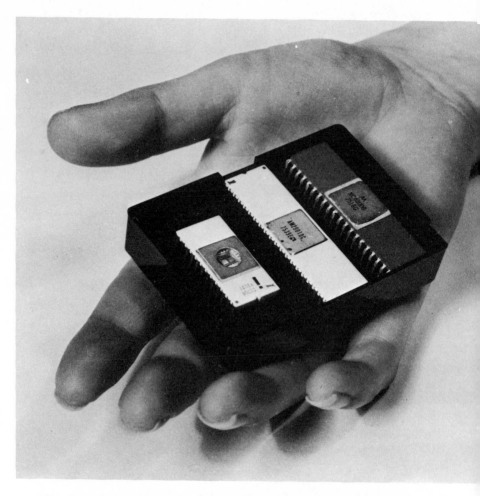

Fig. 1.2(d). **Mid-1970s.** By this time semiconductor technology had so advanced that a processor and memory could be held in the palm of a hand. From left to right, the three integrated circuits shown are an Intel 2708 memory unit of 1K 8-bit bytes; an AMD 2900 central processing element capable of handling groups of 4 bits; and a complete central processor handling 8-bit bytes, the Motorola 6800.

[*Photograph courtesy of Cramer Electronics Ltd.*]

Processing has become faster, and modern production methods have resulted in store being much cheaper and more reliable, many computers being run for twenty-four hours a day with little time lost for maintenance. Integrated circuits have enabled faulty components to be replaced quickly.

Not all of the advances have been used to build bigger and more powerful machines: small specialised computers have also been developed, e.g. those designed to handle input/output for a larger central computer, or to control particular processes. Sometimes several computers may be run linked together, either to provide greater reliability of the total system or because they are processing related jobs which need to share common data.

Nevertheless, despite all these developments, the basic von Neumann concepts of input, storage, manipulation and output remain. We shall now look in more detail at how they are actually organised and used.

Chapter 2

The Computer as a Machine

We have seen in the last chapter that a computer is conceptually a machine which can receive, store, manipulate and yield up information. One of the crucial steps in its development was the realisation that the information which can be stored *and hence manipulated* can include the instructions which the computer obeys in order to perform its tasks. We shall see in this chapter that the physical components from which computers are built fall into these categories: i.e. a modern computer consists of one or more devices which the computer user can employ to present information (both instructions and data) to the machine, one or more of which present the computed results to the user, one or more units store the information while the computer is engaged in the computation; and, at the heart of the machine, one or more units to do the actual manipulation in accordance with the instructions. A unit which fetches the instructions from store, decodes and obeys them is usually called a **processor, central processor, CPU (central processing unit)** or **OCP (order code processor)**. It is often subdivided into sections, one of which decodes and initiates the actions called for by the instructions, usually called the **control unit**, and another which performs the actual manipulations, additions, multiplications, etc., usually called the **arithmetic unit**, more precisely the **arithmetic and logic unit** (ALU), or (following Babbage) the mill. The units which store information are collectively called the **store** or **memory**, though again there is commonly a subdivision which we shall describe shortly. Devices which enable information to be fed into the machine are called **input** devices, while those which yield up information are called **output** devices; we shall use these terms from now on. Some physical units are called **input–output** devices since they are able to perform both activities. Input and output devices are collectively known as **peripheral** devices. In this chapter we shall be discussing the principal units in modern computers for storage, processing, input and output, in that order, with some brief remarks on less common devices and on some which were important in their day but have since been superseded due to technical advances.

2.1 Store

If the processor is the heart of a computer, the store is its foundation, for without the means of storing information the processor has nothing on which to operate. The store associated with a computer can be divided into a number of categories:

(1) **main store** – the store which is directly accessible to the CPU for fetching instructions and data. It is normally faster to use than other storage, but more expensive.

(2) **backing store** or **secondary storage** – used to hold further data and instructions not needed immediately in main store, but able to be transferred there when required. This is usually cheaper than main store and can provide a larger capacity.

(3) **off-line storage** – used to hold information which need not be permanently accessible by the computer, but which can be made available when required. In the majority of computer installations, most data is held in off-line storage.

In some computers there is a further category, of very fast storage associated with the CPU, which enables instructions or data to be brought up in readiness in advance of their actual use. For simplicity we shall not concern ourselves with this variation, though its value when provided should in due course become clear.

The earlier computing machines had only one category of storage, the main store. Babbage conceived his store as mechanical in construction, since this was the basic technology of his day, but a mechanical store is both too bulky and too slow to allow computing of any significant power. Much of the modern history of computers has been the development of faster and faster, and more and more compact, means of storage. In early machines storage was developed using a variety of techniques. Some was electromechanical in character, as in relays or flip-flops, where a small two-position mechanical switch could be electrically triggered to move from one state to the other (corresponding to on–off, yes–no, etc.) or as in ring counters, effectively geared wheels which could be clicked forward one position on receipt of an impulse. This latter technique is still used in, for example, digital clocks. As in Aiken's ASCC, such a counter had ten positions to hold a decimal digit, returning to 0 after reaching 9, and though still basically the Babbage device it was, as we said in Chapter 1, much faster because of its electrical, or later, electronic nature.

Two other early forms of storage were the **Williams tube** and the **delay-line.** A Williams tube (called after its inventor, Professor F. C. Williams of Manchester University) was essentially a cathode ray tube with information stored on it by means of electrostatic charges. As with such a tube in a television set, the charge on a Williams tube dissipated fairly rapidly. The two technical problems to be overcome were therefore those of 'refreshing' the information continually so that it was not lost until replacement was required, and of 'reading off' the information when needed. These problems were successfully dealt with, and the Williams tube would probably have been in use longer had it not been for the invention of the ferrite core, which we shall describe later. The principles behind the Williams tube are now being used in the development of electron beam memory. The delay-line technique consisted of generating sound waves by electronic means at one end of the 'line' (normally a tube filled with mercury, or a bar of nickel), and picking them up again at the other end. These impulses could be made to carry encoded information and when picked up, could be used for processor operations and modified or regenerated (any distortions of the signal being corrected) for re-entry into the line. Neither of these early devices remains in use. It should not be forgotten that 'early' here means 'early in the history of electronic computers'; in fact the Williams tube was constructed in 1948, and delay-line computers continued well into the 1950s.

These two forms of storage are worthy of note because there are fundamental differences between them which we shall encounter again. Delay-line storage is **cyclic,** i.e. the information cycles round and is only available at one point of the cycle. If the information (whether consisting of instructions or data) is not available at the moment it is required, the computer has to wait until that information emerges from the delay line, and is thus slowed down to that extent. Instructing a computer with a delay-line store was often a tricky business in the early days of computers, since much depended upon one's skill in fitting instructions and data into the store so that the minimum time was wasted. The Williams tube, though it could be operated cyclically by scanning the tube surface systematically from start to finish and then resuming, was also capable of being operated **randomly** – i.e. the information could be scattered at will on the tube surface, and the only delay in obtaining a desired piece of information was that involved in redirecting the reading beam to the appropriate area of the surface. **Random access** storage is easier to use and is normally considerably more efficient than cyclic storage. Other factors can also affect the access time (e.g. the actual reading process in the Williams tube was also faster) but only to a minor extent.

Both these methods of storage were limited in capacity when related to size and cost, though through improved technology it is conceivable that in the future new storage devices may be developed based on the Williams tube principle. In the early 1950s, however, it was realised that *magnetic* forms of storage had great advantages. They had speed, since they could be read electronically using reading heads similar to those of an ordinary tape recorder, and similarly could be written on using recording heads. Magnetic storage had compactness, and therefore greater capacity; and it had cheapness, magnetisable materials being relatively easy to produce. The earliest form of magnetic storage device used was the **magnetic drum.**

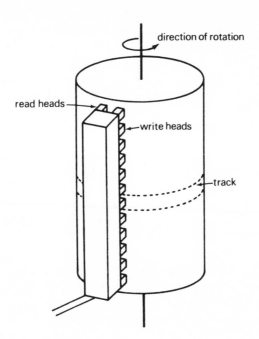

Fig. 2.1. Simplified schematic diagram of a magnetic drum with fixed read/write heads. The drum of the IBM 650 had 40 tracks of 50 words each, and rotated at 12,500 r.p.m.

In a magnetic drum the outside curved surface of a cylinder is coated with a magnetisable material, and the drum is made to rotate very rapidly about its axis of symmetry. Reading and writing (recording) heads are placed close to the magnetisable surface along the length of the cylinder parallel to the axis of rotation, and information is stored on the surface as patterns of magnetisation. The cylinder can be thought of as being divided into circular sections or **tracks** each containing a number of items of information. With some drums each track has its own pair of fixed reading and writing heads, in others the heads are able to move parallel to the axis of the drum and so each pair of heads covers several tracks; here we shall consider only the first kind. At any instant two items of information will become available, one for reading and one for writing. The storage principle for any individual track is cyclic, but the ability to rotate the drum very rapidly means that the access time is fast, and the compactness with which information can be recorded means that the capacity is considerable. A number of the most successful early computers had drum as their main storage, e.g. the IBM 650, the English Electric DEUCE and the Ferranti Pegasus. The DEUCE was one of the first machines to have two 'levels' of storage: the processor had direct access only to delay-lines, information on the drum being brought into delay-lines when required. One snag about this was that the cyclic operations of the delay-lines and the drum had to be synchronised. The IBM 650, where the processor had direct access to the drum, had no such problems, and everything was geared to the drum rotation speed, so that even if the speed varied (i.e. because of voltage fluctuations in the power supply) it was still possible to continue. Nevertheless, the concept of having more than one level of storage was an important one, and most modern computers of any reasonable size have at least two levels of storage.

Despite the advantages we have mentioned, magnetic drum storage still has the limitations which are imposed by the fact that access to its information depends on mechanical movement, which restricts speed of access and compactness, and also increases the possibility of breakdown through wear. The thermionic valve ring counters in ENIAC had no mechanical moving parts and operated at electronic speeds: what was wanted for the main store of computers in the 1950s was something which possessed those qualities, operated by random access rather than cyclic access, yet with reasonably high capacity.

The answer was **magnetic core storage**, which was developed and introduced in the latter part of the 1950s and satisfied all these requirements. It was so

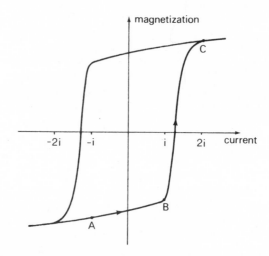

Fig. 2.2. Hysteresis curve (see text).

successful that it was universally adopted for main store for the whole of the next decade, and led to main store being called 'core store' in common computer parlance.

As with many brilliant ideas, the basic principle of magnetic core is simple. Consider a small ring, or 'core', of magnetisable ferrite, with a wire winding which can carry a current. The core can be magnetised in either of two opposite directions, which we shall call positive and negative. The basis of the idea is that the ferrite material exhibits the phenomenon of magnetic **hysteresis**, namely that if a current is passed along the wire winding, the magnetisation of the loop will not be changed unless the current has passed a certain threshold level, after which it will be changed rapidly with only a small increase in current. The magnetisation produced is not, as in other materials, proportional to the current, and it is possible to find two values of the current, one twice the other (say i and $2i$) such that if a current i is passed through the winding the change in magnetisation is negligible whereas if $2i$ is passed the direction of the magnetisation can be reversed.

This is shown in Fig. 2.2, where one can see that if the loop starts with negative magnetisation and the current is reversed in direction but with magnitude less than i (point A to point B), then there is only a slight change in the magnetisation, and its direction is unaltered. It is only when the current is increased to $2i$ that the magnetisation reverses direction (point C).

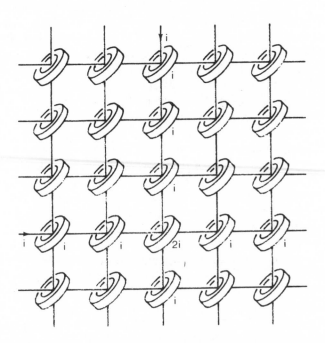

Fig. 2.3. Schematic diagram of a 5 × 5 grid of ferrite cores, showing one core only of the 25 being magnetised by the currents in the two write wires.

The importance of this can be seen when we consider a small grid containing 5 × 5 such loops, or cores, wired up so that each core has two wires threaded through it, one horizontal and one vertical. If a current i is passed through the fourth horizontal and third vertical wires simultaneously, the core at the intersection will have a total current of $2i$ passing through it and so can have its magnetisation changed, but each other core in this row and column will have a current of only i passing through it and so will not suffer any change of magnetisation. Thus by giving 'commands' (in the form of pulses of current) to only 2 wires out of the 10, one can pick out one specific core out of the 25 in which to record a single item of information. It is easy to see that the circuitry can be arranged so that the speed of this operation is independent of the position of the core. The same arguments apply to a grid of any size, whether square or rectangular: for a $64 \times 64 (= 4096)$ grid one picks out two of $64 + 64 (= 128)$ wires.

Each loop has two states, positive magnetisation (or 'yes' or 'on' or '1') and negative magnetisation (or 'no' or 'off' or '0'), and from the above one can see how information in this form can be stored. There remains the problem of reading the information that has been written; this is easy enough in principle, because a magnetised core will affect currents in the wires threaded through it by induction, and in different ways depending on whether the magnetisation is clockwise or anticlockwise with respect to the direction of the current. By passing a current through the two wires intersecting at the particular core, one can detect by the result which state the core is in. Unfortunately this process results in the core being demagnetised, so that if the information is not to be destroyed as it is read, further circuitry, involving further interlacing of wires through the cores, is required to restore the information immediately it is read. All this adds greatly to the expense of core storage.

The cores themselves are cheap to produce, by a process similar to the one which makes medical tablets, but their intricate wiring is expensive. This is why core storage came to be used as main storage but backing store had to be provided for storing the bulk of the information not immediately needed by the processor. Nevertheless for certain kinds of application, where the need for the fastest possible access to large amounts of information is acute, computers have been designed containing many millions of cores, and these cores are sometimes arranged in a 'primary–secondary' hierarchy.

The dominance of core store ensured that the basic unit of information in computers was confirmed as the **binary digit** (1 or 0, yes or no, on or off), something which we shall be going into in detail in the next section. This may well have come about anyway, since such a representation has other advantages, but the fact that a magnetic core naturally represents such an item of information certainly helped. In recent years new forms of random access storage suitable for main store have been developed, based on semi-conductor physics and large scale integrated circuit techniques (the same technology used in the pocket electronic calculators which flooded into the market in the 1970s).

With the advent of core, the magnetic drum was relegated to the role of backing store, and is still used in that role to some extent. The increasing amount of data demanded by the expanding applications of computers demanded further kinds of storage with even greater capacity for a given cost. The two principal ones which were developed, and are still the major forms of backing store, are **magnetic tapes** and **magnetic disks.**

The idea of magnetic tape storage can be easily appreciated by anyone who owns or has used an ordinary tape recorder. As with sound recordings, the storage medium is a length of plastic tape coated with a magnetisable compound and wound on a reel. The most common size is the 2400-feet reel of $\frac{1}{2}$-inch wide tape, though there are a variety of sizes available. Information can be written on to the tape in coded form by passing it under a writing head similar to the recording head on an ordinary tape recorder; this information can be retrieved by the use of a reading head able to pick up and decode the patterns of magnetisation. The principle of this part of the operation is

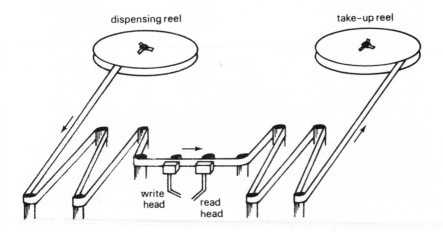

Fig. 2.4. Diagram of the essential features of a magnetic tape drive, viewed from an angle; the axes of rotation of the spools are in fact horizontal (cf. photograph, Fig. 2.5).

identical to that of the magnetic drum, but only one reading and one writing head is needed for each tape drive. The first main difference between drum and tape lies in the fact that tape storage is not cyclic but **sequential**, in that (as in ordinary recorders) normally reading and writing can only be done when the tape is running in a forward direction, so the items of information are stored one after another in sequence. When the end of the tape is reached, the whole tape has to be rewound to get back to the items at the beginning. As with domestic recorders the mechanism is provided with a fast rewind, but even so this is a big disadvantage of magnetic tape storage as compared with drum, since a complete rewind of a 2400-feet reel still takes minutes.

Where tapes score over drums are in compactness, cost, and exchangeability. One standard reel of tape the size of a dinner plate costs only a few pounds sterling and (depending on the density with which the information is stored) can contain anything up to several million characters of written text or their equivalent. The few pounds of course does not include the tape drive on which the reel of tape is loaded. This includes the reading and writing mechanism, and because of the precision and reliability required can cost several

Fig. 2.5. Magnetic tape drive, part of a Data General laboratory monitoring system installed in the Physics Department, Queen Elizabeth College. Between the spools on the left and the read–write mechanism on the right are two vacuum chambers for taking up slack in the tape. When winding forward the tape unwinds from the lower spool, through the left-hand vacuum chamber, and then is guided upwards by pulleys to pass the read–write heads (on the right below the large upper pulley). After passing round this large pulley the tape goes through the right-hand vacuum chamber and finally winds on to the upper, take-up spool. The tape drive controls are between the two spools: below is the front panel of the processor itself, a Data General Nova minicomputer.

[*Photograph by Tony Kerr, Queen Elizabeth College*]

thousand pounds. Magnetic tape achieves its cheapness because it is an **exchangeable** medium, in that (again as in sound recorders) one reel of tape can be unloaded and replaced by another. Big computer installations normally have hundreds of tapes available – the capacity of magnetic tape storage is theoretically limitless, though at any one time only a certain number of tape will be accessible to the computer, namely those actually loaded on to the tape drives.

Two things can be seen from this description. One is that the sequential nature of magnetic tape renders it wholly unsuitable for main store, since the processor often needs information, whether instructions or data, in other than sequential order. The other is that the exchangeable nature of tape means that it is similar in many ways to input-output media such as punched cards or paper tape. Magnetic tapes were for quite a time used as backing store, but they are now mainly used for off-line storage, while the more recently developed magnetic disks are used for backing store.

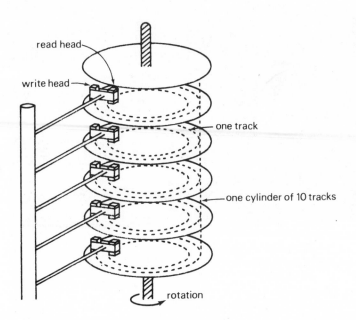

Fig. 2.6. Schematic diagram of a multisurface, moving head disk. The heads can be moved radially towards or away from the centre of the disk to access different tracks. If the arms are completely withdrawn the entire pack of disks can be removed from the spindle and replaced. Note that the two outermost surfaces at the top and bottom are not used; this gives additional precaution against accidental damage.

While tapes resemble sound recording tapes and drums are like old-fashioned phonograph cylinders (though these were 'written and read' sequentially rather than cyclically), disks are similar to modern gramophone records. The disk is made to rotate about its centre, though much faster (3000 rpm is

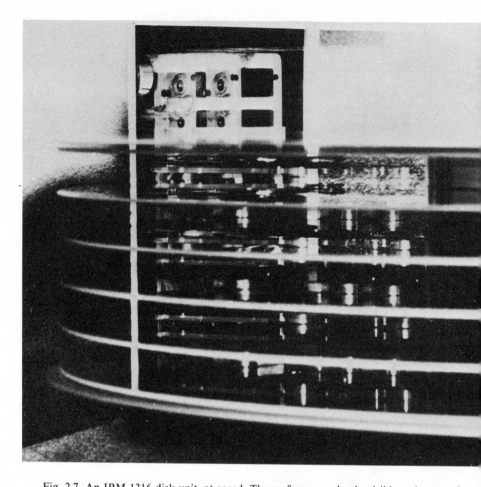

Fig. 2.7. An IBM 1316 disk unit, at speed. The surfaces are clearly visible and some of the read-write mechanism between them can be made out (cf. conceptual diagram, Fig. 2.6). Disk packs of similar size can be seen in Fig. 2.8.

[Photograph courtesy of IBM United Kingdom Ltd.]

typical). As with drums and tapes the recording surface is coated with magnetisable material and is read and written by heads close to the coated surface. The difference between a disk and a gramophone record (like that between drums and phonograph cylinders) is that the information is stored on concentric circular tracks rather than a single spiralling track, or groove (see Fig. 2.6). The storage method is therefore cyclic, like the drum, with all the advantages which this implies.

A simple magnetic disk drive will have one reading and one writing head for each surface, mounted on radial arms so that they can move from track to track as required: thus only one track on each surface will be available for reading or writing at any one time. As with drums, where even the short time taken to change tracks is a handicap, it is possible to have more than one pair of heads for each surface, each head covering fewer tracks. The extreme case is to have one of each type of head for each track thus eliminating head movements altogether.

By having a stack of parallel disks with a common axis of rotation, each surface with its own read and write heads, it is possible to achieve a storage capacity which is comparable to that of magnetic tape, and which is compact, fairly cheap, yet still cyclic. Furthermore, disks can be made exchangeable. Thus disks combine the speed and cyclic access advantages of drums with the exchangeability of tapes, at a somewhat higher cost than tape. Disks have become the commonest form of backing store for modern computers.

Most big computers nevertheless have magnetic tapes as well as disks, which are used for holding data which can be processed sequentially, e.g. a commercial payroll, but the principal use of tape is as tertiary or off-line storage. Magnetic tape is a common form of off-line storage since a reel of tape is considerably cheaper than an exchangeable disk pack, and takes less space to store. It is usual, therefore, to keep frequently used or frequently changed off-line information on disk packs (except where the sequential nature of tape is not a handicap), using tapes for longer term storage of infrequently needed or 'archive' material or where the volume of information is so great that the saving in terms of space or money are significant.

The search for new forms of storage goes on, the aim being to achieve simultaneously all the desirable characteristics – speed, reliability, no moving parts, random access, cheapness and ease of production, large capacity and compactness. An indication of the problem is that designers are now having to face the limitation on speed imposed by the speed of light, which determines how fast information can be transferred from one part of the store to another or to the processor. Completely new kinds of storage are being developed and tested, such as those based on laser technology. It is too early to tell what impact these will have, but a fortune awaits the designers who can produce fast, cheap, bulk, random-access storage.

2.2 Binary Arithmetic

When discussing core store, we pointed out how its development helped to ensure that the basic unit of information in modern computers was what we called the 'binary digit'. We shall now look at this in detail, and in particular its implications for arithmetic and the way in which computers perform their operations.

In the twentieth century our everyday arithmetic is based on a decimal system; that is to say, the values represented by the sequence of characters '161' or '25·071' are determined by the positions of the various digits in relation

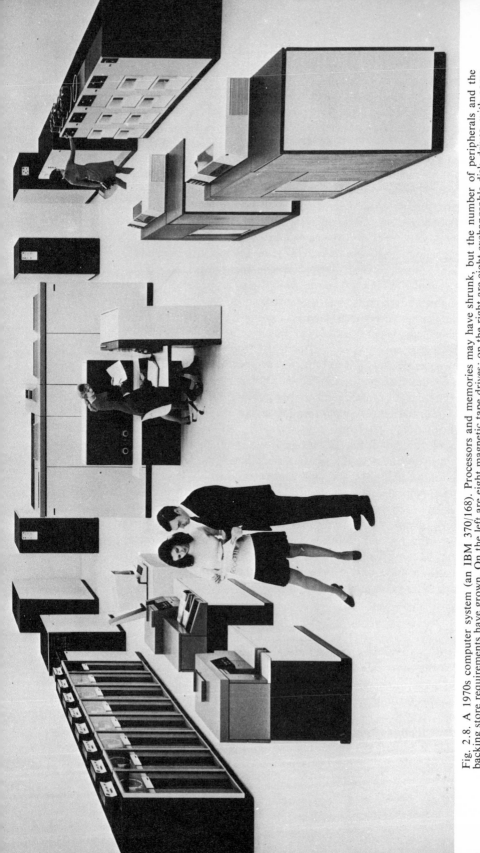

Fig. 2.8. A 1970s computer system (an IBM 370/168). Processors and memories may have shrunk, but the number of peripherals and the backing store requirements have grown. On the left are eight magnetic tape drives; on the right are eight exchangeable disk drives, with some exchangeable disk packs waiting on top of the units and one being held by the operator. Nearest the camera on the left is a card punch, with a card reader and a visual display alongside it. Opposite are two lineprinters. The operator's console is in the centre with the main processor and store in the background.

to an (actual or assumed) decimal point, and weighted by an appropriate power of ten; for example

$$161 = 1 \times 10^2 + 6 \times 10^1 + 1 \times 10^0.$$

Ten is the **base** of our number system, and ten digits (0 to 9) are needed as separate characters (together sometimes with a decimal point) to represent any possible decimal number. However, there is nothing special about the number 10, and any other integer greater than one is suitable to use as the base of a number system. In the past others such as 12 and 60 have been used. In particular, the *smallest* suitable number is 2, which needs only two digit characters. It is natural to use 0 and 1 for these, but they are now *binary digits*, not decimal digits. Any integer can be represented as a sequence of these appropriately weighted by powers of 2:

binary base   decimal base

$$
\begin{aligned}
1 &= \quad\quad\quad 1 \times 2^0 \quad\quad \times \quad = \quad\quad 1 \\
101 &= 1 \times 2^2 + 0 \times 2^1 + 1 \times 2^0 = \quad\quad 5 \\
10100001 &= 1 \times 2^7 + 1 \times 2^5 + 1 \times 2^0 = \quad\quad 161
\end{aligned}
$$

The number system based on the number 2 is called the binary system. This is the natural system when using core since each core can have one of two states, 0 or 1, and hence can be used to store one binary digit. It is also an easy system for the other forms of magnetic storage mentioned above. The natural arithmetic of a computer is therefore binary arithmetic, and this will remain until computers are developed which have as their natural base a number different from 2 and which are superior in speed, efficiency, etc. It is possible to design computers whose number base is not 2 (there are some now with base 3, for instance) but quite apart from the question of storage it is also easier to design electronic circuits to perform binary arithmetic than to perform ternary or decimal arithmetic. For a machine whose main purpose is to perform numerical calculations the binary system is both the most natural and the most efficient one to use. Commonly then, all information storage, transfer and manipulation is done in terms of binary numbers, made up of binary digits (called **bits** for short).

Storage, transfer and manipulation of information is not performed one bit at a time but in groups of bits, the most common of which are **bytes** and **words.** There is no intrinsic difference between a byte and a word apart from length: both can be regarded as binary numbers, and for neither of them is there a universally agreed length. Transfers between main and backing store, between input/output devices and store, and between main store and the processor, will take place in a particular computer system in terms of single bytes or words, or blocks of a specific number of bytes or words. Transfers between main and backing store are normally in terms of blocks of information because the cyclic or sequential nature of backing store make transfer of single bytes or words wasteful of time.

Word - unit of storage holds 1 item of data or 1 instruction.
varies from 12-16 60-64
BYTE - no of bits required to hold 1 character of coded
required info.

44   **The Computer as a Machine**   [Ch. 2

A word is the basic unit of storage in the machine and normally holds one item of data or one instruction, though some machines do allow data items or instructions to be shorter or longer than a single word. The word length varies from 12 or 16 bits for modern small computers (usually known as mini-computers) up to 60 or 64 bits for the largest.

A byte is normally the number of bits required to hold one character of coded textual information (and is sometimes called a character). It is normally 8 bits and can therefore be interpreted as a binary number between 00000000 and 11111111 inclusive, i.e. as a decimal number between 0 and 255 inclusive. A character of text is represented by (coded into) a number in the range 0 to 255. Although in principle this allows representation of 256 different characters, usually only those with an even number of '1' bits are used, a maximum of 128, such values as 4, 7 and 11 (in binary 100, 111, 1011) being discarded. This is to allow for checking against corruption, i.e. the accidental or undesired change of bits through human error or machine malfunction. A human user, or the computer itself, can check for 'parity', i.e. the presence of an even number of '1' bits. A chance error or corruption will be detected unless each single undesired bit change is matched by a second undesired bit change, which is much less likely than a single bit change. For instance, if the probability is 1/1000 that any individual bit in an 8-bit byte is corrupted, then the probability that a second bit in an 8-bit byte is also corrupted is 7/1000, and the probability that there will be an error which will not be detected by parity will be approximately 7/1000000.

The most likely time for information to be erroneous is on first input to the computer, but it is also vulnerable to corruption during transfer from one part of the machine to another as well as during input and output. Machines therefore usually check for parity on transfers. On magnetic tape, in addition to a parity check on each byte, there is a longitudinal parity check on the corresponding bits of each byte in a block of data. There are other forms of parity and checking, designed to give preference to detecting the likelier forms for corruption in a particular system.

Since a byte on its own can represent only numbers in the range 0 to 255, it is words rather than bytes that are of importance. Words are usually considered solely in terms of their working length. An extra bit is often added inside the machine for parity checking purposes, this being made 0 or 1 depending on whether the word proper contains an even or odd number of '1' bits. We shall first consider the representation of numbers in a word of 24 working bits; the parity checking bit we shall ignore as being in the province of the computer engineer rather than the computer user.

Just as a four decimal-digit number can represent anything from 0 to $9999 = 10^4 - 1$, similarly a 24 binary-digit number can represent anything from 0 to $2^{24} - 1 = 16777215$. This is a satisfactorily wide range of whole numbers (or **integers**) except that no negative integer can be represented. The obvious solution is to reserve one of the 24 bits to indicate the sign (0 for positive or zero, 1 for negative) and to restrict the magnitude to the range 0 to $2^{23} - 1 = 8388607$.

In this case the obvious answer is not necessarily the best, and in order to see why we have to consider the nature of addition in binary arithmetic.

Binary addition works by the application of the simple rules:

$$0 + 0 = 0, 1 + 0 = 0 + 1 = 1, \text{ and } 1 + 1 = 0 \text{ and carry } 1.$$

To see these in action one can produce the following addition table of two 3-bit numbers (the reader is advised to produce this table for himself and then check that he has done it correctly).

	000	001	010	011	100	101	110	111
000	000	001	010	011	100	101	110	111
001	001	010	011	100	101	110	111	1000
010	010	011	100	101	110	111	1000	1001
011	011	100	101	110	111	1000	1001	1010
100	100	101	110	111	1000	1001	1010	1011
101	101	110	111	1000	1001	1010	1011	1100
110	110	111	1000	1001	1010	1011	1100	1101
111	111	1000	1001	1010	1011	1100	1101	1110

From this table we can see that in the lower right triangle below the diagonal the sums 'overflow' into a fourth binary place. Suppose that we only have 3 bits into which we can store the result of an addition: the bits printed in **bold** type will then disappear from the table and we are left with results like

$$001 + 111 = 000, \quad 010 + 110 = 000, \quad 101 + 110 = 011.$$

If we define $-n$ to be that integer which when added to n gives 0, then it is not difficult to see that a natural interpretation of '111' is the decimal number -1, since $001 (= +1) + 111 = 000$ (zero), and of '110' is -2 since $010 (= +2) + 110 = 000$. A common mode of representing negative numbers is this 'twos complement' notation, as it is called, all binary numbers beginning with 1 being interpreted as negative and all those beginning with 0 as either zero or positive. This representation has two further advantages: it is easy to test whether an integer is negative or not merely by looking at the leftmost bit; and it is fairly easy to check if overflow has occurred. If it has, then the sum of two positive integers appears negative (beginning with a 1), while the sum of two negative numbers appears positive (beginning with a 0), as in the third example above. Using this representation, a 24-bit word can now hold an integer in the range -8388608 to $+8388607$.

However, it is not enough to have a means of representing integers. Much mathematics needs fractional arithmetic, and we have already seen in Chapter 1 the importance of real number arithmetic. Once again the 'obvious' answer – to assume the existence of a 'binary point', analogous to the decimal point, within the binary number – is not the best, partly because very small numbers would then have very few significant figures. The normal way to represent real numbers in a digital computer is by the **floating point** method, which we shall now briefly describe.

It is easier to understand if we consider floating point first in the decimal system. Floating point representation in decimal is based on the fact that any non-zero real number can be uniquely expressed in the form $a \times 10^b$, where a is a fraction with a non-zero digit immediately following the decimal point, and b is an integer exponent: e.g. 378·23 can be written as ·37823 $\times$ 10³, −0·0002013 can be written as −·2013 $\times$ 10⁻³. Similarly in the binary case any positive real number can be expressed in the form $p \times 2^q$, where p is a fraction with 1 following the binary point and q is an integer exponent. A little thought will show that in the decimal case a lies in the range $0·1 \leqslant a < 1$, and in the binary case p lies in the range $0·1 \leqslant p < 1$ where the numbers in this last inequality are written in *binary*, i.e. $\frac{1}{2} \leqslant p < 1$ in decimal. Similarly, for negative reals, a lies in the range $-0·1 \geqslant a > -1$, and p lies in the range $-\frac{1}{2} \geqslant p > -1$.

This is the basis of floating point representation of real numbers in computers, a certain number of bits being allocated to the fractional part and another number to the exponent part. The only modification is that the exponent q is an integer in twos complement notation, and the fractional part is also in twos complement, where the left hand bit represents the sign and the next is the bit immediately following the binary point. The reader should, by writing down a few examples, be able to convince himself that the fractional part will begin 01 ... for positive reals and 10 ... for negative reals. The exceptional real which has been omitted is zero, which is represented by zero in both fractional and exponent parts. In the 24-bit word that we are using as an example one might allocate 16 bits to the fractional part, thus expressed to 15 binary places (about 5 decimal places) plus a sign bit, and 8 bits to the exponent part, 7 bits plus a sign bit representing the range $-128 \leqslant q \leqslant +127$. Since 2^{128} is about 10^{38} this 24-bit word can hold a very wide range of

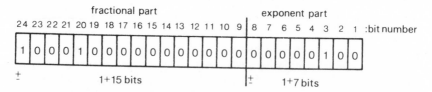

Fig. 2.9. A 24-bit word divided into fractional and exponent parts to hold a real number in floating point format. The leftmost bits indicate the signs of the two parts, and each part will be in twos complement notation. The number represented is −3·75 (in decimal).

real numbers, and all will be expressed to 15 bits accuracy. The floating point representation is therefore superior to the 'obvious' fixed point solution. Often further accuracy is needed and the representation is then spread over two or more words of store; this is usually the case. Using two words in our machine would give 8 bits plus a sign bit to the exponent and 38 bits plus a sign bit to the fractional part (about 12 decimal places).

In general, as can be seen, a real number in floating point form is an approximation only, and real number arithmetic is not exact: what is sometimes overlooked is that a real number which can be represented exactly in floating point decimal may not be exact in floating point binary (the reader is invited to verify this for himself). Note also that if a calculation requires an integer which is outside the range allowed on the machine being used, then representing it by a real number will again in general involve an approximation and, for example, it may not be possible to use it for counting purposes.

2.3 Processors and Instructions

Before turning to the representation of instructions in a computer word it will help to consider the general problem of information transfers. It is possible to transfer the contents of a computer word between devices sequentially, bit by bit, but this would mean that our 24-bit word would take 24 times as long to transfer as a single bit. Thus, as far as possible, transfers are done in *parallel,* e.g. a core store of 8192 24-bit words would not be arranged as a 8192×24 grid (requiring $8192 + 24 = 8216$ wires for writing alone) but as 24 parallel 64×128 grids (requiring $24 \times 192 = 4508$ wires for writing). The 24 bits in corresponding grid positions form a single word and their contents can be transferred *simultaneously* to and from the processor when required. For some transfers the nature of the device concerned are a limitation: for example, magnetic tapes mainly come in 7-track or 9-track versions, i.e. each reading position across the tape carries 7 or 9 bits (6 or 8 bits plus one for parity). A computer designer will normally design his processor, store and input/output devices so that a number of bits are transferred in parallel between the various units.

Computer processors vary in size, design and complexity; whole books have been written on the subject. All we shall do here is point out some of the important features. What all processors have to do is to take in and decode a sequence of instructions. The instructions will be in the main store (leaving aside for the moment the question of how they get there) and so the processor's first need will be to know where to find the succeeding instruction. In the simple case each instruction will occupy one word of store so the processor will need to know which word contains which instruction. Hence each word in the store is allocated a numerical 'address' which identifies it uniquely. There is a crucial difference between the address of a word and the contents of this word, though confusion often arises because both can be thought of as integers. One analogy is the address or number of a house, which is fixed, and the people living there, who can change. To find particular people, you need to know the address where they are currently located; on the other hand, if you keep calling at the same address, you will find that the occupants change from time to time.

Returning to our simple example, the 24-bit word computer with 8192 words of main store, the address of any word in that store can, since 8192 = 2^{13}, be represented by a binary number of 13 bits. These numbers can be conveniently thought of as unsigned integers, thus assigning to the words in the store, numerical addresses ranging in decimal from 0 to 8191. (Note that starting to number the addresses from 0 rather than 1 is a consequence of this: had we tried to start from 1, the final address of 8192 would have required 14 bits for its binary representation.)

To enable it to perform its tasks, the processor will have available a number of **registers.** Each register is able to hold a binary number of some length, and to that extent resembles a part of the store, but has a specific function in the processor's operations. One such register is the **sequence control register**, which holds the address of the next instruction to be obeyed.

In our hypothetical machine the sequence control register will need to be at least 13 bits long, to allow it to hold the address of an instruction anywhere in the main store. Since the length of the sequence control register determines the maximum address which it can hold (i.e. 14 bits allowing up to 16383, 15 bits up to 32767, etc.), it is necessarily related to the maximum size to which the main store can be expanded, though other factors can be involved, which means that the relationship is not always direct. Incidentally, computer main store tends to be supplied by manufacturers in blocks or **modules** where the number of bytes or words is a power of two. Since 2^{10} ($= 1024$) is close to one thousand, a 4096-word store ($= 4 \times 2^{10}$) is often referred to as '4K', 8192 as '8K' and so on.

The sequence control register is used to help control the sequence of operations the computer performs or, more precisely, the instructions it obeys. Suppose that our hypothetical machine has in its sequence control register the address 1043. The order of events is as follows. Firstly a copy of the word at address 1043 is transferred to the processor from the main store, and it is placed in another special register, the **control register.** The control register is another special register, which holds one instruction for the processor to decode. Once the instruction word has been obtained, two things occur. One must clearly be the decoding and execution of the instruction in the control register, which we shall deal with in a moment. The other is that the sequence control register is increased by 1, to 1044. Usually instructions are held in consecutively addressed locations in the store, so 1044 is the address of the instruction which will be normally needed next. The sequence control register is ready to help to bring in the next instruction without delay after the current one has been obeyed, provided nothing happens to interrupt the normal sequence. The sequence control register and the control register are the two essential components of the control unit within the processor, which is itself the heart of the computer. Some machines have more sophisticated ways of fetching instructions and data from main store and decoding the instruction, allowing more than one instruction to be processed simultaneously.

To consider the decoding of an instruction in the control register it is necessary to examine how the instruction is represented in a machine word. For most instructions there are two essentials: part of the word must specify the operation which the computer is to perform; and there must be at least one address specifying data which is to be involved in the operation. Thus the control register must be able to split up the instruction word into various parts or **fields**, including a **function field** specifying the operation and at least one **address field** referring to data, each field consisting of a specified number of bits of the machine word. The length of the address field in an instruction and that of the sequence control register also help to determine the limits of direct (i.e. main storage) addressing. (Some machines with short word lengths have special techniques to overcome apparent limits on main storage implied by the length of the address field, but we shall not go into this variation.)

In our hypothetical machine there is room in a 24-bit word for only one 13-bit address, leaving 11 bits for the function field and other purposes. One-address instructions are sufficient even for operations such as addition which, as we shall see, require two operands. An addressing range of only 8192 is very small, and one may want to extend the machine later by adding extra main store, so we shall assume 15 bits for the address field. Of the remaining 9 bits, 6 bits allow for up to 64 different operations and 3 bits are left available for other uses. 6 or 7 bits give an ample range of different functions

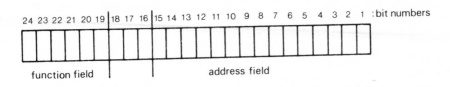

Fig. 2.10. A 24-bit divided into fields to represent an instruction. The three unallocated bits (16–18) will be used to specify special registers to be used in particular instructions (see text).

on many computers; some minicomputers use only 4 bits for the function field, providing a mere 16 different operations. There are a number of different kinds of functions; the four main ones are those for performing arithmetic, those for transferring information internally within the computer system, input and output instructions to enable the computer to communicate externally, and control instructions.

For arithmetic operations, at least one extra register is needed inside the processor to accumulate results of calculations, e.g. the sum of a set of numbers; this is usually called the **accumulator**. The accumulator is normally of one word length, often with an additional 'overflow' bit. A typical one-address function would add a copy of the contents of the address given in the instruction to the current contents of the accumulator, the result being left in the accumulator and the contents of the specified address being unchanged.

Other common instructions are those for subtracting from the accumulator, and for negating the contents of the accumulator. Circuitry for performing such operations is simple: computer designers in the past have tended to work with basic electronic devices called 'gates' which perform simple operations on the electrical pulses submitted to them. Gates are built up from diodes; a diode permits current to flow in only one direction, and only then if there is a

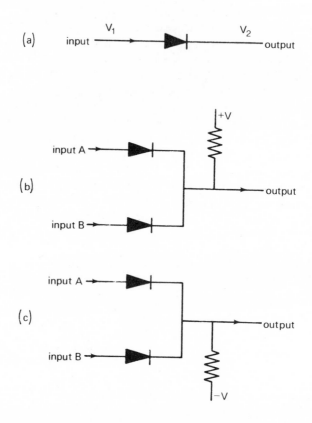

Fig. 2.11. Diodes and gates: (a) diagrammatic representation of a diode. Current flows through the diode only if $V_1 > V_2$; (b) AND gate: there is an output only when the sum of the two input potentials is greater than V, i.e. when there is input on both A and B; (c) OR gate: there is an output when there is an input on at least one of A and B.

voltage drop across the diode. An **AND** gate has two inputs and one output, an output signal being transmitted only when two input signals are received simultaneously. Similarly, an **OR** gate also has two inputs and one output, and transmits an output signal whenever at least one of the inputs provides a signal. Some simple gates and simple circuits employing them are illustrated in Figs. 2.11, 2.12 and 2.13 indicating how the computer designer can build up operations on single bits into operations on bytes or words.

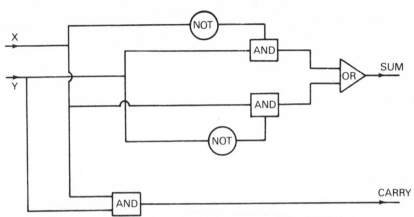

Fig. 2.12. A two-input adder circuit, usually called a half-adder. It accepts two binary inputs X and Y and outputs sum and carry digits. AND and OR gates are shown in Fig. 2.11; a NOT gate produces an output in the absence of an input, but not in the presence of an input.

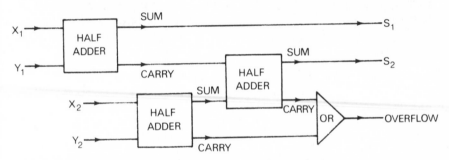

Fig. 2.13. A full adder for two 2-bit binary integers X ($=X_2X_1$) and Y ($= Y_2Y_1$), using three half-adders as shown in Fig. 2.12 and an OR gate. The adder generates the sum S ($= S_2S_1$) and also an overflow bit. The reader may like to work through the adder using different inputs.

Addition or subtraction of integers may result in overflow of one place (in both binary and decimal),

e.g. $99 + 99 = 198$ (decimal), $111 + 111 = 1110$ (binary).

The extra overflow bit on the accumulator is used to indicate that such overflow has occurred. Multiplication can sometimes result in a product of twice the number of places of the original numbers,

e.g. $99 \times 99 = 9801$ (decimal), $111 \times 111 = 110001$ (binary).

Processors normally have additional registers, called **auxiliary registers,** to hold the double length result of a product without any loss of accuracy. Our hypothetical machine would have a 24-bit auxiliary register as well as a 24-bit accumulator. Division would be performed with the dividend at double length held in the accumulator extended by the auxiliary register, the divisor at single length in the machine word specified in the instruction, leaving the resulting quotient in the accumulator.

All these operations refer to integer arithmetic. Because of the importance of real number arithmetic in mathematical applications, computers designed for scientific work, unless cheapness is the main priority rather than speed, also have functions for floating point arithmetic. The circuits required are comparatively complicated and expensive, and extra registers may be required, so in computers not primarily intended for scientific work, or in low-cost minicomputers, floating point arithmetic has to be performed by sequences of more basic functions. This is much cheaper, but also much slower. Computers can also have a variety of instructions used to perform non-arithmetic operations, e.g. on bits or bytes instead of whole words, which is why the term 'arithmetic unit', collectively meaning the accumulator and other registers for data manipulation, and the associated circuits, is to some extent misleading, and why 'arithmetic and logic unit' is sometimes used instead.

Other necessary operations involving the accumulator obviously include transferring information to and from the main store. Thus a sequence of instructions to add together the integers stored in the locations with addresses 1473, 1474 and 1475, leaving the result in the location with address 3006, might read

```
LD    1473   (LD = load a copy of contents of location 1473
                   into accumulator)
ADD   1474   (ADD = add a copy to contents of accumulator)
ADD   1475
ST    3006   (ST = store copy from accumulator)
```

where we have put the addresses in decimal form and replaced the function codes by shorthand alphabetic mnemonics. The comments in brackets are not part of the instructions but explanations of the functions.

Some control instructions also involve the accumulator. Control instructions are those which modify the sequence control register mentioned earlier. An **unconditional jump** instruction is one which specifies the address of the next instruction to be obeyed. A **conditional jump** has the same effect, *provided that a specified condition is satisfied.* Among the conditional jump instructions commonly available are 'jump if accumulator zero' and 'jump if accumulator negative', while others could include 'jump if overflow bit of accumulator is 1'. Control instructions enable the computer to take decisions.

There is one further kind of register which must be mentioned because it provides one of the most powerful and sophisticated tools that a programmer has at this level. We shall give merely a brief introduction to it and an example of one of its uses. We have seen above a simple sequence of instructions to find the sum of three numbers in consecutive store locations. This technique may be used to total many more numbers, but at the cost of a long sequence of

ADD instructions, one for each addition – a wasteful use of main store. An alternative is to use a loop of instructions, repeatedly obeyed while scanning through the sequence of locations containing the numbers until the sequence is complete. In early computers this had to be done by bringing, in each cycle, the instruction containing the 'add contents of address' into the accumulator, treating it as if it were a *number* rather than an instruction, changing the address part by arithmetic operations and checking every time until the final address was reached. This technique is so dangerous that some modern computer systems do not allow it for normal user programs. The modern solution is at once more elegant, more efficient, easier to use, and a great deal safer; its invention was a major step forward made by the Manchester pioneers of the 1950s.

This solution involves the use of yet another type of register, called an **index register.** Modern computers have at least one and sometimes several of these, and their function is to facilitate the kind of address modification we have been discussing. If there is one index register, one bit of each instruction word is set aside as the **index field**: it will be recalled that in the instruction word of our hypothetical machine there were 3 spare bits left over after we had allowed for the function and address fields, and at least one of the three will be used for this purpose. If this 1-bit index field is left zero, everything is left as we discussed it earlier, but if the index field is 1, then the contents of the index register are added to the address field of the current instruction *after* it has been loaded into the control register but *before* that instruction has been obeyed. Thus the effect of the index register is to enable the address field of the instruction *as obeyed* to be modified as required, without either needing to use the accumulator or altering the contents of the instruction word in the main store.

To show this kind of address modification in action, here is a typical set of instructions to sum the sequence of integers in the consecutive locations addressed 1473 to 1572:

1039	LD	2212	(2212 contains integer zero, this initialises the sum)
1040	LDR	7311	(7311 contains integer -100; LDR = transfer copy to index register)
1041	ADD:M	1573	(M = modified by contents of index register)
1042	ADDR	7312	(ADDR = add to index register; 7312 contains integer $+1$)
1043	JRNZ	1041	(JRNZ = jump if index register non-zero)
1044	ST	3006	

The numbers on the left indicate the main store addresses of successive instructions and are included only so that the instructions can be followed more easily. The JRNZ instruction is a conditional jump which resets the sequence control register if the index register is non-zero, so that the next instruction obeyed is the one specified (that in 1041) instead of the instruction in 1044, which is not obeyed until the whole sequence has been summed. The reader will probably not appreciate the importance of modification unless he actually works through a few cycles in the above example, obeying each instruction as if he were the processor, tabulating the successive contents of each register on a sheet of paper.

We have only discussed superficially the problems of machine design. In our hypothetical computer, where a 24-bit instruction word contains a 6-bit function field and a 15-bit address field, we can provide a 3-bit field specifying one of 8 ($= 2^3$) independent accumulators (or their associated auxiliary registers), or a 3-bit field to specify one of 7 independent index registers (assuming that the field value 000 indicates that no modification is required). There are machines which have several registers within the processor and can perform operations which involve two or more of these registers. Other machines have independent processors, each with its own control, sequence control, index and accumulator registers, all of which can collaborate and signal to one another. As we shall see, very often the individual computer user does not need to know in such detail the particular structure of his machine.

2.4 Input and Output

We now turn to input and output devices. If all input and output to and from computers had to be in the form of word-length binary numbers, using computers would be very difficult since human beings, even mathematicians, are unused to thinking in such terms. Thus input and output, except in a few special applications, is normally in the form of text readable by human beings. The user can therefore present his input data in a way convenient for himself: numerical data in ordinary decimal form, other information using alphabetic and other characters. Normally the numerical data will have to be translated on input from decimal to one of the binary forms described. Very big processors sometimes have small 'slave' processors working for them which do all the handling of input and output: but in the simpler case where the main processor does the handling itself, sets of instructions will be needed to handle the various forms of input and perform any necessary conversions such as decimal to binary. Some computers have function codes and operations specifically designed to aid the commonest forms of conversions, and in any case computer manufacturers normally supply with their machines sets of instructions for handling standard kinds of input.

There still remains the problem of getting *instructions* into the machine. This is achieved by a 'bootstrap' process; a few initial instructions are first input, which are used to input further instructions, and these in turn can then handle input and output from actual users. In early computers the initial instructions were directly placed in the main store by an operator using keys on the computer's control panel; nowadays it is usual for these initial instructions, often called the **initial program loader**, to be built permanently into the computer. The operator simply has to initiate the execution of these instructions in order to load some basic programs into the machine, often from backing store. These basic programs are also supplied by the computer manufacturer, and control the input and running of users' programs. With this in mind we can now look at the forms of input available to users.

One of the most convenient forms of input for users is a keyboard, rather like an ordinary typewriter keyboard; usually the computer operator has a keyboard as part of the control equipment. Unfortunately the fastest human speeds for keyboard operation are far too slow for the slowest electronic computers, causing unacceptable waste of computer time. There are two main ways to overcome this problem. The first method, used on the earlier machines, was for the instructions and data to be typed at a keyboard **off-line** from (i.e. not connected to) the computer and recorded on some intermediate medium, suitably coded, which is then used for input to the computer at faster speeds. The second is the **multi-access** approach, mentioned in Chapter 1, where several users are provided with keyboards on-line to the computer, and each are allocated a share of the computer store.

The off-line method is commonly done by professional data preparation staff and is useful for large amounts of data or instructions. It relieves the programmer of the chore of typing (most are not good typists), and enables errors to be detected and corrected before input to the computer. One intermediate medium is punched cards, which have already been mentioned in Chapter 1; the other main one is paper tape. Both have advantages and disadvantages. Punched cards are bulky and heavy, and if a deck of cards is dropped it is laborious to reassemble them in the correct order. Equipment for card punching and handling tends to be large and expensive. On the other hand, an error can be easily corrected by substituting a correctly punched replacement card, and each card can carry a human-readable record of its punched information. In contrast, reels of paper tape are light, compact and cheap, and the information cannot get out of its correct order, though there is a danger of tape becoming tangled or torn during handling. Also, paper tape punching and handling equipment is cheap and compact. Correcting an error may involve repunching a whole tape or splicing in a correction, both error-prone processes, and any printed record of the contents of the tape will be separate from the tape itself.

In recent years methods of using exchangeable magnetic media have been developed, i.e. direct key-to-tape or key-to-disk systems. Though more expensive in terms of equipment, the greater compactness and the avoidance of slow speed entry to the computer via card or paper tape readers make such systems viable for commercial applications involving large amounts of data.

The forms of input discussed so far have equivalent forms of output, and again sets of instructions will be provided to handle the output and perform the necessary conversions back from machine form to human readable form. Thus a computer may output on punched cards or punched paper tape, or send output character by character to a teletypewriter or to an alphanumeric display, i.e. a cathode ray tube capable of displaying alphabetic, numeric or other textual characters. The normal kind of multi-access terminal is a keyboard together with printing or display facilities: it is thus an input–output device capable of carrying information to and from the computer. The normal output device for a computer is a **line printer**, which outputs textual information a line at a time (usually over 100 characters) rather than a single character at a time. Many line printers operate at more than 1000 lines a minute, which is more compatible with the speed and amounts of output which computers tend to generate.

Numerous other forms of input and output have been developed, particularly for special applications. One which is of importance for certain kinds of scientific work is the **incremental plotter**, a machine which enables results to be presented in the form of graphs. A human will draw a graph by holding a pen over a sheet of paper and lower the pen, raise it, or move it in different directions in either the raised or lowered position. A plotter works on the same principle of raising and lowering a pen, though commonly the required movements are produced by a combination of moving the paper backwards and forwards on rollers, and moving the pen laterally in an orthogonal direction. All the movements of pen and paper are controlled by computer output: since this is digital the instructions are discrete rather than continuous (hence 'incremental') and the graph is drawn as a sequence of short straight lines; but usually the step length is so small (less than a millimetre) that the lines look smooth to the unaided eye. The value of such a device where the result of a computation is best expressed in graphical form is obvious.

A cathode ray tube can be adapted to present graphical results, the screen being divided into a grid for this purpose. As with television pictures, the resolution depends on the size of the grid and the size of the screen: a 1024 × 1024 grid on a 17-inch screen is acceptable to most eyes. Graphical displays usually have an associated form of input, either a moving spot on the screen which can be controlled from the keyboard, or a **light pen** which the user can physically pick up and point with to the desired place. In either case the coordinates of the grid point (the nearest in the case of the light pen) are transmitted to the computer for analysis and use.

Among other forms of input are devices to detect marks on cards or paper forms, to recognise characters printed in magnetic ink or, optically, printed in ordinary ink; many readers will be familiar with the oddly shaped but still human-readable characters printed in magnetic ink at the bottom of cheques. Other developments are still in their infancy, such as speech recognition for input and speech synthesis for output. One important form of input and output, which we shall discuss later, is where measuring instruments can submit information (as digital approximations) to a computer system, and the computer system can return signals which control various kinds of apparatus. For the time being we shall assume that input and output can be arranged in any desired form, and look in more detail at how the computer can be instructed to perform the desired calculations on the input data.

Chapter 3

The Computer as a Problem Solver

In the first two chapters we explained briefly what a computer is in principle, and some of the ways in which these principles are embodied in actual machines. We now turn to the main purpose of the book, which is to describe how computers are used.

The essence of using a computer is to ensure that the problem which it is required to solve is in a form such that the computer can automatically correctly compute the desired result. That is, the computer must be presented with a set of instructions which will, when obeyed, produce the correct output. Such a set of instructions is called a **program**, and the human activity of devising the instructions is called **programming.** The American (and original English) spelling of 'program' is customary, and convenient when one wants to distinguish between, say, a research programme, and a computer program which is used in the research programme.

The designing and writing of computer programs can vary considerably in difficulty, depending on several factors, e.g. the complexity of the problem, the design of the computer, the help from the computer manufacturer, and so on. A major proportion of the cost of a computer system lies not in the physical machines themselves (called the **hardware**) but in the cost of producing the programs (the **software**). This has become much more marked over the years, as the production costs of hardware have dropped while on the other hand the labour costs of software have increased: and whereas at one time a computer manufacturer would give away a great deal of software to anyone who bought their machine, now it is much more common to buy software items separately from hardware, whether from the manufacturer or from independent firms called **software houses** specialising in program writing.

When presented with a problem, a computer programmer should not expect to be able to sit down at once and start writing a program to solve it, still less to produce a program correct in every respect at the first attempt. Writing other than the most trivial of programs involves several stages of development.

First, he must understand the problem, making sure that both the problem and the nature of the solution is clearly defined. Although this appears to be common sense, failures at this initial stage are frequent, and can often lead to difficulties later when the program has gone into use. The recommended procedure to adopt, especially if the problem is a complex one difficult to grasp in its entirety, is to try to divide it into a set of tasks, which though interdependent can be considered separately; then to divide each task into subtasks in the same way; and to repeat this process until the subtasks become of manageable proportions. Experience has shown that this helps to get the various difficulties into perspective, leads to better understanding of the problem, makes it easier to develop the program and to isolate errors, and will eventually produce a better program which will be easier to modify should changed circumstances require it.

Secondly, the programmer has to determine if an algorithm exists to solve the problem (or each subtask, if he has subdivided the problem). **Algorithm** is a term used to denote a finite set of rules, specified in advance, which will after a finite number of steps produce a solution to the problem to which it is applied; we shall come across a number of examples of algorithms in this and succeeding chapters. Often the programmer will work with other people, they providing the algorithm and he providing the computing skills: he does not have to understand the theory behind the algorithm.

At the third stage he starts the actual task of programming, translating the algorithm into a set of instructions which will be accepted by the computer. He then reaches stage four, trying out the program with sets of carefully chosen test data until it is working correctly. The more complex the problem the more difficult it will be to both get the algorithm right and to write correctly the program which represents it. A large amount of time can be spent on this stage, often caused by inadequate care in the design of the algorithm. This is where breaking a big problem up into a number of subtasks can be helpful, because it is then often possible to test the various sections of program separately. Another point to note is that to some extent the picture we have given is oversimple, since the algorithm can be affected by the available instructions and facilities of the particular computer that is to be used, causing interaction between the third and fourth stages. We are here mainly concerned with stage three, and we shall illustrate various aspects of programming by taking some simple, common problems which arise in scientific applications, and show how the algorithms for solving them are translated into computer terms.

3.1 A Simple Problem

Our first example will be the solution of a system of simultaneous linear equations, a problem which arises in many areas. For our purposes it is sufficient to take the simplest case of two equations in two unknowns, e.g.

$$ax + by = c$$
$$dx + ey = f$$

are to be solved for x and y. An algebraic solution runs as follows: eliminate x by multiplying the first equation by d and the second by a:

$$dax + dby = dc$$
$$adx + aey = af$$

and then subtract:

$$dby - aey = dc - af$$

giving:

$$y = (dc - af)/(db - ae),$$

which, when substituted into the first equation gives:

$$ax + b(dc - af)/(db - ae) = c$$

which can be rewritten as:

$$x = (bf - ec)/(db - ae)$$

thus giving the necessary solutions for x and y.

At this stage we can see that there are two distinct possible algorithms for the solution of this problem: (1) follow through the process used above of eliminating the first variable, solving for the second and then substituting back into one equation to find the first variable, or (2) apply the above derived formulae directly. Solution (2) is simpler and we shall follow it (note that the programmer does not have to know how these formulae were obtained), though (1) is more general since the process of successive elimination of variables and then substituting back can be applied to any number of equations, not just to two.

We see that applying the derived formulae involves the calculation of three quantities – the two numerators and the denominator, which is the same in each expression. Hence we can rewrite the solution as:

Calculate $r = db - ae$
Calculate $x = (bf - ec)/r$
Calculate $y = (dc - af)/r.$

This is now broken into more detail and takes us quite close to the actual operations of the computer:

Multiply a and e and call the result t
Multiply d and b
Subtract t and call the result r
Multiply e and c and call the result t
Multiply b and f
Subtract t
Divide by r and call the result x
Multiply a and f and call the result t
Multiply d and c

Subtract t

Divide by r and call the result y.

Note the repeated use of t for the storage of intermediate computations. After its first value (ae) is subtracted from db it is no longer required and so can be re-used in later parts of the calculation. This kind of technique is very common in computer programming and saves using an unnecessary amount of store.

Finally, using the last form of the solution we can write out every step the computer is to take in the calculation, using alphabetic mnemonics for the function codes as in the previous chapter, and also using names instead of numerical addresses:

LD	A	(A = address of location in store containing the value a)
MUL	E	(MUL = multiply)
ST	T	(store result since accumulator needed for another calculation)
LD	D	
MUL	B	(db in accumulator)
SUB	T	($db - ae$ in accumulator)
ST	R	
LD	E	
MUL	C	
ST	T	(re-use T to keep ec)
LD	B	
MUL	F	
SUB	T	($fb - ae$ in accumulator)
DIV	R	(DIV = divide)
ST	X	
LD	A	
MUL	F	
ST	T	(re-use T to keep af)
LD	D	
MUL	C	
SUB	T	($dc - af$ in accumulator)
DIV	R	
ST	Y	

For the solution of this very simple problem we have already used 23 steps, although we have ignored the fact, mentioned in the last chapter, that multiplication and division usually use an auxiliary register as well as the accumulator, and we have not covered the tasks of input of the values of a, b, c, d, e and f, or the output of the values of x and y which have been calculated. Even if this can be done, the mnemonics for function codes and addresses have to be replaced by actual codes and numerical addresses, and the whole program has to be entered into the computer to be run. It should be clear by now that if the programmer is forced to do all this himself then programming even quite simple algorithms can be a lengthy, often tedious, and frequently error-prone process. Mis-copying a function code or address, omitting one instruction, losing track of the purpose of the computation in a mass of detail, are all too easy when sheet after sheet of paper is being covered by instructions. Over the years various techniques have evolved to minimise these problems and we shall be introducing some of them in this chapter.

3.2 Algorithms and Flow Diagrams

The first aid to the programmer that we shall consider is a diagrammatic method of representing an algorithm; some examples are given in Figs 3.1–3.3 and in Chapter 4. Most (though not all) programmers find that it helps them to keep in mind the overall structure of the algorithm, and hence the program, if they represent it in **flow diagram** form. A flow diagram (also called a **flow-chart**) consists of a set of differently shaped boxes, each step of the algorithm being written in a box, the different shapes indicating different types of activity. For example, a parallelogram is used for input/output, a rectangle for normal processes such as arithmetic operations, a diamond for decisions. These boxes are joined by connecting lines, and the reader charts a path along the lines (usually from top to bottom of the page), picking the appropriate exit from a decision diamond.

Flow diagrams can be used to represent the algorithmic solution of a problem at any of the levels of detail to which it is analysed. A programmer often draws several flow diagrams, of increasing detail, during the design of his algorithm. Each box of the most detailed flow diagram is then translated into a set of instructions. A well-documented program, i.e. one provided with a complete description of its purpose and functioning so that anyone with a minimum of computer knowledge can understand and use it, will often come with a series of flow diagrams showing the operation of the program, and the algorithm it represents, at varying levels of detail.

One useful feature of flow diagrams is their ability to show clearly the various decisions or branches in the program structure, and depending on the conditions, the different courses of action which will be taken. The flow diagram for our simultaneous equations problem is simple but it ignores the possibility of r being zero. In this case the problem cannot be solved, since either the two equations are inconsistent or one is a multiple of the other and they are the same equation, making it impossible to determine x and y. Without modification the program would 'crash' in this case when asked to divide by zero, something which computers find no easier than human beings.

It is a basic principle of good program writing that the algorithm should work for any set of data. This is not the same as requiring that it should always produce a solution, since a solution may not always exist, but the program should guard against errors by testing and take appropriate action, e.g. by outputting a warning message. In our example we should check if the value of r is zero as soon as it has been computed; if it is, we should output an appropriate message, such as 'DENOMINATOR ZERO', and then jump to the end of the program.

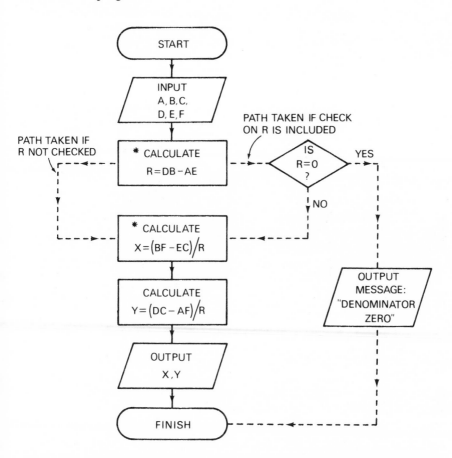

Fig. 3.1. Flow diagram for solution of two simultaneous equations. Two alternative paths are shown for the routes between the two asterisked boxes. The direct path, on the left, omits the check on the value of R, and the next calculation will fail if R is zero. The path on the right enables a check to be made on R and the calculation continues only if the division by R is possible. Note the different shapes of boxes for different kinds of activity.

There may be several alternative algorithms for the solution of a single problem, and the one most suitable for human use may not be the one most suitable for a computer. In Chapter 1 we gave the familiar rule for extracting the square root of a decimal number. While this could be programmed for a computer, it would not be particularly efficient. Since most computers work in binary rather than decimal notation there is no easy correspondence between the decimal digits and the groups of binary digits. Also, many computers, especially those designed for numerical scientific work, are not well equipped for the digit-by-digit manipulation on which this rule depends. The alternative algorithm (Fig. 3.2) is much more suitable; the repetitive nature of the computation, considerably more than in the first solution, is tedious for

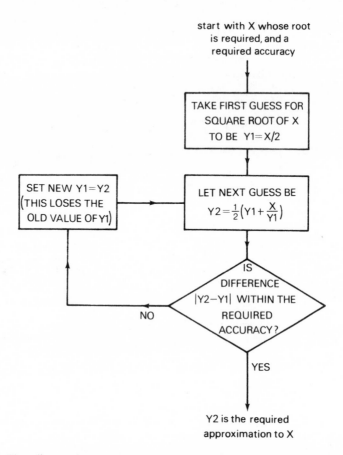

Fig. 3.2. Flow diagram for calculating a square root. The calculation depends on the fact that if Y1 is too small an approximation to X, X/Y1 will be too large (or vice versa), and Y2, which is their mean, will be a closer approximation than either. The loop will be repeated as many times as necessary to reach the required accuracy, e.g. if X is 36, successive calculations to 3 significant figures will give Y1 = 18·0, 10·0, 6·80, 6·05, 6·00 giving a final Y2 = 6·00. This flow diagram would form a part of a complete flow diagram for a bigger calculation.

humans but is easy to program for computers and is quickly executed by them. Incidentally, it is much easier to see from the algorithm why it produces the result.

A programmer should not necessarily work from the first algorithm which occurs to him. As mentioned before, it is often worthwhile putting in more thought on the algorithm to see if improvements or better alternatives can be found. One can be lucky, and the standard algorithm is obviously 'right'. Much depends in programming on individual judgement and style, which is why it is often called an art as well as a science.

3.3 Assemblers

We now turn to the practical considerations of getting a program, together with any accompanying data, into a computer and getting the answers out. The essence is to be able to produce the bit patterns representing the program instructions and the data into the words of memory. If we consider our hypothetical 24-bit word computer, we could punch the bit patterns for each word in three 8-bit positions on a paper tape or two 12-bit columns on a punched card, and similarly obtain the bit patterns for the computer words representing the answers as the 'output' action of the program. However, this is impractical for humans; even if each possible 8-bit pattern is interpreted as a separate written character, a 24-bit word would be output as three characters: whereas if it represented an integer, a user would prefer it to be output as a $+$ or $-$ sign followed by up to eight digit characters.

A programmer who wants to make his output easily readable by humans will need, once he has reached the stage in the program where he has the computed answers in binary form, some further program instructions which will take these binary answers and convert (or encode) them into bit patterns which will enable the output characters, whether punched on tape or cards, printed on a lineprinter, etc. to appear in easily readable form. For example, if the contents of a location are 00 . . . . 0010111 in binary ($= 23$ in decimal) and the user wants to output these as an integer on a tape punch, then his instructions must produce the 8-bit patterns in paper tape code for the decimal characters '2' and '3' in that order. By means of suitable program instructions at the input-of-data stage, the input can also be represented in human-readable character form and then decoded, so that, for example, a sequence of decimal digit characters is converted into the bit pattern representing the corresponding integer. Fig. 3.3 gives a flow diagram for inputting a signed integer in decimal and translating it into the binary form needed for arithmetic inside the computer.

This task of converting data from human form to computer form and back again could place a massive additional burden on the programmer. However this kind of decoding and encoding will occur in almost all programs and after the necessary sequence of instructions has been worked out by one programmer, then they can be taken and used by any other programmer. Thus, as we said in Chapter 2, the manufacturer of a modern computer system will normally supply a library of sets of standard instructions as part of the software. These sets of instructions are known as **subprograms** or **subroutines.** They are so written that users can incorporate them into their own programs, and among them will be subroutines for the input and output of data. The subroutine concept can be carried much further, and we shall return to it soon.

We have considered the problem of input and output of data from a program

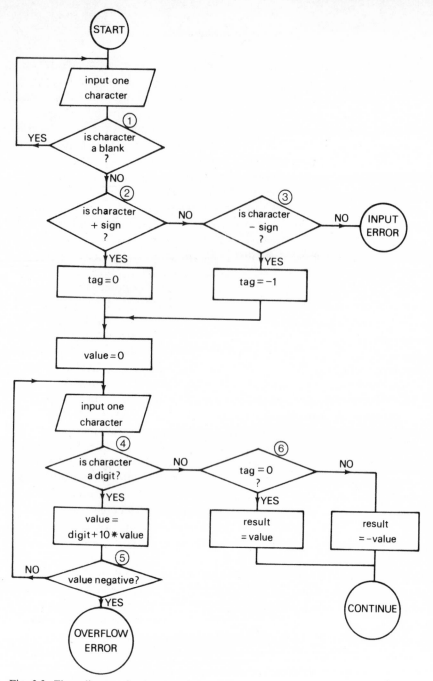

Fig. 3.3. Flow diagram for input and conversion of signed decimal integer. Note the various tests, numbered in the diagram: (1) allows for leading blanks before the sign; (2) tests for positive sign; if the first non-blank character is not a + sign (3) tests for − sign and gives an error if it is not; (4) tests that the next character is a digit and takes a non-digit character as terminating the number; (5) tests that the accumulated value in the binary twos-complement notation is not apparently negative, but shows an overflow error if it is; (6) tests the 'tag' which records whether the original sign was + or − and produces the result accordingly. Note that not every possibility is covered, in that a sign followed by a non-digit character will give a zero result rather than an input error. The reader may like to modify the diagram to allow for this possibility.

while it is running but there still remains the question of how to get the program into the machine to start with. By extending the solution for the input and output of data it should be possible to write a program which will take in instructions in coded form, and convert them into bit-patterns in the form required for instructions inside the computer. The coded program text itself becomes the input data for another program which performs the translation into internal machine instructions. This program, like the subroutines for input and output, has only to be written once by a skilled programmer: afterwards, all other programs can be written in coded form for translation by it into machine form. Such a program is called an **assembler** and the internal instructions are called **machine code.** A computer manufacturer normally supplies assemblers with the machine, together with a specification of the form of coding to be used for the instructions.

In the simplest case, such coding will take the form of direct decimal equivalents to the various parts of the instruction words: one for the function code, one for the address part, and so on. Translation by the assembler will then merely involve the conversion of the decimal numbers into binary and then putting together ('assembling') the required instruction words. Translation is nearly as easy if simple mnemonics, using letters as well as digits, are used for the function codes rather than decimal codes whose functional equivalents have to be memorised. The earlier examples of pieces of program are of this form, and with a suitable assembler such instructions could be directly loaded into a computer store.

Further facilities are included in assemblers to make programming even easier. In some examples we have given the actual machine addresses for instructions and data. It is normal for assemblers to accept alphanumeric identifiers instead of numerical addresses. An identifier is used to label a specific instruction or item of data. When the assembler reads a labelled instruction it associates with the label the address of the location in which it is storing the instruction and keeps a record of the label and address; it uses a similar technique for data. When the label is encountered as an address part of an instruction, the assembler replaces the label by its associated actual address. One advantage of using identifiers instead of actual addresses is that the instructions are now independent of where in store the program has been loaded.

A coding notation such as this, in which the programmer can write his instructions, is called a **language.** There are many different languages, offering different facilities. The sort that we are looking at now, where each instruction that the programmer writes is translated into a single instruction in machine code, is called an **assembly language.** An assembly language often has more facilities than mnemonics and labels and, to show some of these features, we give below part of a program in our hypothetical language for the input of signed integers from a tape reader. The flow diagram for this example is given in Fig. 3.3.

	. . . .		(previous instructions)
	. . . .		
FIND	INCH	PTR	(input one character from the paper tape reader)
	ATOR		(copy contents of accumulator into index register)
	LD:M	DICT	(pick up code from dictionary – see below)
	ADD:L	1	(:L directs the assembler to interpret the address part of the instruction as literally the value shown, i.e. here we are adding +1 to the accumulator. The result will be zero if the character was blank, i.e. its code was −1)
	JZ	FIND	(go back to read another character to find sign)
	NADD:L	11	(negate accumulator, then add 11, giving zero if + sign, −1 if − sign, positive for anything else)
	JP	ERR	(jump if positive, as first non-blank is not + or −)
	ST	TAG	(the 0 or −1 in the accumulator sets the tag)
	LD:L	0	(zero in accumulator)
	ST	VALUE	(initialise value to zero)
LOOP	INCH	PTR	
	ATOR		
	LD:M	DICT	(same sequence as before to pick up code)
	JN	RESULT	(negative code terminates)
	SUB:L	9	
	JP	RESULT	(codes 10 or 11 – another sign – also terminates)
	ADD:L	9	(restore to original code, now certainly digit)
	ST	DIGIT	
	LD	VALUE	
	MUL:L	10	(multiply previous value by 10)
	ADD	DIGIT	(new value)
	JN	OVER	(jump if negative, since overflow occurred)
	ST	VALUE	
	J	LOOP	(jump back for next character)
RESULT	LD	TAG	
	JZ	MORE	(sign was positive so VALUE correct)
	NEGS	VALUE	(negates the contents of VALUE)
MORE	. . . .		(calculation continues with required integer in location VALUE)
	. . . .		

Various labels are used in this example, including meaningful identifiers for instructions in the program (FIND, LOOP, RESULT, MORE) and for data items (TAG, VALUE, DIGIT). Somewhere in the complete program the data item labels will have to be 'declared', i.e. space reserved in the store for holding these items. The positions of some labelled instructions appear in the example, but ERR and OVER are assumed to appear elsewhere, in sections of the program dealing with error conditions. The label PTR in the INCH instructions is a label corresponding to a 'pseudo-address', referring not to that address in the store but instead being a code identifying a paper tape reader as the source of input.

Of critical importance is the label DICT, which points to the beginning of a list of codes, which will also have to appear somewhere in the complete program. The modified instruction

LD:M   DICT

adds the numerical value (say i) of the 8-bit pattern of the character just read from the paper tape reader and copied into the index register, to the actual address corresponding to DICT, thus picking out the ith item in the list following DICT. This item contains the code corresponding to that character. The program works on the basis that each digit character 0 to 9 has its own value as its code, blank is coded as -1, a $+$ sign as $+10$ and a $-$ sign as $+11$. All other characters have negative codes. This method of coding is chosen to simplify various tests, though others are possible and the reader may like to try to devise others, remembering that what is obvious is sometimes best, but not always.

Note in the above example the use of **literals**, arithmetic constants expressed in decimal notation. The assembler interprets these as implied declarations of items of data of the required form. Data declared explicitly, or implicitly such as by the use of literals, may also be of non-arithmetic forms, e.g. coded textual characters or actual bit patterns.

Usually an assembly language program will also have instructions, or **directives**, to the assembler. These will not directly generate machine code instructions, but instead provide information to the assembler about action to be taken during the assembly of that program. A typical example is a directive to output a list of identifiers that have been declared in the program.

So far we have considered a situation in which each assembly language instruction translates into one machine instruction in the assembled program; or none at all in the case of directives. The designer of an assembler can also provide assembly language instructions which correspond to more than one machine code instruction. This is an important point because, as we have seen, the step-by-step coding of even a quite simple calculation is a lengthy business. Writing in an assembly language rather than machine language may make the program easier to understand and may reduce the chance of errors, but it does not shorten the text: with directives it may even lengthen it. More sophisticated assemblers contain **macro** facilities. The use of a macro, which appears in the assembly language to be a single instruction, generates a set of machine instructions. Some standard macros will be provided, but the assembly language programmer will be able to invent, define, and use others for himself. For instance, he may define the macro SWAP which interchanges the contents of two locations specified when the macro is used in the program. A typical use, or call, would be

SWAP X,Y

which would generate the set of instructions

LD   X
LDR   Y
ST   Y
STR   X   (loading and storing the index register do
                not affect the accumulator).

This can be used to swap the contents of any two locations by using the identifiers for the locations in the call of the macro.

A more important method of reducing the amount of program text is by the use of subroutines, or procedures as they are also called. The process of reading in a numerical item of input data in decimal form and decoding it will take a large number of machine instructions – let us suppose 100. To write out this set each time a number is to be read in would be tedious, as the input of ten numbers would take 1000 instructions. The use of a standard macro for input would reduce the number of assembly language instructions to 10 *but* the generated program would still use 1000 machine code instructions. The programmer could easily run out of available store if the problem involved a great deal of input data.

No sensible programmer would want to do this; instead he would write the input instructions only once (by macro or not) and then jump to these whenever he wanted to input a number in his program. Such jumps might take place from various points in his program for different input items. There is a snag to this: after the input has taken place the programmer will want to return to the main part of his program, but to different places in it at different times, depending on where the jump was made from on each occasion.

Hence a method is needed to decide which part of the main program to return to, i.e. a *link* must be created before the input instructions are entered (it cannot be done after the jump is made, as by then it is too late and the necessary information is lost) and then used when the input is complete to return to the right place. A set of instructions that can be called from different places in a program and, after being obeyed, automatically causes a return to the point of call, is called a **subroutine** or **procedure.** This technique, invented early in the history of stored-program computers (it is attributed to Stanley

Gill, one of the Cambridge EDSAC team), is so valuable that computers normally have special instructions and/or hardware to make its use easy and efficient. Subroutines can be organised so that other information as well as the link can be transferred between the subroutine and the main program in either direction: for example, in the case of the input subroutine we have been discussing, the programmer could specify to the subroutine at each call, the address of a location in the store where the particular number to be input at this call is to be placed.

The concept of subroutines is so important and fundamental that we have had to spend some time explaining it, but the details of how they are implemented must be left to more specialised books. As far as the users of computers are concerned, subroutine facilities are normally available whatever computer language they are using, both standard subroutines provided as part of or in combination with the language, and means for the programmer to specify further ones for his own particular needs.

3.4   Concept of High-Level Languages

Even the maximum use of macros and subroutines is not sufficient to make assembly language programming a really simple matter: an assembly language program still tends to be lengthy and prone to errors, and to be restricted to a particular computer. In the 1950s, as computers became more widely used, more sophisticated programming languages became necessary, and much of the subsequent history of the use of computers is concerned with the development and exploitation of these languages. The key was to break away from the limitation that an instruction in the language should have a simple relationship to the corresponding machine code instructions. The principal aims in designing languages have been to make them easier to use and understand, to give them more powerful facilities, and to make them less dependent upon any particular computer: though these aims are not altogether compatible. Such languages are called **high-level languages** in contrast to assembly languages and machine code (called **low-level languages**), where the direct connection between language instructions and machine instructions has not been broken.

We shall indicate some of the properties of high-level languages by programming two of the earlier examples in this chapter in one of the earlier major high-level languages, ALGOL 60. This is still in considerable use and has been influential in the design of later languages. A complete ALGOL 60 program for the simultaneous equations problem follows below:

```
begin
    real a, b, c, d, e, f, x, y, r;
    input (a, b, c, d, e, f);
    r: = d*b − a*e;
```

> if $r = 0$ then goto *unsolvable;*
> $x: = (b*f - e*c)/r; y: = (d*c - a*f)/r;$
> *output* $(x, y);$ **goto** *finish;*
> *unsolvable: output* ('denominator zero');
> *finish:* **end**

This shows many of the features of the language, even to someone who has never seen ALGOL 60 before.

line 1 (and elsewhere): the language contains several basic words, printed in heavy type to distinguish them from the names the programmer has invented himself

line 2: the reservation or declaration of space in store for data and work space, labelled by the programmer

line 3: the use of a standard input procedure

lines 4 & 6: the ability to calculate complicated arithmetic expressions and to assign the result to a variable in a single instruction

line 5: testing a condition and a jump (**goto**) to a warning message if the condition $r = 0$ is satisfied

lines 8 & 9: labelling of instructions

lines 7 & 8: use of a standard output instruction which can output both numbers and characters (text).

One warning about ALGOL 60 is essential: the language does not include standard input and output instructions, which the language designers left to those who were to implement facilities for using the language on each machine. The reader is therefore likely to come across ALGOL 60 examples elsewhere whose input and output instructions look quite different.

The second example is of a procedure (the standard name for subroutines in ALGOL 60), to calculate the square root using the flow diagram in Fig. 3.2 to within 0·00001.

> **real procedure** *root*(x); **value** x; **real** x;
> **begin real** *y1, y2;*
>   **if** $x < 0$ **then goto** *error;*
> $y1: = x/2;$
> *loop:* $y2: = (y1 + x/y1)/2;$
>   **if** $abs(y1 - y2) < 0·00001$ **then goto** *result;*
> $y1: = y2;$ **goto** *loop;*
> *result: root:* $= y2$
> **end**;

In the first line, *root* is the name of the procedure. When the procedure is used it will need to be provided with the value of a real variable, since this value cannot be known in advance it is called x in the definition of the procedure. When the procedure is used or 'called' in a program, x will be replaced by the actual value of the variable at the point of call. **real** in the first line indicates that the procedure will supply to the program a real value which can then be used in arithmetic expressions. The setting of links between the program and the procedure is done automatically and the programmer does not have to worry about it. A typical call of the procedure would be

$$z: = 1 + root(2*b)$$

(If the value of b was 2 then z would be given the value 3.) Note that the test against taking square roots of negative numbers is included in the procedure rather than in the program.

We do not expect the reader to understand every part of these two examples, but they should be sufficient to give some indication of the power of high-level languages, both in conciseness and readability. There is a price to be paid. Translating a program from its original high-level language form (or **source code**) to its final machine language form (or **object code**) is far from simple, and the verb 'assemble' with its connotations of mere slotting together of ready-made components, has been abandoned for the more general 'compile'. A compiler for a high-level language is a very complex program and (depending on the language) is unlikely to be able to translate the source code directly into object code. Instead it may have to 'scan' the whole program more than once before the program structure can be ascertained and the object code generated. This is often called a **multi-pass compilation**. The compiled program is unlikely to be as efficient in terms of running speed and store utilisation as one written in an assembly language: to overcome this to some extent, some compilers have extra 'passes' after the program is fully compiled to improve the efficiency of the object code.

For any particular computer there are usually compilers available for a variety of different languages, provided by the manufacturer or in some cases written by a programming team in a software house or a user installation. The majority of programs are now written in high-level languages because it is much easier to express algorithms in them than in assembly languages and because a good compiler will clearly indicate many kinds of routine error, though not logical errors due to incorrect formulation or expression of the algorithm or to incorrect analysis of the original problem. Every programmer should expect his programs to contain errors when they are first written; the compiler should detect any errors in the use of the language (**syntax errors**), but only the programmer himself (or another human who knows the problem he is trying to solve) can detect the **semantic errors**. Semantic errors are errors in *meaning*, where the program does not do what was intended, either through mistakes in individual instructions or because of an incorrect logical structure. As with assembly language programs, such errors have to be found and eliminated by running the program with several (sometimes many) sets of test data, carefully chosen so that all parts of the program will be fully tested. A well-designed program will be written so that such testing is facilitated. Some compilers are partially corrective, i.e. they not only identify syntax errors in a user's program, but also try to work out what the user probably meant, and correct the program on that assumption during compilation. This can be helpful, but can also introduce further semantic errors, since no computer is a mind-reader; and no corrective compiler will correct semantic errors the programmer himself introduced. Programmers are advised not to lean too heavily on such facilities.

The other main advantage of common high-level languages is that they are nearly machine independent, allowing exchange of programs and subroutines between users of completely different machines. We say 'nearly' because compiler writers sometimes add extra ideas of their own to the language, taking advantage of specific features of their particular computer. This has led to the growth of 'dialects' of languages, and any use of non-standard features can create problems in moving programs to different machines. An extreme example is the case of ALGOL 60 where, as mentioned earlier, input-output is not standardised. For this reason alone, almost every machine with an ALGOL 60 compiler has its own dialect. Despite all this, high-level language programs are still relatively easy to transfer from machine to machine, and published algorithms are often expressed in them rather than, say, in flow diagram form.

3.5 Brief Survey of High-Level Languages

The earliest successful high-level language was FORTRAN (short for FORmula TRANslator), developed by IBM in the mid-1950s for ease of expression of scientific formulae. Since then it has undergone a number of revisions which have extended its scope and power, and it is still the most widely used scientific language. The other main scientific language, ALGOL 60 (ALGOrithmic Language) was designed by a working party of IFIP – International Federation for Information Processing – around 1960. As mentioned before it has been very influential upon the subsequent design of languages and is still in considerable use, more in Europe than the United States.

One factor in the continued success of FORTRAN has been that, unlike ALGOL, it does have standard specifications for input and output, making FORTRAN programs more easily transportable between machines. Another factor has been that, while ALGOL is on the whole a much more flexible and readable language, imposing far fewer restrictions on the programmer than FORTRAN, there is a penalty to pay in that the resulting object code tends to be less efficient, an important factor in some applications. Certain special features also make FORTRAN more attractive for some kinds of scientific work, such as the existence of built-in complex number arithmetic.

Both ALGOL and FORTRAN were designed for programmers with scientific problems, and as computers became more widely used outside this area the need arose for different types of languages. The most successful of these has been COBOL (COmmon Business Oriented Language), designed as its name implies for commercial applications such as payroll and tax calculations, etc. COBOL, like FORTRAN, has been extended and revised several times since it emerged about 1960. (It is often difficult to determine exactly when a language came into being.) Most computer installations are for commercial work and COBOL is at present the world's most-used programming language. It is a good example to show that high-level languages need not be concise: COBOL programs tend to be rather 'wordy' since the language has an English-like syntax.

Attempts have been made to devise general-purpose languages which are suitable for both scientific and commercial work (the distinction between the two areas is not always clear). The first major attempt was PL/I (Programming Language I), produced by IBM in the mid-1960s and incorporating many features from ALGOL, COBOL and FORTRAN. The authors have a personal preference for ALGOL 68, which is a later IFIP product dating from 1968 though revised in 1974. It is not an extension of the earlier language but a new language based on the same design principles, including many more powerful and wider-ranging facilities, and eliminating the deficiencies of ALGOL 60.

Programs in all of these languages are normally processed in the conventional 'compile, link-edit, run' variety that we have been describing: the program is first translated, or compiled, into machine form; then if necessary 'link-edited' to add standard, already translated subprograms; and then actually obeyed. Other languages have been devised to deal with different needs. For example the multi-access use of computers, mentioned before as being of increasing importance, has led to the development of special languages for **interactive** work, where the programmer directly types his instructions into the computer and the compile and run stages are closely interwoven. The best known such languages are BASIC and APL. BASIC (Beginners All-purpose Symbolic Instruction Code) is a very simple high-level language and is often considered to be a good, easy first language to learn. APL (A Programming Language) is capable of very succinct and powerful expression of algorithms using only a few symbols. It achieves this partly by using a much wider range of symbols than other languages (it started as a mathematical notation rather than a programming language), and so has the disadvantages of ideally needing a special keyboard device and of being virtually unreadable to the uninitiated. Nevertheless in an interactive situation there is an advantage in being able to express a complicated algorithm rapidly by typing only a few characters, and the language has an enthusiastic, if still relatively small, following.

Other computer uses which are becoming increasingly important and are not well suited to conventional languages are the direct control of processes, for instance traffic flow, laboratory experiments, or industrial activities. In these situations it is important for results to be produced at the correct time, or within given time limits. For such **real-time** applications some special languages have been developed, e.g. CORAL 66, though the bulk of real-time programs are still written in machine or assembly languages. We shall return to these applications in Chapter 6.

There are at present over 200 high-level languages in use and the number is growing each year. We have deliberately not made any attempt to give a comprehensive list, or to teach a particular language, or to examine any of them very critically. All of these areas are covered by more specialist books, a selection being given in the reading list at the end of this book.

Languages have their own characteristics, and each has usually been designed for specific purposes. A programmer must therefore decide which language is most suitable for his particular problem, and hence should know a variety of languages, not merely one. A word of warning – a programmer should make sure that the languages he knows, he knows well, rather than a smattering of many. Otherwise, he will not be able to program in any language efficiently, and the point of knowing more than one language will be lost.

Whether or not any language ever will be truly universal, the one fundamental problem, the discovery and detailed specification of the algorithm to be programmed, will always remain. It is here rather than in the details of design of computing or programming languages that the understanding of the art of using computers lies. It is to this that we now turn.

Chapter 4

The Computer as a Number-cruncher

In Chapter 1 we mentioned that Babbage called the part of his Analytical Engine which actually performed the numerical computations the 'mill'. **Number-crunching** is an expressive term with similar connotations, a piece of computer jargon which neatly describes one very common use of computers. Briefly, number-crunching is the kind of computing where the principal activity is a very great deal of numerical computation, though not necessarily involving large amounts of data. The prime requirements of a computer used for number-crunching are the fastest possible central processor and the capacity for accurate performance of arithmetic operations on floating point numbers (see Chapter 2) to a large number of significant figures. A typical example of a number-cruncher – a computer specifically designed for this kind of work – is the Control Data Corporation's 7600 which has a 60-bit word length, 12 bits for the exponent part and 48 for the fractional part of a floating point number, and is capable of performing about 4 million floating point multiplications per second (by hardware, not software). The same company's Star 100 computer, due to come into service in the second half of the 1970s, is designed to perform 80 to 100 million multiplications per second.

The examples of number-crunching we shall be giving in this Chapter will be simple, not involving a great deal of data, but sufficient to impart the flavour of this kind of computing. For many readers, this chapter is the central core of our book, since most scientific computing is number-crunching in some form.

4.1 Iteration and Errors

We have already met one number-crunching example, the square-root calculation in Chapter 3. This is so simple that many computer people would not regard it as number-crunching at all, but it exhibits some of the features on a small scale. It involves a good deal of computation, certainly in relation to the amount of initial data which is a single number. This quantity of calculation is achieved by means of an **iterative process**, which consists of a loop, i.e. a sequence of instructions repeatedly obeyed until the desired result is achieved.

The idea of iteration is central to many algorithms for numerical computation, and we shall see it many times. Iterative algorithms are particularly suitable for computers because the reduction of a process to repeating a sequence of simple steps decreases the chance of error in devising or in programming the algorithm, reduces the amount of coding, and occupies less space in store. This last factor is important when a lengthy program and a large amount of data have to fit into store.

There are essentially two different kinds of iterative processes, those which are finite and those which are not. A finite iteration will be terminated, either by counting the number of times the process has been performed and stopping when the count reaches a specified number, or because the algorithm guarantees that the process will stop. For example one can determine whether an integer n is prime by trying to divide by all integers starting from 2 and terminating either when a factor is found or $\sqrt{n}$ is reached, in which case n is prime. (This is an inefficient algorithm and the reader should be able to see some ways of improving it.)

Most iterative processes are not inherently finite and should not be terminated by counting. A potentially infinite iteration must instead be terminated by applying some criterion of the form 'we have not reached the exact answer but the approximation we have reached is close enough'. The square root algorithm (Fig. 3.2) is an example of this: the square root of most numbers cannot be calculated exactly, so the algorithm was terminated if the difference between two successive approximations was sufficiently small. In this case the algorithm is such that after each iteration the new approximation will be nearer to the true answer than the previous one, and also such that the difference between two successive approximations will be greater than the difference between the approximation and the true value. We shall see that this is not true of algorithms. Many are not as simple as this, nor is there any general criterion which will work for all algorithms. The construction of algorithms, and their analysis to determine whether and what extent they can be guaranteed to arrive at a 'nearly enough' correct answer, forms a large branch of mathematics called **numerical analysis.**

An iterative process generates a sequence (usually infinite) of successive approximations, and the **convergence** of such sequences has been studied by mathematicians for several centuries. The reader has probably met the idea of the convergence of a sequence when studying infinite series. A series $\sum_{r=1}^{\infty} a_r$ converges if the sequence of partial sums $s_n = \sum_{r=1}^{n} a_r$ (s_n is the sum of the first n terms) converges to a limit, i.e. gets arbitrarily close to a real number for large enough n. It is not always true that the sequence arising from an iteration does converge, or that testing that the difference between two successive approximations is small will guarantee convergence. For example the infinite series

$$1 + \tfrac{1}{2} + \tfrac{1}{3} + \tfrac{1}{4} \ldots + \tfrac{1}{n} + \ldots$$

does not converge, but the difference between two successive approximations does get arbitrarily small, this difference being just a_n. After 100 terms the difference between two successive partial sums will be 0·01, after 1000 terms the difference will be 0·001 and so on, yet the partial sums become arbitrarily large.

There are other problems associated with iterations, but first we must describe some of the kinds of error that can arise in numerical computing. By 'error' we do not mean that the computer adds 1 and 1 and gives 3 as the answer, but errors inherent in the processes that are being used. There are two main types, **rounding errors** and **truncation errors**.

Rounding errors are errors due to the approximate nature of floating point arithmetic. Real numbers cannot be stored exactly, but only approximately to a certain number of significant figures, and the rounding error is this error in representation. Every time operations are performed on these approximations the answer will also be an approximation to the true answer. For example if reals are stored to 4 significant decimal figures then $1/3 \cong 0\cdot3333$ has a rounding error of 3×10^{-5} (0·01%) and $1/4 = 0\cdot2500$ is exact. The difference $1/3 - 1/4 \cong 0\cdot0833 = 0\cdot8330 \times 10^{-1}$ in floating point is correct to only 3 significant figures. A programmer should try to write his computations in forms which will minimise the effect of rounding errors, for example by avoiding differencing two almost equal numbers. To give one instance,

$$\frac{1}{n} - \frac{1}{n+1} \quad \text{should be rewritten as} \quad \frac{1}{n(n+1)},$$

and the reader is invited to recalculate $\tfrac{1}{3} - \tfrac{1}{4}$ by this method in floating point decimal.

During a long computation, rounding errors can accumulate to become large in total even though each individual error is quite small. This can be illustrated by calculating cos 0·7 not directly but recursively by using the formula

$$\cos(n+1)x + \cos(n-1)x = 2\cos x \cos nx$$

By putting $C(n) = \cos nx$ this can be rewritten as

$$C(n+1) = 2\cos x\, C(n) - C(n-1).$$

$C(n+1)$ can be calculated if the values of $C(n)$ and $C(n-1)$ are both known, cos x needs only to be calculated once. If we take starting values for $C(0) = \cos 0$ and $C(1) = \cos 0\cdot1$ and use this relation to calculate cos 0·2, cos 0·3, etc. each time working to 5 significant figures, we obtain the table:

	calculated	error $\times 10^{-5}$	
C(0)	1·00000	—	starting values
C(1)	0·99500	—	
C(2)	0·98005	2	
C(3)	0·95530	4	
C(4)	0·92100	6	
C(5)	0·87749	9	
C(6)	0·82521	12	
C(7)	0·76468	16	

This shows clearly the cumulative effect of rounding error. In this case the individual errors increase not linearly but exponentially, and as early in the sequence as $C(6)$ the result is not accurate to even 4 significant figures. In most cases it is possible to minimise the effect of such errors by reorganising the computation, and a programmer should try to do this when designing his algorithm.

Truncation errors, the second major form, are errors which arise when an infinite process is replaced by a finite one, and will always occur when using non-finite iterations. For example, the series

$$1 - \tfrac{1}{2} + \tfrac{1}{3} - \tfrac{1}{4} + \tfrac{1}{5} \ldots$$

converges with sum log 2 but converges very slowly. The difference between two successive partial sums is $1/n$, so that after summing the first fifty terms the difference between two successive approximations will be 0·02. In this series the partial sums oscillate and so at best the actual value of the sum will be half-way between two successive approximations, and hence the truncation error at this stage will be at least 0·01 and could be worse. This illustrates one of the problems of iterations; even if there was no effect from rounding errors at least 5000 terms are needed in this instance simply for 4-figure accuracy. This will involve 5000 divisions, and 2500 additions and subtractions, all in floating point arithmetic, and it is extremely likely that the rounding errors from all of these will completely swamp the truncation error. The other main disadvantage of slow convergence is the long time taken to execute large numbers of iterations. Many functions are evaluated by power series (including the standard functions like 'sin', 'exp', etc.) and when an algorithm is being designed care should be taken to try to make convergence rapid. If there are several iterations in a long calculation then the truncation errors can build up the same way as rounding errors can.

There are other forms of error in addition to these important ones, but instead of discussing them in general terms we shall introduce them in the context of some of the following examples.

Study of the behaviour of errors, especially truncation errors, in numerical algorithms is an important area of numerical analysis called **error analysis.** It can be argued that error analysis is the most important area of numerical analysis, since merely quoting a numerical answer without any indication of its accuracy makes the answer worthless. Sometimes a problem is too difficult to analyse and hence the programmer does not know how reliable his results are – we shall make some general comments on this at the end of this chapter.

4.2 Roots of Equations

The need to find some or all of the roots of an equation is a common situation in scientific work. Despite its apparent simplicity this will illustrate some of the points we want to make. In some cases there may be an explicit non-iterative formula for the roots, but these are rare: for instance, there is no general formula for the zeros of a polynomial of degree greater than 4. Usually one has to use iterative methods and obtain approximate roots. A variety of methods exist, some for specific types of equations such as polynomials, some more general, some only find real roots, others find complex roots and so on. We shall consider one of the earliest methods, still commonly used, for finding the real roots of the equation

$$f(x) = 0$$

when the derivative $f'(x)$ of the function $f(x)$ can be found. This is the **Newton-Raphson** method.

The Newton-Raphson method is based on the following idea. Consider the graph of the function $y = f(x)$ (Fig. 4.1): then the roots of the equation $f(x) = 0$ will be the points where the curve cuts the x-axis. If the function is reasonably smooth and regular near these points, then over small intervals the tangent to the curve will give a close approximation to the curve. If we have an approximation to a root, then the tangent to the curve at this point will intersect the x-axis at a point which should be much closer to the actual root.

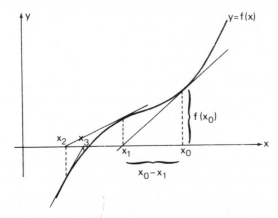

Fig. 4.1. Newton-Raphson approximation to root of equation $f(x) = 0$.

If the initial approximation is x_0 and the new approximation is x_1, then the gradient is given by

$$f'(x_0) = \frac{f(x_0)}{(x_0 - x_1)}$$

which, on rearrangement gives the formula

$$x_1 = x_0 - \frac{f(x_0)}{f'(x_0)}$$

which gives the next approximation x_1 from the initial x_0. By repeating the process one obtains a sequence x_2, x_3, ... of approximations which will approach the actual root. (The result can be proved by using either the Mean Value Theorem or the Taylor series expansion for f.)

One criterion that could be used for terminating the iterative process is that used in the square-root algorithm, namely when two successive approximations are close together. (Note that the formula for the square root is just this method applied to the equation $x^2 - a = 0$.) It can be proved that the iteration will always converge for the square-root algorithm, but in this more general case it may not always work. Before we discuss this further, the method is applied to finding the real root of $x^3 - x - 1 = 0$ using an initial value of $x = 2$. The table below gives the steps in the iteration, which converges quite quickly.

r	x_r	$f(x_r) = x_r^3 - x_r - 1$	$f'(x_r) = 3x_r^2 - 1$	$f(x_r)/f'(x_r)$
0	2	5·0	11·0	0·45
1	1·55	1·17	5·75	0·204
2	1·346	0·0926	4·44	0·0208
3	1·3252	0·00206	4·27	0·00048
4	1·32472	0·0000086	4·26	0·000002

root to 6 significant figures = 1·32472
Steps in calculation of root of $x^3 - x - 1 = 0$ using
a starting value of $x_0 = 2·0$

As with most numerical methods several things can go wrong with this method, and Fig 4.2 illustrates some of these. In (a) there is false convergence, the difference between two successive approximations being small but not near the root: if the iteration were continued then this difference would increase before converging to the true root. In (b) there is no convergence and the approximations oscillate; in (c) there is again no convergence and the approximations diverge further and further away from the root; and in (d) there is convergence but to a different root than the one wanted.

Using more or different criteria may help, but there will always be some cases where the method fails, and extra criteria will also mean testing within

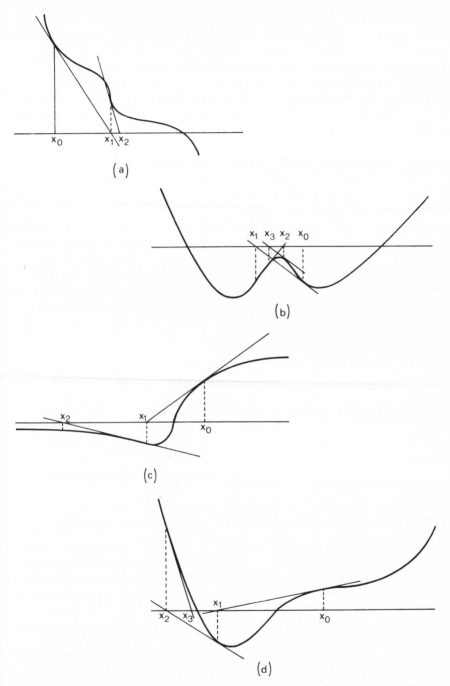

Fig. 4.2. Illustrations of various types of breakdown in Newton-Raphson convergence: (a) false convergence; (b) oscillation; (c) divergence; (d) convergence to different root.

each loop of the iteration. There are two main causes of failure. One is when the derivative of the function is small at the point where an approximation is made, giving a small denominator in the expression for the next approximation and so a big 'jump' along the x-axis. This is the main weakness of the Newton-Raphson method, and the best that a programmer can do is to include a test in his program to detect when this occurs. If it does, avoiding action can be attempted in the same program or, alternatively, execution can be terminated with a suitable warning message and information output about where the trouble has occurred, so that the programmer can then decide what to do, such as reprogramming using a different algorithm.

The second cause of failure is when the first approximation is not very close to the root. We have not yet mentioned how to choose this starting value. One way is to use the Intermediate Value Theorem, which states that if the values of a continuous function at two points are of different sign, then the function must have a zero between these two points. One method of locating zeros is to evaluate the function at several points and to detect changes in sign. If this occurs then a zero occurs between, say, a and b. If the function values at a and b are joined by a straight line the point of intersection with the x-axis can be taken as a first approximation to the root. This is shown in Fig. 4.3.

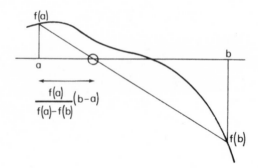

Fig. 4.3. Straight line intercept giving first approximation to a root of $f(x) = 0$.

In the iterative loop a check can be made to prevent approximations diverging or converging to another root, by testing that each new approximation lies in the original interval. If it does not, then a closer initial approximation could be found by looking at the value of the function at the midpoint of the interval and finding in which of the two new intervals the root lies. (This should only be used for first approximations since it is a very slow process.) Oscillations can be guarded against by including a count of the number of iterations performed and stopping if this exceeds some specified number. These precautions do not cover every case, but they indicate the sorts of problems which can arise, their cause, and the sorts of tests that can be used to detect them. These have been included in the flow diagram in Fig. 4.4.

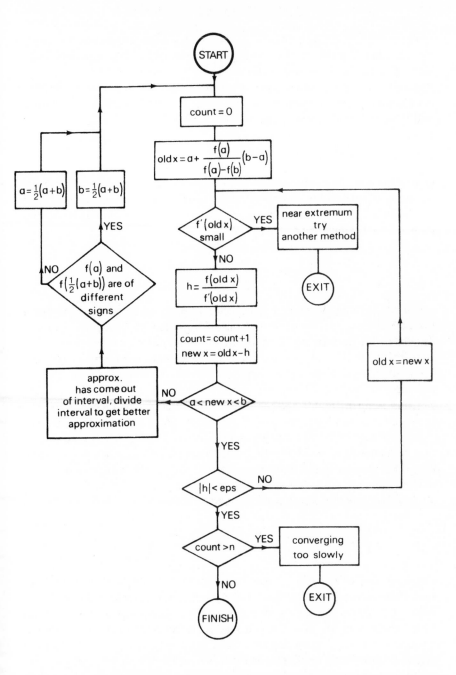

Fig. 4.4. Modified Newton-Raphson method for locating root of $f(x) = 0$ in the interval $a < x < b$. Note the inclusion of checks against: (1) new approximation lying outside interval; (2) convergence too slow, in more than n iterations; (3) approximation near to an extremum. The initial approximation is found by a straight line through $f(a)$ and $f(b)$.

The reader should be warned that this method of locating zeros by looking for changes of sign can be very inefficient, and should not be used unless some idea of their position has been obtained by other, possibly theoretical, methods. The idea of using one method to obtain a reasonable first approximation and a separate method to refine this is typical in numerical methods and we shall come across it again.

4.3 Numerical Integration

One of the most frequent needs in scientific work is to perform an integration. Methods of integrating functions analytically have been extensively studied for centuries but many important functions exist which cannot be so integrated. One example is the error function

$$\text{erf}(x) = \frac{2}{\sqrt{\pi}} \int_0^x e^{-t^2} \, dt$$

which comes from the normal distribution in probability theory. Long before the advent of the computer as we now know it, many methods had been developed for performing integrations by numerical approximations. These were intended for hand computation, sometimes assisted by a desk calculator. They tended to be direct methods, involving a single evaluation of an approximation formula, of varying complication depending on the nature of the function being integrated and the accuracy required. Only in recent years have the iterative methods more suited to computers properly come into their own.

Probably the best known of the simple, direct rules for numerical integration is **Simpson's Rule**. The formula for the approximate value of the definite integral of the function $f(x)$ over the interval $a \leqslant x \leqslant b$ is expressed in terms of the value of the function at three points, the two end points of the interval, a and b, and the midpoint, $\frac{1}{2}(a + b)$, and is

$$\int_a^b f(x)dx \sim \frac{(b-a)}{6} \left\{ f(a) + 4f\left(\frac{a+b}{2}\right) + f(b) \right\}$$

The Rule can be derived by approximating to the function by a quadratic (parabola) passing through these three points and integrating the quadratic. Hence if the function is a polynomial of degree 2, then Simpson's Rule is exact. Error analysis shows that this can give remarkably good results despite its simplicity. One surprising feature is that it is also exact for polynomials of degree 3. There is a modified version which uses three values all at points within the range of integration, instead of using the endpoints.

There are superior integration methods but Simpson's Rule has the advantage of simplicity and familiarity. The formula is easy to program, and in itself would be of no interest to us, but we shall consider what to do if a simple

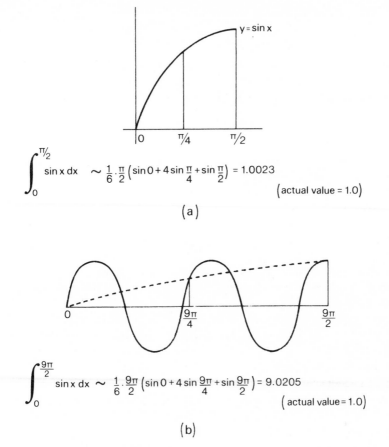

$$\int_0^{\pi/2} \sin x \, dx \;\sim\; \frac{1}{6} \cdot \frac{\pi}{2} \left(\sin 0 + 4 \sin \frac{\pi}{4} + \sin \frac{\pi}{2} \right) = 1.0023$$

$$\left(\text{actual value} = 1.0 \right)$$

(a)

$$\int_0^{9\pi/2} \sin x \, dx \;\sim\; \frac{1}{6} \cdot \frac{9\pi}{2} \left(\sin 0 + 4 \sin \frac{9\pi}{4} + \sin \frac{9\pi}{2} \right) = 9.0205$$

$$\left(\text{actual value} = 1.0 \right)$$

(b)

Fig. 4.5. Integration using Simpson's Rule: (a) a good approximation; (b) a bad approximation. The quadratic approximation through the mid and end points is shown by a dotted curve.

application of Simpson's Rule is not accurate enough. Fig. 4.5 gives two examples, one where the Rule gives a good approximation and the other where it fails badly. This failure is because the three points at which the function is evaluated are not properly representative of the whole function (the dotted curve indicates the quadratic approximation). The obvious solution is to use more than three points, either by using a more complicated formula or by dividing the range of integration into strips and applying Simpson's Rule separately to each. For the reason given earlier, and because of its flexibility, we shall choose the second course.

The 'extended Simpson's Rule' is easy to derive. If the range of integration is divided into m equal strips there are $2m + 1$ points where the function must be evaluated. (There are three points for each strip, the last point of each being the same as the first for the next except for the final strip.) If the distance

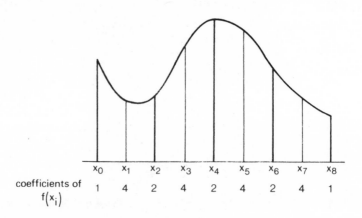

Fig. 4.6. The extended Simpson's Rule, using eight strips. See main text for discussion.

between each pair of points is h (making the width of each strip $2h$), then the points are $x = a, a + h, a + 2h, ..., a + 2mh = b$ (see Fig. 4.6). For the first strip Simpson's Rule gives

$$\int_a^{a + 2h} f(x)dx \sim \frac{h}{3} \left\{ f(a) + 4f(a + h) + f(a + 2h) \right\}$$

for the second it gives

$$\int_{a+2h}^{a+4h} f(x)dx \sim \frac{h}{3} \left\{ f(a + 2h) + 4f(a + 3h) + f(a + 4h) \right\}$$

and so on, ending up with

$$\int_{a + (2m-2)h}^{b} f(x)dx \sim \frac{h}{3} \left\{ f(a + (2m - 2)h) + 4f(a + (2m - 1)h) + f(b) \right\}$$

for the mth and final strip. Adding all these together gives

$$\int_b^a f(x)dx \sim \frac{h}{3} \left\{ f(a) + 4f(a + h) + 2f(a + 2h) \right.$$
$$+ 4f(a + 3h) + 2f(a + 4h) + \ldots\ldots\ldots$$
$$+ 4f(a + (2m - 3)h) + 2f(a + (2m - 2)h)$$
$$\left. + 4f(a + (2m - 1)h) + f(b) \right\}$$

(The pattern of the coefficients of the function values is 1, 2, 4, 2, ..., 2, 4, 2, 4, 1.)

This extension is not wholly satisfactory, because the number of strips m has to be specified in advance, and it is difficult to determine in advance how many strips will be needed to obtain an answer to the desired accuracy. Figure 4.7

gives a flow diagram for the extended method where the number of strips used is increased until the results obtained satisfy the now familiar criterion, namely that two successive calculations do not differ by more than a certain amount. This is a double iteration, a finite iteration inside an inherently infinite one.

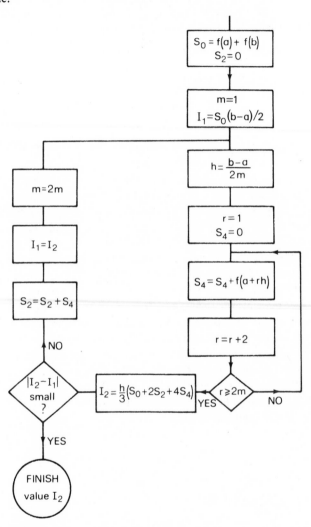

Fig. 4.7. Flow diagram for extended Simpson's Rule. The interval length is halved at each stage. All the terms with coefficient 4 have to be evaluated at each iteration; they then have coefficient 2 on the next and subsequent iterations.

While this criterion cannot be guaranteed to succeed any more than in the Newton-Raphson case, it is an improvement' on applying the formula just once and hoping for the best. There are extra difficulties which did not arise in the earlier example. On each Newton-Raphson iteration the same amount of computation is required but here, even if we re-use the values calculated at a previous iteration rather than work them out again, the amount of calculation increases each time. The most efficient re-use of function values occurs if the number of strips is doubled each time, 1, 2, 4, 8, etc. rather than increased linearly 1, 2, 3, 4, etc. The table below shows the result of using this iterative method on the integral in Fig. 4.5(b) which failed on a single application.

Evaluation of $\int_0^{\frac{9\pi}{2}} \sin x \, dx$ by repeated Simpson's Rule.

(values to 4 decimal places)

Number of strips	h distance between function values	Calculated value of integral
1	7·0686	9·0205
2	3·5343	−3·3129
4	1·7671	1·0840
8	0·8886	1·0037
16	0·4443	1·0002
32	0·2221	1·0000

Notice how the approximation only becomes reasonable when there are enough points to represent the function adequately. This example is typical in that the function, $\sin x$, cannot be evaluated explicitly but must be evaluated iteratively, e.g. by a power series, and there will be a truncation error from each evaluation of the function. As the number of strips increases so does the number of evaluations. Hence the rounding errors will tend to increase at each iteration, though this may not be troublesome if the convergence in Simpson's Rule is rapid. A second consequence of this iterative method is that the time taken for each succeeding iteration will increase. Even though the numerical convergence rate may be satisfactory, this slow computational convergence rate could be unacceptable.

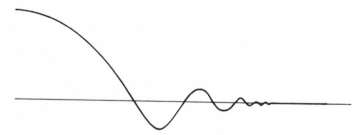

Fig. 4.8. Example of a function which oscillates in only part of its range. When calculating the integral over the interval shown only a few iterations will be needed in the Simpson's Rule method for the ends of the interval, but more will be required in the middle where the function varies more rapidly and narrower strips are necessary to obtain a good approximation.

Note that a slow convergence rate and a large number of iterations may occur simply because the function being integrated 'misbehaves' in only part of the range of integration, and for the rest of the range only a few strips are needed for an accurate result. This could be cured by testing at each stage the result from one strip at the previous iteration against the sum of the results from the two strips which replace it, and not subdividing the strip in further iterations if the two are sufficiently close. This adds to the complexity of the algorithm. This example indicates that a method which is attractive at first sight can turn out, on closer inspection, to contain hidden problems.

We said earlier in Chapter 3 that a programmer should not necessarily pick the first algorithm which comes to mind. Using computers sensibly involves a good deal more than feeding in data and having a button pushed for you. It may seem that we have tended to concentrate on the pitfalls: but one can only use a method successfully if the difficulties are appreciated.

4.4 Differential Equations

While the functions which can be integrated analytically are limited in kind, there are even fewer differential equations which can be solved explicitly. Thus most differential equations have to be solved by numerical methods. This includes most ordinary differential equations as well as almost all of those involving partial derivatives. Because of the great variety of equations there are many different methods: here we can only scratch the surface by looking at one particular type.

The simplest differential equations are those which can be written in the form

$$\frac{dy}{dx} = f(x, y)$$

with the condition that the solution $y = y(x)$ passes through a specified point (x_0, y_0). This is known as an **initial value problem.** It can be geometrically interpreted as picking, from the family of curves which are solutions of the differential equation, the curve which passes through the specified point. A number of standard methods exist, both iterative and non-iterative, but probably the commonest are the Runge-Kutta formulae. There are several such formulae and we shall now give the simplest of those in frequent use.

The basic idea is that the differential equation can be used to obtain a Taylor series expansion for the solution curve $y = y(x)$. If the differential equation is differentiated with respect to x, i.e.

$$y'' = \frac{\partial f}{\partial x} + \frac{\partial f}{\partial y} y',$$

then the second derivative can be evaluated and by repeating the process the higher order derivatives can also be obtained. If the solution $y = y(x)$ is expanded in a Taylor series about the point x_0,

$$y(x_0 + h) = y(x_0) + hy'(x_0) + \tfrac{1}{2}h^2 y''(x_0) + \dots$$

then one can find the value y_1 of the solution at the point $x_1 = x_0 + h$ near to the initial point $x = x_0$. This new point (x_1, y_1) can be used as a new starting value; and so the next point on the solution curve is then found. The solution curve is then obtained by going forward, step-by-step. The normal, or fourth-order, Runge-Kutta formula gives the solution value y_{n+1} in terms of the previous value y_n at the point $x_n = x_0 + nh$ by the formula:

where
$$\begin{aligned}
y_{n+1} &= y_n + \tfrac{1}{6}(k_1 + 2k_2 + 2k_3 + k_4) \\
k_1 &= hf(x_n, y_n) \\
k_2 &= hf(x_n + \tfrac{1}{2}h, y_n + \tfrac{1}{2}k_1) \\
k_3 &= hf(x_n + \tfrac{1}{2}h, y_n + \tfrac{1}{2}k_2) \\
k_4 &= hf(x_n + h, y_n + k_3)
\end{aligned}$$

(This is obtained by truncating the Taylor series after terms of the fourth order.)

The table below gives several steps in the iterative solution of the equation

$$y' = 1 + y^2$$

with the initial condition $y(0) = 0$, and using a step size of $h = 0.2$. The calculated results are compared with the actual values (the true solution is $y = \tan x$). (Calculation to 5 significant figures.)

n	x_n	y_n	k_1	k_2	k_3	k_4	y_{n+1}	$\tan x_{n+1}$
0	0	0	0·2	0·202	0·20204	0·20816	·2027	·2027
1	0·2	0·2027	0·20822	0·21883	0·21948	0·23564	·4228	·4228
2	0·4	0·4228	0·23575	0·25847	0·26095	0·29350	·6841	·6841
3	0·6	0·6841	0·29361	0·33810	0·34559	0·41207	1·0296	1·0296
4	0·8	1·0296	0·41202	0·50535	0·52884	0·68575	1·5573	1·5574
5	1·0	1·5573	0·68510	0·92196	1·0148	1·5232	2·5709	2·5722
6	1·2	2·5722	1·5219	2·4203	3·0593	6·5400	5·7411	5·7979

The Runge-Kutta algorithm is simple and easy to program; most of the difficulties lie in deciding how to apply it. At first glance it appears that the method has the same deficiency as Simpson's Rule in that it only uses a few points as being typical of the function. However, Runge-Kutta includes information about derivatives up to the fourth order, and hence can cover many oscillations, etc. in the function. Thus a single application of the algorithm, with a suitable step size h, can give excellent results. Serious problems do not normally start to arise until the formulae have been applied for several successive iterations.

If, starting from an initial point, the value at just one other point is required, a single application of the algorithm can be used, but if the step size is large the result may not be accurate enough. In our example above, finding the value of y at $x = 1$ by a single step $(h = 1 \cdot 0)$ gives $y(1) = 1 \cdot 5359$, which is considerably less accurate than taking a step size of $0 \cdot 2$ and performing five iterations, as in the table. Thus once again we encounter the problem that reducing the step size can increase accuracy, but involves more calculation and more potential rounding error.

There are two factors which make this a much more serious problem than with Simpson's Rule. Both result from the fact that each evaluation after the first depends on a previous iteration — k_2 depends on k_1, k_3 on k_2, k_4 on k_3, and the next iteration on all of the k_i from the previous iteration. One factor is that if one attempts to achieve greater accuracy by halving the step length, as in Simpson's Rule, the previously computed values (except at the starting point) are no longer of any use. The other factor is that the rounding error is not only increased by performing further calculations, but is transmitted from each evaluation to the next through the k_i. Since the value of y in each successive evaluation of $f(x, y)$ contains an error arising from previous evaluations, it is possible for the computed solution to diverge rapidly from the true solution.

It is frequently the case that a solution is required not at a single point but at a succession of points – i.e. a solution curve is required over a range of the independent variable. This defect of the Runge-Kutta method is then even more serious. Fig. 4.9 illustrates the divergence from the true solution caused

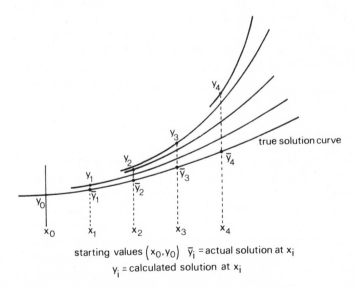

starting values (x_0, y_0) $\bar{y}_i$ = actual solution at x_i

y_i = calculated solution at x_i

Fig. 4.9. Runge-Kutta. Divergence from the true solution due to the accumulation of rounding errors.

by a succession of errors which are small individually but which each take the computed solution on to a neighbouring curve and further away from the original correct solution curve. A similar feature can be seen in our tabulated example, where the errors are insignificant until $x = 1.0$, when the solution curve ($y = \tan x$) becomes steeper and the errors start escalating. This property of escalating rounding errors is an inherent feature of the particular differential equation, and is usually known as **instability.**

Thus the Runge-Kutta method is full of pitfalls for the unwary. The cautious programmer will keep reducing the step size until he is sure he has sufficient accuracy or finds that he has insufficient computer time to carry the iteration forward any further. The irresponsible programmer will ignore any checking and merrily obtain the solution step by step without any cares about possible errors. Both approaches are bad. When the Runge-Kutta method is good it is very good but when it goes wrong it can go badly wrong. It is very accurate for a small number of steps, and it needs no information other than one initial value, i.e. just *one* point on the solution curve. When 3 or 4 iterations have been performed then there is more than one point known and Runge-Kutta will waste all of these except the last. There are other methods available to continue the solution from this point – they are just as accurate, require less work and indicate the likely error size quite easily – but they do need several points on the solution curve to have been computed beforehand.

These are known as **predictor-corrector** methods and work on the following principle. First, use the differential equation and the last calculated point to obtain an approximation to the next point on the solution curve. Then iteratively use several of the previous points to correct this prediction and, when two successive iterations are sufficiently close, then move along one step. This illustrates a point that we made earlier that the solution to a particular problem often requires a combination of methods. Here it occurs on two levels – first use Runge-Kutta to obtain an accurate start to the solution, and then use a predictor-corrector method to continue: and the predictor-corrector itself consists of two methods.

4.5 Simultaneous Equations

Our last example is again important, and is the solution of simultaneous linear equations, of which we saw the simple case of two equations in two unknowns in Chapter 3. We were able then to write the solutions explicitly and program them, but obviously an algorithmic solution is needed if it is to be able to cope with any number of equations. There are various methods, both direct and indirect. A direct method is Cramer's Rule, which uses determinants. The $n = 2$ case essentially uses that method, but it is unsatisfactory for several reasons. Another method comes from writing the equations in matrix form and then inverting the matrix of coefficients. This raises many interesting problems, but the necessary mathematics may not be known to all our readers. Hence we shall discuss a direct method, one of elimination and back-substitution. This is a finite rather an an infinite iterative process, and so does not involve convergence problems: as we shall see, there are problems enough without that, though infinite iterative algorithms also exist.

The method is basically the same as was used in Chapter 3 to obtain the direct algebraic solution, and is easily described in its general form. Starting with the system of equations

$$a_{11}x_1 + a_{12}x_2 + \ldots + a_{1n}x_n = y_1$$
$$a_{21}x_1 + a_{22}x_2 + \ldots + a_{2n}x_n = y_2$$
$$\cdot$$
$$\cdot$$
$$\cdot$$
$$a_{n1}x_1 + a_{n2}x_2 + \ldots + a_{nn}x_n = y_1$$

the variables x_1, x_2, ... , x_{n-1} are eliminated one by one. Eliminate x_1 by dividing the first equation by a_{11} and then subtract this equation multiplied by a_{21} from the second equation, subtract it multiplied by a_{31} from the third equation, and so on. This will leave only one equation involving x_1; now divide the second equation by the new coefficient of x_2 and subtract suitable multiples of it from the third, fourth, etc. equations. This process is continued until the system now has the form

$$x_1 + b_{12}x_2 + \ldots + b_{1n}x_n = z_1$$
$$x_2 + \ldots + b_{2n}x_n = z_2$$
$$\cdot$$
$$\cdot$$
$$\cdot$$
$$b_{nn}x_n = x_n$$

The last equation can be solved for x_n, the solution substituted in the previous equation to obtain x_{n-1} and this back-substitution continued to obtain x_{n-2}, ... , x_2, x_1.

If this is applied to the system

$$2x_1 + 2x_2 + x_3 = 1$$
$$2x_1 + x_2 \qquad = 0$$
$$3x_1 + 2x_2 + x_3 = -1$$

then one obtains
$$x_1 + x_2 + \tfrac{1}{2}x_3 = \tfrac{1}{2}$$
$$x_2 + x_3 = 1$$
$$\tfrac{1}{2}x_3 = -\tfrac{3}{2},$$

and the back substitution gives $x_3 = -3$, $x_2 = 4$, $x_1 = -2$.

This method is known as **Gaussian elimination**. There is a modification (Jordan's variation) where each variable is eliminated from all but one of the equations and not just from those succeeding it. In the example above the eliminated system would be

$$
\begin{aligned}
x_1 &= -2 \\
x_2 &= 4 \\
x_3 &= -3,
\end{aligned}
$$

and the solution can be obtained immediately without any back-substitution. This modification appears to make the method simpler, but if a count is made of the number of operations involed then Gauss uses approximately $\frac{1}{3}n^3$ operations while Jordan's requires about $\frac{1}{2}n^3$. Hence the unmodified Gauss procedure is usually preferable. The determinants method of solution, incidentally, involves at best n^4 operations when the determinants are evaluated efficiently.

As can be expected, this large number of operations can lead to cumulative rounding errors badly distorting the solution, the errors in the last few variables to be evaluated often being the worst. One way to minimise this is the method of **pivoting.** This means that, instead of using the first equation to eliminate x_1 from all the others, the equation with the largest (in magnitude) coefficient of x_1 is chosen. This avoids the risk of trying to divide by 0 if x_1 is missing from the first equation, and it also reduces the effects of rounding errors by trying to avoid as much as possible divisions by small numbers, and differencing two almost equal numbers. Fig. 4.10 gives a flow diagram for Gaussian elimination using pivoting.

Pivoting will not eliminate the effect of rounding errors, but will only reduce it. There is a second potential source of error, namely inexact data. A small error in the input data can sometimes give rise to errors in the computed solution which are out of all apparent proportion to the original error. An example of this is the system:

$$
\begin{aligned}
x_1 + \tfrac{1}{2}x_2 + \tfrac{1}{3}x_3 &= 0 \\
\tfrac{1}{2}x_1 + \tfrac{1}{3}x_2 + \tfrac{1}{4}x_3 &= 1 \\
\tfrac{1}{3}x_1 + \tfrac{1}{4}x_2 + \tfrac{1}{5}x_3 &= 1
\end{aligned}
$$

This has the exact solution $x_1 = -6$, $x_2 = 12$, $x_3 = 0$. If an error of 1% is introduced into the right hand side of the second equation so that it now becomes

$$
\tfrac{1}{2}x_1 + \tfrac{1}{3}x_2 + \tfrac{1}{4}x_3 = 1 \cdot 01,
$$

then the exact solution is

$$
x_1 = -7 \cdot 56, \; x_2 = 13 \cdot 92, \; x_3 = -1 \cdot 80.
$$

A problem where either errors in input or rounding errors produce disproportionate errors in its solutions is usually called **ill-conditioned.** Ill-conditioning can occur however many equations are involved, and it is seldom obvious without the use of tests that it will happen. Therefore the programmer *must* include some checks to detect its presence.

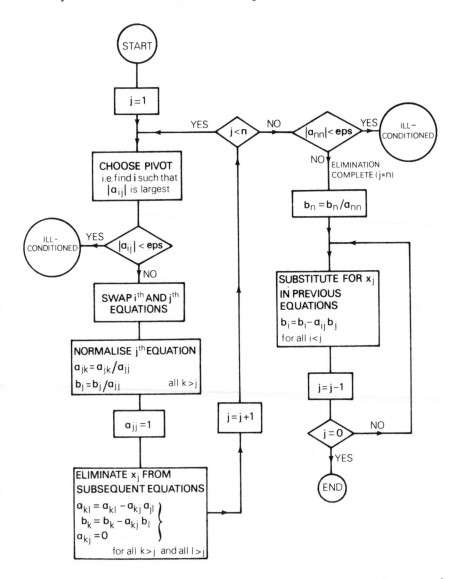

Fig. 4.10. Flow diagram for Gaussian elimination with pivoting to solve the system of simultaneous linear equations.

$$\sum_i a_{ij} x_i = b_j \qquad (j = 1, \ldots, n).$$

The final values of the b_i are the required values of the x_i $(i = 1, \ldots, n)$.

(In the case of simultaneous equations there is a straightforward test. If the equations are written in matrix form $\mathbf{Ax} = \mathbf{y}$, then solving the equations is the problem of finding the inverse matrix $\mathbf{A}^{-1}$. Ill-conditioning will occur when the matrix is nearly singular, which can be detected by looking at a normalised form of the determinant of $\mathbf{A}$.)

Ill-conditioning can also arise in other types of problems, for example in finding the roots of a polynomial equation.

The equation $\qquad (x + 1)(x + 2) \ldots (x + 20) = 0$
i.e. $\qquad\qquad x^{20} + 210x^{19} + \ldots + 20! = 0$

has roots -1, -2, ..., -20. If the coefficient of x^{19} is changed to
$$210 \cdot 0000001192$$
then the roots are widely displaced, e.g. three of them become (to 2 decimal places) $-16 \cdot 73 \pm 2 \cdot 81i$ and $-20 \cdot 85$. In this case, to guarantee 2 significant figure accuracy in the answer, all the computations must be exact to at least 10 significant figures!

4.6   Avoiding Programming Pitfalls

In this chapter we have not tried to give a catalogue of methods for solving particular problems. Our examples were chosen to illustrate the sorts of problems that arise in numerical methods, and we have omitted many areas, e.g. least squares fitting. We also chose the particular methods in the examples because they are in common use, even though often misused.

There is a popular misconception that programs and data can be put into a computer and everything that comes out will be correct – that is, the machine will do all the thinking. Unfortunately this misconception is not confined solely to the uninitiated: it is sometimes found in programmers. Although in most cases this is simply the result of laziness, this kind of programmer is the most dangerous, since his results could be used by others who may be unaware of their unreliability. On the other hand the ideal solution (having chosen the algorithm) of performing a complete error analysis is usually impossible even for specialists. What, then, is the programmer to do? He certainly cannot abandon the problem, since it has to be solved.

In fact there are several things the programmer can do, and since many of them are applicable to using computers in any context they are worth listing:

1   As mentioned at the start of Chapter 3, he must arrive at a clear definition of the problem he has to solve. Having done this, and before going any further, he should ask himself if he really does need a computer. Useful though the computer is, it is not the best tool for every job: even in the numerical field it is not infrequent for the computer to be used, say, for finding roots of an equation which could have been found just as easily by inspection, or for inverting an orthogonal matrix. (One of the authors once marked some written mathematics which ended with ' $= 4/2 = 2 \cdot 0$, approximately, by slide rule'. The same attitude nowadays sometimes exists towards computers.)

2   The programmer should next look for standard algorithms, or other evidence that the same or a similar problem has been solved on a computer before. This is where the program library comes in, as well as the literature of his subject. Any computer installation will have a program library, and he should search it for relevant programs or subprograms. As well as saving time and effort, he is quite likely to find a better and more efficient program than he could write himself, as the library programs are probably written by professional programmers who (in the case of numerical methods) may also be professional numerical analysts or have been advised by them. Nevertheless he should take nothing on trust, but should read all the small print in the program description: it may have been written for a problem differing from his own, only slightly, but sufficiently so to mean that checks necessary in the present case were omitted. Further, not all library programs are perfect, and not all are written by professionals: a good rule of thumb is to avoid any whose descriptions do not clearly state the conditions under which its use is appropriate, situations in which it should not be used, and the checks which are included in it. In the case of numerical algorithms the description should include discussion of the errors: if such discussion does not appear, the program is almost certainly badly written and should be avoided. Also, numerical methods by computer have made such advances since the 1950s that the date of the program and the algorithm on which it is based can also be a guide.

3   Assuming that the programmer has to write much or all of the program himself, he must try to list as comprehensively as possible all the things that can go wrong. Also, though a complete error analysis may well be impossible, any analysis at all which can be carried out is usually worth the effort. Having done this, he should not try to work out ways of getting round all the different kinds of bad behaviour that might occur (there is no point in anticipating trouble and, if he is lucky, most or even all of the types of bad behaviour might not arise), but he should include in his program checks to detect each of the various kinds should they in fact happen.

4   If, after the initial syntax errors have been removed from the program, it takes a long running time in execution, the programmer should include the output of intermediate results, even although they will not finally be needed. These can help in various ways: in checking results and detecting semantic errors; in indicating the behaviour of the solution and speed of convergence where appropriate; in possibly enabling greater efficiency, faster convergence, or slower accumulation of error to be achieved. Where possible, such results should be designed to enable computation to be resumed from any stage, thus avoiding the need to go back to the beginning every time to start again. Doing this saves a great deal of human and computer time: and nothing annoys a programmer more than a program which eats up half an hour of processor time and then gets ejected for exceeding its time allocation without producing any useful results.

5   Some computers allow the user to choose the number of significant digits to be used in the computation. This facility is useful but must be used with discretion, matching the accuracy to the requirements of the problem. In particular the programmer should resist the temptation to work to too many figures, especially when the input data is only accurate to a few figures, but also when the final answers are not needed to be very accurate. In this context, it is a common fault for programmers to output results to the limit of the working length within the computer, regardless of accuracy of input, accuracy required, or likely errors generated by the computation.

6　As mentioned before, the program must be run with test data which will check all parts of it thoroughly. However, in the case of numerical computation in particular, the programmer must remember that this will not guarantee that the program will work every time; where program behaviour (including accumulation of error) can depend critically on the data, it is highly unlikely that test data (whose results by definition have to be able to be checked by hand) will exhibit the same characteristics as the real data.

A common failing of programmers is a reluctance to seek help, an unwillingness to admit (to oneself or others) that one's program might be deficient. It is a mark of a good programmer that he will readily seek help, and indeed try to get someone to check his work or find faults in it even when he is sure in his own mind that everything is right. If he will tell a joke on himself about how long it took him to find an error, it does not mean that he is a bad programmer. Thus no one should be diffident or nervous about seeking help from professionals, whether programmers or numerical analysts. Computer installations normally have formal or informal advisory services where people are glad to help all who are willing to learn. No good programmer will scoff at a beginner's mistakes, as he will know how easy they are to make. Even more, a numerical analyst will be aware of the problems of picking a suitable algorithm, and will encourage anyone who thinks about his problem and seeks guidance.

Chapter 5

The Computer as a Data Handler

Most computing done today is in the commercial rather than the scientific field. Many computers are devoted solely to commercial work and therefore a lot of effort has been spent on solving problems and developing techniques specific to this area. These techniques are often useful in other areas of computing, so an understanding of them is useful for anyone engaged seriously in computing.

One of the main tasks in commercial work is the handling and storing of large quantities of data. In most commercial applications the algorithms for processing the data are relatively simple, but the technical computing problems of handling the data are often extremely complex. The main requirements of the data handling are that the data should be (a) input accurately, (b) held securely, (c) processed efficiently, and (d) selected items should be easy to output. As an example, consider one of the most common commercial applications – the company payroll, which we shall examine in more detail in the next section. Data is input on a regular basis (weekly or monthly): it gives details of the employees, the hours they have worked, and so on. As their pay depends on this input information, its accuracy is important. It must also be held securely: these details must not be corrupted or lost during processing or again incorrect pay will result. Processing must be efficient, because the employees must receive their pay by a specific time each week. There will be several sets of output such as pay slips, lists of bank transfers, etc.

Commercial computing is motivated by cost. A company will only install a computer when the result is financial gain for the organisation, and it will therefore prefer methods which have been thoroughly tested and which are unlikely to involve unpredictable and potentially large costs. Commercial computing developed later than scientific computing, because potential commercial users were reluctant to use prototype methods and machines before they had been proved. Nevertheless commercial work was found to entail special difficulties which the commercial users (especially the pioneers) had to solve, with or without the help of the computer manufacturers.

Early commercial computers replaced manual systems. The changeover sounds relatively simple; many manual systems merely involve routine calculations on standard data, but almost all rely to some extent on human judgement. A human will recognise 'suspect' items in the data that he is handling, for instance a timesheet which says that a worker did 450 hours in one week, will query this and have it verified. In practical applications there are usually a considerable number of such exceptional items. In order to replace the manual system the programmer must therefore explicitly program to recognise and deal with each exception. There can be so many, that this part of the program often takes longer than does the part dealing with normal cases. In the early days there was a tendency to expect some human intelligence from computers, and this resulted in insufficient checking, which unfortunately still persists today. Many computer 'jokes', e.g. about gas bills of incredible magnitude, or cheques for £0.00, arise from the failure to carry out proper checks.

In order to use a computer for a commercial application, the problem to be solved must be thoroughly understood by someone who also understands computers and their capabilities. This is the job of the **systems analyst**, who tries to bridge the gap between people in the commercial company who want a job done but are not concerned how it is done, and programmers who understand the computer but sometimes do not appreciate what the users require from it. The systems analyst must make sure he understands all the requirements, including exceptional cases and other points which the user thinks are obvious and therefore not worth mentioning, but which will need explicit programming. The good systems analyst will spend time finding out what the user actually wants, which is not always what he says or thinks he wants; and he will also identify areas where extensions may be needed later, and allow for them in his design.

Having thoroughly understood the user's problems, he must then decide how to use the computer to solve them. The most important problems here concern the data: what data is input and output; what form and order this will take; and most important of all, the form of the data while it is held in the computer. This problem is complex and depends on many factors, including the quantity of data; how secure it must be; in what order it is needed during processing. In the early days and on most current installations, all the data is divided into sets of data items of the same type called **files**, by analogy with ordinary office files, and many of these files may be kept off-line for most of the time. In a stock control system, for example, there may be one file containing a record for each type of stock item, and another for the address of each warehouse.

The information contained on these files can be related. In a complex installation many of the files can be interrelated, and this led to the idea of considering all the data at an installation as a whole, i.e. forming one large data base. In a **data base**, all the data is defined together rather than each file being defined separately. The data base is then 'managed' by a supervisory program which controls the actual use of the information by user programs. Each user program, depending on its function, will probably be allowed by the supervisory program only a restricted view of the data base, limiting access only to the information it needs. (Note again here the emphasis on security.)

5.1 Company Payroll Example

To introduce some of the typical problems in commercial computing we shall look in a little more detail at the case of a company's weekly payroll. The calculations are simple and there are standard rules for dealing with most of the exceptional cases and special circumstances, e.g. overtime, part-time working, various rates of taxation, productivity bonuses, superannuation, etc. The essential purpose of the program is to calculate the amount to be paid to each individual. This is tedious routine, and the real complexity and interest lies in the various layers which surround the core.

The systems analyst has to work backwards, first considering what is wanted from the computer, then what is needed to produce this. Each employee, as well as receiving a pay slip, will also expect actual payment. Some may be paid in cash, some by cheque, some by bank transfer. If hundreds of cheques are involved it may be worth considering printing them by computer control. In the case of bank transfers, different banks may be involved, for each of which a separate record of account numbers and payments must be produced. Throughout, records will need to be kept of the totals paid out; more important, data relating to individual employees must be updated and kept for the next run of the program. For example, information like the total tax paid by an individual so far in the current tax year is needed when calculating future tax payments. Thus, every time a single employee is dealt with by the payroll program, several quite distinct items of output may be involved, perhaps on separate output devices.

Two main kinds of input are required. One is transient, relating to the week (or pay period) concerned: hours worked, bonus earned, whether on holiday or off sick, and so on. The other input is semi-permanent: whether an employee is to be paid by cash or cheque, etc., tax deduction codes, cumulative pay and tax totals, his address within the company for sending his pay slip, and so on. The weekly file will have to be prepared, checked and entered every period. The rest of the input, after the first week, can be carried forward by means of an output file produced by the previous run of the program. The semi-permanent file is therefore likely to be kept on magnetic tape or disk and can be kept off-line except while the payroll is being processed. Hence the weekly output will consist of this updated file on magnetic tape or disk, and printed lists on lineprinters.

If the number of employees is very large then the weekly file and the semi-permanent file may be too large to be held together in main store. Nevertheless, for the pay calculations for any one employee to be performed, both of the above records relating to him will have to be in main store simultaneously.

It is therefore necessary to arrange for records to be read from backing store in the same order from each of the two files.

There will be no problem if the transient file can be created each week in the same order as the semi-permanent file; but this may not be easy to organise. If the files are differently ordered, at least one of them will have to be sorted by the computer to make their ordering the same, or one file will have to be searched each time a record from the other is processed, in order to find the record which matches it. Sorting and searching files are important operations in commercial computing and their efficient running is a significant problem which has received a lot of attention and which also is of mathematical interest. We shall look at them shortly in Section 5.4.

For maximum efficiency both files must be ordered the same way. If the semi-permanent file is ordered initially, this order can be preserved each time it is updated. This raises an important question – how is the information going to be kept on this file so that it can be easily processed, so that searching and sorting is minimised, and so on? We shall examine this problem in Section 5.3, assuming for the present that we have a sorting routine which will sort the weekly input file into the same order as the semi-permanent file the best order in this case is to arrange the records in order of increasing employee number.

Each week a new version of the semi-permanent file will have to be created, updated with information about the current week in readiness for the next week's run of the program. This file will normally be kept on magnetic tape rather than disk because of cheapness and compactness. The 'obvious' solution to updating the file is to replace the new version of each record back into its place in the original file after processing. This would involve backspacing the tape after each record has been input to the main store, ready to receive the updated version, but this is inefficient and dangerous since backspacing does not always position the tape accurately enough for writing the new block to exactly the right position. Magnetic tapes and handlers are usually the least reliable part of a system, and a good rule is that an input tape should never be destroyed until it is known that all of its contents have been successfully processed. Hence a completely new version of the file must be created on a separate magnetic tape using another tape handler.

After the run, both the old and the new files will be in existence. The old one could be erased as being no longer needed, but it is wise not to do this too quickly. Computers are very reliable by human standards but are not wholly infallible; human errors in programming or operating may mean that the new file is defective in some way; and there is always the chance that it may be lost or corrupted before in turn it is updated on the next run. It is common practice in commercial computing to adopt a 'father and son' policy of retaining both the new file, the son, and the old file, its father, until the son has fathered the next version by the next run of the program. A copy of the input file which was used to create the son from the father must also be retained, so that if anything should happen to the son it can be recreated. Usually three generations are kept: the current son, its father, and its grandfather, with the appropriate updating files. Even this may not offer enough security if the payroll includes both weekly and monthly paid employees, because an error in the monthly update may not be discovered until one month later. The grandfather file, only 2 weeks old, would not then make recovery possible; hence some files of older generations will have to be kept as well.

There is another aspect of security. If the run is very lengthy (a number of hours) and an accident occurs, one does not want to have to restart from the beginning of the program. There are two practical solutions to this. One is to have periodic breakpoints when enough information is 'dumped' (e.g. output to disk) in order to enable the run to be restarted from this point instead of from the beginning. This information will have to include positions of files at the breakpoint so that the magnetic tapes can be correctly repositioned on restart; the maximum time lost will then be the time between two breakpoints. The other solution is to duplicate, using two identical versions continually updated and processed in parallel, which although needing more processing time and extra devices, much reduces the chance of time being lost in re-running.

Turning now to the execution of the program, the easiest way to handle the payroll calculations is to input both records for one employee, or group of employees, perform the calculations followed by the output operations, and then repeat for each employee or group. The difficulty is that these events will occur in sequence, the CPU waiting while the input and output occurs, and hence the total running time will be the sum of the input, processing and output times. This situation can arise in many areas of computing, which has led to the development of facilities whereby the CPU and the input–output devices can be used simultaneously by the same program. This is done by using **buffers**, which are areas of main store such that a device could be transferring data to or from one buffer at the same time as the CPU is processing data in other areas. In the simple case of **double buffering** there are

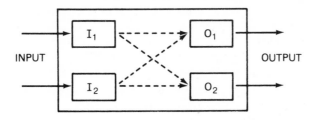

Fig. 5.1. Schematic diagram showing the principle of input–output buffering. See main text for full explanation.

two input buffers I_1 and I_2, and two output buffers O_1 and O_2. Initially the first record or block of records is input to buffer I_1. At the next stage the second block is input to buffer I_2 and simultaneously the first block is processed from I_1 to O_1. Then the third block is input into buffer I_1, the second is processed from I_2 to O_2 and the first block is output from O_1, all occurring simultaneously. This is now continued with input, output and processing all occurring at the same time. In this case the running time will be the maximum of the input, processing and output times, rather than the sum of all of three.

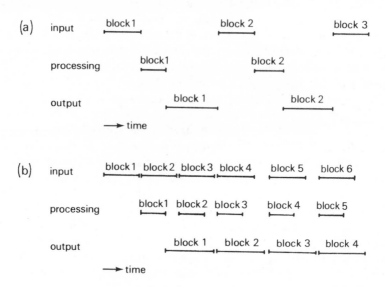

Fig. 5.2. Time chart demonstrating the input, processing and output of blocks of information (a) without input-output buffering and (b) with input–output buffering. The greater efficiency of (b) clearly appears, although gain obtained will depend on the relative sizes of the input blocks, the output blocks, and the processing time which each requires.

This technique of buffering is often extended to utilise more buffers. The program designer has to juggle with the sizes of the blocks, the available store and the times for the various operations to arrive at the most efficient solution for each particular case. Buffering is in common use to make the best use of commercial systems and often occurs in other contexts.

We now turn to the input data – none of the payroll system will work properly if there are errors in this input. First the data must be prepared in a form which is suitable for input to the computer. Hence it must be transcribed from clock cards onto punch cards, paper tape or other media. This is a slow and costly process and is inevitably error-prone; hence an important area of commercial work is data preparation. There are two main sources of error – errors in the original clock cards, and errors produced in the preparation stage by mistyping or misreading. The input data must be checked to detect both types of error, which are quite common, and the detection of the errors should occur before the data is sorted and processed. If errors are not detected until later, the run will have to be stopped while the errors are corrected and then may have to be restarted from the sort stage with the corrected data. As much checking as possible must therefore be done between the preparation and the start of processing. There is an alternative: to avoid the problem by eliminating the transcription entirely. We shall look at both of these strategies in more detail in the next section.

We have now covered the main features of the payroll program, which can be summarised as a flow diagram (Fig. 5.3), and is suitable in many commercial applications.

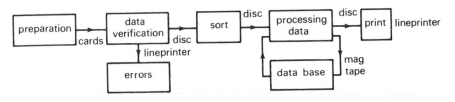

Fig. 5.3. Flow diagram indicating the main features of the payroll program discussed in the text.

5.2 Data Preparation

As mentioned in the last section, data preparation is one of the most important areas in commercial work, and it is desirable that errors are detected before processing the data. The data is normally checked in two stages; first by verification, and then by a vetting program which is run before the sorting and main processing.

Usually there are source documents (such as timesheets or clock cards) which have to be transcribed into machine-readable form, e.g. keyed on to punch cards or paper tape. Two kinds of error can arise in this process: misreading and mistyping, such as the transcriber reading a 3 for an 8, or typing 46 instead of 64. It is standard practice to follow the transcribing or keying stage by **verification**, where the same data is keyed again from the same source documents and compared character by character with the original keying. If there is any discrepancy, the verification system stops and the operator checks what the correct entry should be. Since the same individual often tends to repeat the same misreading or mistyping, it is better to have different operators to do the keying and verifying. Keying the same data twice doubles the time and cost of data preparation, but this is easily justified in the savings of time, cost and trouble caused in correcting errors after they have passed through the sorting stage.

The method of verification adopted will depend on the input medium. In the case of punched card or paper tape input, special machines have been devised which do the verification while the second copy is being typed. As with a simple punching device such as can be used for the first copy, there is a keyboard with a feed and punch, but there is in addition a reader for the first punched copy of the original data. Each keystroke is compared, character for character, with this first copy by means of this reader. If the character read is the same as the character keyed, it is punched on the blank card or tape in the feed which produces the verified version, otherwise the keyboard locks and the operator is forced to check what the correct punched character should be. Obviously the second operator is just as likely to make keying errors as the first, but (especially with different operators) the chance of an identical repeated error is greatly reduced. Note that verification will also pick up errors such as the omission of characters or the insertion of spurious additional ones.

Similar principles apply to systems in which the data is written directly to a magnetic medium, such as tape or disk. If the key-to-tape or key-to-disk system is computer-controlled, whether independently or as part of a multi-access system, a number of other checks can be made which might otherwise have to be made separately. An example of this is the **direct data entry** facility on the ICL 2903, a small-to-medium sized commercially oriented computer introduced in 1974. While processing other programs, the 2903 can simultaneously support a number of VDU terminals for direct entry of data on to disk. Each terminal operator can enter data in accordance with a prescribed format, display it on the screen for visual checking, or carry out a verification. Extra protection is given by the safeguard that such data cannot be used directly by a program, but must be copied, and the system will query any command to copy unverified data. Such key-to-disk activity need not be confined to the machine on which the data is to be used. Commercial systems of 1960s vintage tended not to have the multi-access facilities which make it viable and hence the development of off-line key-to-tape and key-to-card systems. The advantages of multi-access data preparation are obvious, and hence this trend is likely to gather momentum.

Verification will not detect all transcription errors and will not detect errors in the source documents. A second phase is needed in checking data, which will normally be in a program run before the main processing. Several checks can be made, some of which are sometimes included in the verification. Extra items may be added to the data to help to detect errors which may arise at later stages of the processing. We shall just mention a few of the types of checks that can and should be made.

Range checks: These verify that the data items lie within sensible limits, e.g. that the hours worked before overtime lie between 0 and $42\frac{1}{2}$.

Batch totals: The sum is formed of one particular data item in each record from a batch of records. For example, the clock keeper gives the total time worked by all the employees in a section, and the sum of their individual hours worked is compared with this total at various stages of the processing. A missing record can be easily detected by batch totals. This can and should be used for large numbers of records, forming batch totals for groups of say 30 each, and it is best if a data field is chosen whose value varies from record to record.

Format check: This is often used at the verification stage, and requires that each data item must occur at specific places in the input record – e.g. the hours worked must occur in columns 11 and 12 on the punched card and columns 13 and 14 must be unpunched.

Check digits: Here a critical number in a record has an extra digit added according to a specified rule, an extension of the idea of parity. For instance the employee number could have an extra digit added so that the sum of the digits is 4. To give an example, 4638 has digit sum $= 4 + 6 + 3 + 8 = 21$ and $2 + 1 = 3$; hence the check digit for this number is 1 and the final employee number is 46381. All employee numbers in the data base will already have this check digit included. The employee number is an important case because it is a 'sensitive' part of each record, identifying an individual person. Without a check digit, a mistranscription of 4638 as 4658 might cause employee 4658 to receive 4638's pay. Check digits are obviously useful in identification numbers of all kinds (the ISBN numbers which all books, including this one, are now given, include them), and many rules have been devised for their creation which enable different kinds of errors to be detected.

Checking and verification do not form the only possible answer to the input problem. Another course is to avoid the problem. This means trying to avoid the transcription stage by designing the source documents so that they can be input directly. It is not surprising that a good deal of attention has been paid to this. As well as avoiding transcription errors, direct input saves time taken by keying and verification. There is a range of possibilities: one can try to build machines to read the source documents, or devise source documents so that machines can read them, or seek a compromise.

There are optical character readers, designed to recognise and input ordinary alphabetic, numeric and other symbols on ordinary documents. At present these readers are expensive and only reasonably reliable when used with specially designed type fonts, whereas many human source documents are handwritten or produced on ordinary typewriters. There is no point in eliminating human error, only to replace it by machine error, and hence such optical readers have as yet been successfully used only in a few specific areas, often when the source documents are specially designed.

A variation on this method comes from replacing optical recognition of characters by magnetic recognition. The characters are still legible to humans, but a special magnetic ink is used to print them. The commonest example is the printing of magnetic ink numerals at the bottom of each cheque when issued, which identify the bank branch, account number and cheque number. The amount for which the cheque is written must still be keyed in manually when the cheque is being cleared, but much of the transcribing has been avoided.

An example of source documents which are pre-prepared and involve no transcription are Kimball-tags. These are used for stock control, for example, of dresses, shoes, etc., and consist of tags which carry information in the form of punched holes. The tags are perforated so that they can be split into separate input documents at different stages. For instance, if a retailing chain receives 500 identical dresses at its warehouse, an operator sets up details of a dress (size, code number, price etc.) and a machine will punch out 500 tags for the dresses. One tag is put on each dress, and whenever a dress leaves the warehouse a strip is removed from its tag and is used as input to the stock control program. When the dress arrives at a branch, another strip is removed and processed and similarly when the dress is sold, leaving one strip which can be used as a customer receipt. Because of its cheapness and simplicity this type of preprepared document is becoming common in many areas.

We can apply this idea to our payroll example. The employees' clock cards could be produced from a computer with each employee's number, etc. pre-punched, and the clock card machine modified so as to punch data directly on to the card as well as the usual printing.

There are also intermediate forms of documents including pre-scored or mark-sensed cards. Pre-scored cards have punching positions partially punched so that a hole in a given position can be easily completed by piercing the card with a suitable instrument such as the end of a ballpoint pen. The cards can then be read by an ordinary card reader, which is obviously a useful advantage. On mark-sensed cards there are indicated positions which may be filled in with a soft pencil; they are read by a device which uses the graphite in the pencil mark to complete a circuit. Other forms include documents which are optically read for marks (instead of for specific characters), which is clearly simpler technically than optical character recognition. Such devices are used for computerised counting of ballot papers in elections in some American States. While such direct input documents can be and often are specifically designed and printed to assist humans to complete them, the fact remains that they are unfamiliar in form and are sometimes frightening for the uninitiated to fill in, often for psychological reasons. Quite apart from the management problems which this method can cause, it may also affect the computer system since difficulties in completion will result in more errors, thus reducing the advantage of omitting the transcription stage.

Unless and until optical character reading becomes completely effective, the solution to the data entry problem is likely to lie in the use of pre-prepared documents such as Kimball-tags, or by professional data preparation staff working at direct data entry keyboards.

5.3 Filestore

We now turn to the important problem of how the data is to be arranged in files so that it may be processed efficiently. Data in a commercial installation is normally held in a number of files in permanent storage. **Filestore** is the name for this storage used to hold data files, most of which will normally be held off-line; this is different from secondary store which is an extension of main store. A file consists of a number of **records**, each record being the basic unit of data which the user sees, e.g. a record could contain all known data about one employee in a payroll file. If these records are small and each is written separately to a storage device there can be a considerable waste of space in that the computer system has to attach some internal information to each, and in an extreme case this 'book-keeping' information may need more space than the original records. In practice, therefore, the unit of data written to a device is a **block**, which may contain several records, or just one, or even part of one if the record is large. Some devices allow blocks of different sizes to be held on them; others use a fixed block size. Even when variable block sizes are allowed, it is often convenient if one standard block size is used throughout a file. Filestore is held on devices such as magnetic tape, disks and drums, and the way that data is held in files depends, to some extent at least, on the device used.

Magnetic tapes are normally read or written one block at a time in a forward direction. To find a particular record, the user must usually read each block in turn until the block containing that record is found. It is possible to backspace, but this is normally slow; magnetic tapes should not be used when the records are accessed randomly since the time taken to find each record is too high. As mentioned earlier, when updating a file held on magnetic tape it is usual to copy all of the information to another tape since overwriting blocks is error-prone. Magnetic tapes allow any sized blocks to occur (normally up to a specified maximum) along their length. Between each block is an **interblock gap**; the blocksize is normally chosen so that undue space is not wasted on the magnetic tape and also so that an excessive amount of main store is not required for buffers. Note that a file on magnetic tape may extend over more than one reel, in which case it is called a multi-reel file; or several files may be on one reel, which is called a multi-file volume.

A file on magnetic tape is **sequential**, i.e. each record is read in sequence one after the other. In lots of commercial applications a sequential file is the obvious type to use, such as in the payroll file where the records are stored in sequence of employee numbers. The advantages of magnetic tapes were discussed when we discussed the payroll example.

Magnetic disks are the second commonest device for storing data; their physical characteristics were described in Chapter 2. Here we shall consider the disk as it appears to the programmer. The most frequent form is the exchangeable disk pack, with one read/write head for each surface. A **cylinder** is that part of the disk pack which can be accessed without moving the read/write heads, and a **track** is that part of a cylinder which can be accessed by one read/write head, i.e. a part of a cylinder belonging to just one surface. The read/write heads move together so that tracks in corresponding positions on each surface form a cylinder. (The reader may like to refer back to Fig. 2.6.) Each track can hold a number of blocks of information; blocks are of fixed length on some computers, but the majority allow variable length blocks on disks.

Any information on a cylinder can be accessed in the time that it takes for the disk to spin round once, but information on other cylinders cannot be accessed until the heads move to the appropriate cylinder, which takes longer than the spin time. For efficient use of disks the information should be arranged on them so as to minimise the head movements. However, any block on a disk can be accessed in a relatively short time (of the order of milliseconds), whereas it may take seconds or even minutes to find a block on a magnetic tape. Disks are therefore usually used when random access to records is required. Also, the transfer of information from a magnetic disk is faster than from magnetic tape. When fixed head disks are used then random access is even faster, since there is no head movement. Magnetic drums also provide these facilities.

In the rest of this section we shall be concerned with files on those devices which allow random access, with particular emphasis on files held on standard exchangeable disks.

The simplest method of holding information on magnetic disk is to read and write the records serially, i.e. accessing them in the physical order in which they occur, first the blocks from cylinder 1, track 1, then cylinder 1, track 2 and so on. The disk is then being used as fast but expensive magnetic tape. Because of the large capacity of disks it is normal to hold a number of files on one disk and this will require an index showing what files are on the disk. It is totally unacceptable, because of search time, to use the magnetic tape approach and to read serially through the whole disk until the appropriate file is found. Thus an index is needed which contains more than simply a list of the files on the disk: it must also give the position of each and, as we shall see, contain additional information on the position of free space on the disk.

This brings us to the problem of where a file should be placed on the disk. It is more efficient if all the records in a file are in adjacent cylinders in order to reduce head movements while the file is being processed. But a file need not be of a fixed size, because records may need to be added to it or deleted from it. If enough space is allocated for the maximum size to which the file might grow, there may be a large amount of wasted disk space. On the other hand, if space for a file is allocated to it when needed, then after a time the file is likely to consist of small fragmented areas of disk. The free space on the disk will be similarly fragmented and a disproportionate amount of time will be spent in allocating and releasing space. This allocation problem can be solved in different ways depending on the nature of the file, e.g. how frequently changes will be made. For large data files, the usual approach is to allocate a large area of the disk when initially creating the file, and to allow extension by adding further areas as required.

Having allocated space for a file, it becomes necessary to decide how to store and access data within it. If only serial access is wanted there are no particular problems, but usually the user will want to access the data randomly. He will refer to a record by a record number or **key** (a record may in fact be identifiable by more than one key, for different purposes); means are therefore required, whereby from the record or key number used, the block containing that record can be identified. The simplest case is when fixed-length, consecutively numbered records are stored in fixed-length blocks which are also consecutively numbered. It is then easy for the file handling software to find the block concerned from the record number, by using the formula

$$\text{block number} = \left[\frac{\text{record number}}{\text{number of records per block}}\right]$$

where the square brackets denote 'integral part of'. (Blocks and records are numbered from 0.) Use of this method requires that space will have to be allocated for all potential records whether or not they actually exist. In our payroll example the employee numbers, with check digits removed, will act as the keys and are unlikely to be consecutive, though correctly ordered. Apart from any other factors, staff turnover would in time mean that several possible key numbers are unused. Therefore some other method of finding the record is needed.

The commonest technique, the use of **index sequential files**, is designed for files which are normally accessed sequentially, i.e. in order of increasing key number, and which may also be accessed randomly. Most forms of index sequential filing allow new records to be inserted into the file or existing records deleted, such as for new or departing employees.

Index sequential filing is usually used for large data files, extending over several consecutive cylinders, and stored in order of increasing key number so that they can be accessed sequentially in an efficient manner, with minimal head movements. To access the file randomly there are a number of levels of indexes, a **cylinder index** which gives the highest key numbers in each cylinder and a set of **track indexes,** one for each cylinder, which give the highest key numbers in each track of the cylinder. The cylinder index is held on the first cylinder of the file: when the file is first accessed this index is copied into main store and held there all the time the file is being processed. When the user specifies the key of the record that he requires, the file handling software uses the cylinder index to locate which cylinder contains the record. The appropriate track index is then input (in some implementations it may already be in main store) and the track which contains the record is identified. Sometimes there is also a **block index** on each track to locate the block required, which is then read into store and the particular record extracted. Fig. 5.4. shows this arrangement of indexes. It can be seen that any record in the file can be found by using a small number of disk accesses. Once the record has been read it may be updated and (assuming that its size has not been increased) written back to disk simply by over-writing the old version.

As well as accessing existing records the user may want to insert new records or delete old ones. When an index sequential file is first created and the initial version of the file written to it, it is usual to specify a **packing density**. This means that the data will not be written so as to use all available space; instead a proportion of space on each track will be left free. When a record is to be inserted, the track on which it should be held is located and then the block where it should be included is found. That block is read into store,

cylinder number	highest key number in cylinder
15	1326
16	17151
17	24310
18	38193
19	42000

(a)

track number	highest key number
1	2611
2	4200
3	4513
4	5374
5	6398

(b)

block number	highest key number
1	4213
2	4219
3	4234
4	4369
5	4383

(c)

Fig. 5.4. Tables indicating the form of a hierarchy of indexes associated with a file held on cylinders 15 to 19 of a disk pack. Table (a) shows the cylinder index which gives the range of key numbers held on each cylinder; cylinder 16 holds records with keys in the range 1327 to 17151. Table (b) shows part of the track index for cylinder 16, which indicates similarly how the key numbers in this range are sub-divided between the tracks on that cylinder; track 3 holds the records with keys in the range 4201 to 4513. Table (c) shows part of the block index for track 3, which indicates similarly in which blocks on the track the actual records are stored. To find a given record (e.g. with key 4376) it is simply necessary to scan these indexes in turn, giving cylinder 16, then track 3 then block 5, which can then be searched to find the record with that key.

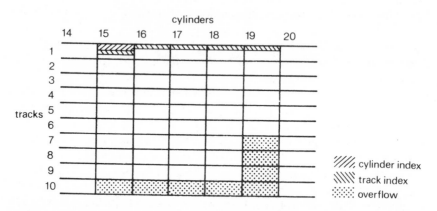

Fig. 5.5. Diagrammatic representation of the file discussed in Fig. 5.4, showing cylinder index, track indexes and overflow areas. The disk pack has ten surfaces and hence there are ten tracks per cylinder; the file is held on cylinders 15 to 19.

the new record added if possible, and the block written back. This may mean that a record at the end of the block must now be written into the next block on the track, and so on. Normally the packing density is such that the record will fit on the track. If it does not, blocks should not be transferred between tracks, which would involve altering the track indexes and also possibly cylinder indexes. In such cases the record is put into an **overflow area** and information is stored in the appropriate block saying where the record is. There is usually one track in each cylinder providing an overflow area for tracks in that cylinder. There may also be an additional overflow area at the end of the file, consisting of one or more cylinders. After the file has been in use for some time, it may be 'tidied' to bring all records into the main tracks of the file; clearing all the overflow areas, closing gaps where records have been deleted, returning to the standard packing density, and updating the indexes.

Note that the updating of index sequential files is done by over-writing records rather than copying them. This is a common method with many direct access files, especially in a multi-access systems when a user at a terminal asks for one particular record to be updated. It is obviously impractical to copy the complete file each time this happens; it is also undesirable to wait for a number of similar requests and process them together as this would give an unacceptably slow response to the terminal user. This raises the question of how to maintain the security of the data. There are a number of solutions, the commonest being periodically to take a copy of the complete file and then keep copies of all updates. If the main file fails, the copy can be reinstated and the updates reapplied.

Another method of providing security of data is to use **duplex files** where both files are updated in parallel. If an error occurs on one copy, the second continues in use and the erroneous copy is reconstituted while the system is still running.

We have now considered cases where the data is usually accessed sequentially and is stored in a sequential or index sequential file, though the index sequential file also allows random accessing and insertion, deletion and updating without copying. When records in a file are normally accessed in a random rather than a sequential order, there is no reason why the records need be stored sequentially provided there is a method of finding the required records and being able to update, insert and delete them. The obvious way is to keep a complete index of every record in the file and always to use this index to access records. This is usually inefficient, especially when the number of records is large. In some cases one record may refer to others, e.g. a record about seats on a plane will refer to records about the individual passengers. In such circumstances it may be more efficient for the reference to be to the block containing the record, rather than to the record itself. This method needs to be used with care, because if there is a corruption in the file that is referred to, and the file is reconstituted, either all the records in the file must be replaced in their previous positions, or all references elsewhere to records in the file must be located and changed.

Another method of randomly accessing records is by **hashing**. A hash is an algorithm which generates a number from the record key. This number is then used as a block number and the record placed in that block, or retrieved from it if it already exists. To be useful, a hashing algorithm must satisfy three basic requirements: (1) it must produce a wide spread of block numbers; (2) the number of records in each block should be approximately the same, i.e. there should not be many blocks which are either nearly empty or nearly full; and (3) it should be easy to calculate. Hashing removes the necessity of searching and maintaining indexes, and we shall look at it in more detail in the next section. As in the index sequential case, overflow must be allowed for, even though this will be infrequent if the hashing function is chosen carefully. Again overflow areas are used, and again the block in which the record should have gone must contain some indication of where the overflow area is.

There are a number of other methods of accessing data, e.g. there may be multiple indexes where records may be accessed by more than one key. Developments in data bases have led to more complex methods of cross-referencing and techniques for handling them.

When records are inserted into or deleted from files fairly frequently, the method of allocating space should not involve the records being held physically in the order of their keys. In such cases information is kept indicating where the free space in the file is. This may be in the form of a **map**, e.g. one bit representing each position in the file and set to 1 if the position is free and set to 0 otherwise. A more common method is to **chain** or **link** the free blocks together, where each block contains book-keeping information pointing to the next free block in the chain (and sometimes also to the previous block). When space is needed, a block is allocated from the chain: when records are deleted, space is returned to the chain. There may be separate chains, one for each cylinder, so that related records can be arranged to be on the same cylinder.

This technique of chaining can be used to allocate records within a file and can be used as a pool of free space for allocation of space to a number of files whose size is unpredictable but not large, e.g. files of programs. Space is allocated to the files as and when needed; this avoids the waste of space which is likely to result if the person creating the file has to guess its size, since he will naturally err on the safe side. Chaining can also be used for data files, and the blocks allocated from the free space can each contain book-keeping information pointing to the next block in the file, so that the file can be accessed sequentially without the use of indexes and without the blocks having to be in sequence.

The organisation of filestore is a wide and interesting area on which the systems analyst must spend a lot of time, for upon it will depend the efficiency of his whole system.

5.4 Sorting and Searching

The sorting problem is simple to state: given a file of records, each record having a key, e.g. an employee number, we want to order the file so that the records are in increasing or decreasing order of keys. The records may have more than one key, in which case the file can be sorted on different keys. Similarly the searching problem is simple to state: given a file of records, find the record with a particular key number.

The two tasks are clearly interrelated, because the method of searching for a file will depend on how it has been sorted. We shall find that neither problem is as straightforward as it seems.

There are various estimates on the amount of computer time spent on sorting: it is likely that it is at least 25 %. This suggests that sorting is very important, or that it is done when it should not be, or that it is done inefficiently. In fact all are true: sorting is very important, but it is sometimes done unnecessarily and is often done inefficiently. Whether sorting is necessary in a given instance depends on the nature of the program. Deciding this forms part of the general analysis of the given application: sorting is obviously pointless if the time taken is not justified by, for example, later savings in search time. Here we shall give the reader a feeling for the features of sorting and searching: it must be realised that there is no single 'best' (i.e. fastest) method of sorting. Different algorithms are more suitable in different situations, depending on many factors, some of which we shall point out in our examples. The programmer must be aware of the main factors which are likely to apply to his problem, and use his judgement to select which method to use.

Sorting can be divided into two main types, **internal sorting** and **external sorting**. Internal sorting is when all the records can be held together in main store; this allows flexibility in accessing the records, and we shall be mainly concerned with this type of sorting. External sorting is necessary when the file is too large to be held entirely in main store at one time, and hence imposes stringent conditions on the task of accessing the records. This type of sorting is common in commercial computing and we shall consider one method of this type.

There are several ways in which a file can be sorted into key order:

(1) *Physical sorting:* The records can be physically rearranged so that their keys are in order. This is suitable only if both the keys and the records are small.

(2) *Address table sorting:* A table of link addresses pointing to the records is constructed, and these link addresses are manipulated instead of moving the records themselves. This is suitable when the records and the keys are large.

(3) *Key sorting:* The keys from the records are also included in the table of link addresses. This is faster than address table sorting and is suitable for large records with small keys.

(4) *List sorting:* An additional link field is included in each record. These links are manipulated so that after sorting each link points to the following record, but the records themselves are not moved. This is also suitable for large records.

If tables or links are used, then the records can in principle be physically rearranged after sorting, but this is unnecessary since in most applications the tables or links are adequate for subsequent handling of the sorted file.

We shall now look at different methods of sorting, and concentrate on the first type where the records are rearranged. The methods can be easily modified to deal with the other types. First we must introduce some notation that we shall use throughout the discussion:

Let
$$n = \text{number of records to be sorted}$$
$$C = \text{time taken to compare two keys}$$
$$W = \text{time taken to write one record}$$
$$W' = \text{time taken to write one key}$$

The records in a file will be denoted by $R_1, R_2, \ldots, R_n$ with corresponding keys $K_1, K_2, \ldots, K_n$.

It will help the reader to stop at this point and think of different methods of human sorting and searching, e.g. how would he sort a pack of cards or a collection of books, how would he find a name in a telephone directory?

(A) *Insertion:* This is a common method by which some card players sort a hand, where they pick up each card in turn and insert it in the appropriate place in their hand. In this method the sorted file is kept separate from the original. The first record from the file is placed in the first position of the sorted file. If the first $j-1$ records have been sorted, then the jth record is taken from the file and its key is compared with each key in the sorted file in turn. When the appropriate place in the new file is found, the record is inserted there and all the subsequent records in the new file are pushed along one position. This is illustrated in the table below, only the key numbers of each record being shown:

	old file						new file				
	R_1	R_2	R_3	R_4	R_5						
unsorted:	71	43	67	68	19						
initially											
step 1		43	67	68	19		71				
step 2			67	68	19		43	71			
step 3				68	19		43	67	71		
step 4					19		43	67	68	71	
step 5							19	43	67	68	71
					sorted:		R_5	R_2	R_3	R_4	R_1

The analysis of this method is not difficult. At the jth step, when R_j is being inserted into the sorted file, there are on average $\frac{1}{2}(j-1)$ comparisons, and $\frac{1}{2}(j-1)$ records in the sorted file will be written into new positions. R_j will also be written into the new file, and hence the total time to insert R_j will be

$$\tfrac{1}{2}(j-1)C + \tfrac{1}{2}(j+1)W$$

Since the file consists of n records, the average total time to sort the file will be

$$\sum_{j=1}^{n} \left\{ \tfrac{1}{2}(j-1)C + \tfrac{1}{2}(j+1)W \right\} = \tfrac{1}{4}n(n-1)C + \tfrac{1}{4}n(n+3)W \sim \tfrac{1}{4}n^2(C+W)$$

(We are deliberately ignoring overheads, e.g. testing of loops, etc.)

As with most sorting methods there are a number of possible variations. For instance the first record can be placed in the middle of the new file, thus creating space for subsequent records on both sides of the first and reducing the number of records to be moved at each step. The running time is approximately halved but the programming is more complicated.

(B) *Selection:* In this method the procedure is to scan through the whole file to find the smallest key, and then transfer the corresponding record to the first position in the new file. The process is then repeated over and over again, picking up the smallest key and adding that record to the new file each time, until the whole file has been dealt with. For the method to work, the key of the copied record must be changed each time: otherwise the method will continually pick up the same record. One solution is to replace the key of a copied record by a dummy key, a key whose value is greater than all of the others, and hence on each scan there will always be a record whose key is less than the dummy key. For example, if the keys consist of three alphabetic characters and are to be sorted into alphabetic order, then the dummy key could be ZZZ, provided that ZZZ is not a key of an actual record in the file.

Each scan will require $n-1$ comparisons and two writes, one for the record and one for the dummy key. Hence the total time for this selection method will be $n(n-1)C + n(W+W') \sim n^2C + n(W+W')$.

Instead of using a dummy key, the smallest record can be replaced by the last record in the file, so that after each scan the records still to be sorted are at the front of the file. On each scan the number of comparisons will be reduced by 1, and hence the total time is approximately $\frac{1}{2}n^2C + 2nW$. This variation is illustrated below:

old file					*new file*				
R_1	R_2	R_3	R_4	R_5					
CAT	MAN	GNU	AUK	DOG					
CAT	MAN	GNU	DOG		AUK				
DOG	MAN	GNU			AUK	CAT			
GNU	MAN				AUK	CAT	DOG		
MAN					AUK	CAT	DOG	GNU	
					AUK	CAT	DOG	GNU	MAN
					R_4	R_1	R_5	R_3	R_2

The comparison between the selection and insertion methods appears to be straightforward, depending only on the size of the file and the time taken for the various operations. But the time needed for the selection method is fixed for all possible arrangements of records in the file, while the time needed for the insertion method is only an *average* time. For some arrangements of the records the time could be much longer. There is a strong argument for quoting not simply the average time for a sorting method but also the maximum time;

we shall not do so here, but the reader is invited to calculate it himself for each of the methods that we give. This example serves to illustrate the point that, when choosing a sorting method, the programmer should if possible determine what arrangements of records are most likely to arise, which will help him to select the most appropriate algorithm.

Both insertion and selection involve creating a new file which is separate from the previous one. To conserve storage space it is usually preferable, and often necessary, to sort a file within its own length, and this will involve exchanging records. Two records, X and Y say, can be exchanged by the following operations:

> write X into a temporary space in store,
> write Y into the place originally occupied by X,
> write X into the place originally occupied by Y.

Thus an exchange involves 3 writes, so that the time for one exchange is $3W$.

Both insertion and selection can be modified so as to sort a file within its own length. For example, in selection the procedure is to scan through the file and exchange the largest record with the last, then to scan the first $n-1$ keys and exchange the largest and the $(n-1)$th. The process continues until one record is left, which now has the smallest key. This is illustrated below; at the ith step there will be $n-i$ comparisons and one exchange, and hence the total time taken will be

$$\tfrac{1}{2}n(n-1)C + (n-1)3W \sim \tfrac{1}{2}n^2C + 3nW.$$

initial file	CAT	MAN	GNU	AUK	DOG
after 1st step	CAT	DOG	GNU	AUK	MAN
after 2nd step	CAT	DOG	AUK	GNU	MAN
after 3rd step	CAT	AUK	DOG	GNU	MAN
after 4th step	AUK	CAT	DOG	GNU	MAN

(C) *Exchange* or *bubble sort:* This method starts by scanning the whole file, and comparing the key of each record with that of its successor. If two consecutive records are in the wrong order, i.e. the smaller key is second, then these records are exchanged. An exchanged record will thus move down the file until it meets a record which should stay after it in the final order. Hence after one scan of the file the record with the largest key will be in its correct place at the end of the file. Scanning the file is repeated until there are no more exchanges, the scan stopping one record shorter each time. The number of comparisons on the ith scan will be $n-i$, and there will be an average of $\tfrac{1}{2}(n-i)$ exchanges giving an approximate average time of $\tfrac{1}{2}n^2C + \tfrac{3}{4}n^2W$. One minor modification that can be made: after any scan, all the records (after and including the last one to be exchanged) must be in their final positions, and hence need not be compared on subsequent scans. Thus if a note is made of where the last exchange took place, the scan may stop more than one record shorter next time.

If the file is initially almost in order, e.g. updating a football league table by adding in one set of results, then the exchange method is very efficient and will provide a sorted file in only a few scans, because the records will not stray very far away from their ordered position. Sometimes, on the other hand, all $n-1$ scans will be needed to sort the file even if only one record is out of place, e.g. if the record with the smallest key is last in the file, as it will only rise up one place on each scan. In this case the total time will be $\frac{1}{2}n(n-1)(C+3W)$. To overcome this one can scan the file alternately in opposite directions, so that on the first scan the 'heaviest' record sinks to the bottom and on the next scan the 'lightest' record rises to the top: this is the origin of the name 'bubble' sort. Our example uses this variation and is given in Fig. 5.6. The analysis for the average time of a bubble sort is difficult but even with refinements it can be shown to be of the form $Kn^2C + K'n^2W$, where K and K' are constants, i.e. proportional to the square of the number of records.

		file after each scan					
initial	1st scan	2nd scan	3rd scan	4th scan	5th scan	6th scan	7th scan
EMU	DOG	AUK	AUK	AUK	AUK	AUK	AUK
DOG	CAT	DOG	CAT	CAT	CAT	CAT	CAT
CAT	COW	CAT	COW	COD	COD	COD	COD
COW	EMU	COW	DOG	COW	COW	COW	COW
GNU	GNU	EMU	EMU	DOG	DOG	DOE	DOE
PIG	PIG	GNU	GNU	EMU	EMU	DOG	DOG
RAT	AUK	PIG	COD	GNU	DOE	EMU	EMU
AUK	MAN	COD	MAN	DOE	GNU	GNU	GNU
MAN	HEN	MAN	HEN	MAN	HEN	HEN	HEN
HEN	DOE	HEN	DOE	HEN	MAN	MAN	MAN
DOE	COD	DOE	PIG	PIG	PIG	PIG	PIG
COD	RAT	RAT	RAT	RAT	RAT	RAT	RAT
number of exchanges	8	9	6	6	2	2	0

Fig. 5.6. Example of a bubble sort with alternating direction of scan. The direction of each scan is shown by the arrow, and the dashed lines indicate the start and finish of each scan. The example shows how these can be moved by more than one position after a scan, by taking into account where the last exchange occurred. It also shows that the method may move an item away from its correct position before finally returning it there.

(D) *Shell's sort:* The last internal sorting method that we shall briefly look at has been included to give some indication of the complexities that can arise in the search for better sorting algorithms. This method is named after its inventor and was designed to get over the problem which arises in exchange algorithms like the bubble sort, where a minimum of m exchanges is needed to move a record m positions in the file. Shell's method is to group together records which are well separated but at constant intervals apart. The intervals are constant so that the program to access the records in each group is easier to write. For example, for 12 records the 1st and 7th could form a group, the 2nd and 8th, the 3rd and 9th and so on, making six groups of two each. Each group is then sorted separately. The method will be easier to follow if we apply it to the example that was used to illustrate the bubble sort:

	1st	2nd	3rd	4th	5th	6th
Before:	EMU	DOG	CAT	COW	GNU	PIG
After:	EMU	AUK	CAT	COW	DOE	COD

	7th	8th	9th	10th	11th	12th
Before	RAT	AUK	MAN	HEN	DOE	COD
After:	RAT	DOG	MAN	HEN	GNU	PIG

The 2nd has been exchanged with the 8th, the 5th with the 11th and the 6th with the 12th, and the others remain still.

The next step is to divide into groups again, but with a *smaller* interval. This will give fewer groups (the same number as the size of the interval) with more records in each. These are again sorted separately, using a simpler method. The process is repeated, with fewer groups of more records each time, until eventually there is just a single group of all the records – the original file which had to be sorted. At each stage the sorting processes involve files which are either comparatively short or relatively well ordered. Continuing our example using 4 groups of 3 each, then 2 groups of 6, and finally the whole file, we obtain:

interval size	number in group											
6	2	EMU	AUK	CAT	COW	DOE	COD	RAT	DOG	MAN	MAN	GNU	PIG
4	3	DOE	AUK	CAT	COW	EMU	COD	GNU	DOG	MAN	HEN	RAT	PIG
2	6	CAT	AUK	DOE	COD	EMU	COW	GNU	DOG	MAN	HEN	RAT	PIG
1	12 (final)	AUK	CAT	COD	COW	DOE	DOG	EMU	GNU	HEN	MAN	PIG	RAT

The speed of the method depends heavily on the choice of the sequence of intervals, and the reader may like to experiment with different group sizes, working out the number of exchanges that each involves. The mathematical analysis of this and the many other sorting algorithms is interesting and though it is by no means trivial, there is still wide scope for the mathematically minded to experiment with various methods and try to analyse them.

(E) *Balanced sort:* We now give an example of external sorting, used where the number of records in the file to be sorted is too large to be held in main store. The difficulty is the slowness in accessing records from backing store. The case that we shall consider is where the file is held on magnetic tape. The basic idea is to sort as many records as possible at a time by a series of internal sorts, thus forming a set of sorted subfiles. These subfiles are then merged together, possibly several times, to obtain the final sorted file.

Merging two sorted subfiles is simple. Two pointers are set, to the first record of each subfile. Whichever record has the smaller key is copied into a new subfile and the corresponding pointer is moved to the next record in that subfile. The process is continued until one subfile is empty and then the remainder of the other is copied on to the end of the new subfile. The length of the new subfile is the sum of the lengths of the original subfiles. This method can be used for internal sorting and the time taken is $n \log_2 n \, (C+W)$.

The simplest external sort with magnetic tape is the balanced two-way merge, where four tape reels are used. During the first pass through main store, subfiles of records from tape A are internally sorted and output alternately on to two tape reels B and C. These are then rewound and the sorted subfiles from B and C are merged to obtain new subfiles which are twice as long as the previous ones, the new subfiles being output alternately on to tapes D and A as they are formed. During merging, the whole subfile does not have to be in main store at one time – it can be read in blocks. The process is continued until the entire sorted file is output on to one tape. This is illustrated in Fig. 5.7.

The method can easily be modified to permit more working tapes, which will reduce the rewind time. If a file is contained on more than one reel, then each reel should be sorted first and merged afterwards.

The reader should be aware that files which are to be sorted will be much larger than the examples we have given, and the sorting times can be substantially different. For example, for a relatively small file of 1024 records which is being sorted internally, the approximate average time by insertion will be $524288(C+W)$ and by merging will be $10240 \, (C+W)$, differing by a factor about 50. The quoted times should only be used as a rough indication of the relative speeds of the different methods, since they depend on the initial arrangement of the records and take no account of the book-keeping within the sorting program.

We now turn to the problem of searching a file, i.e. finding which record or records have a specified key, so that the rest of the information contained in the record can be obtained. Most searches have to allow for the case when the record is missing, e.g. when the key number is incorrectly given. In the previous Section (5.3) we introduced the idea of having indexes, consisting of keys with pointers to records or secondary indexes. The reader has probably met this idea before when using a thumb index on a dictionary. The main advantage of using indexes is that not all of the records need to be held in main store; thus a search is commonly done on the index, not the complete file, and this is the type of searching that we shall discuss.

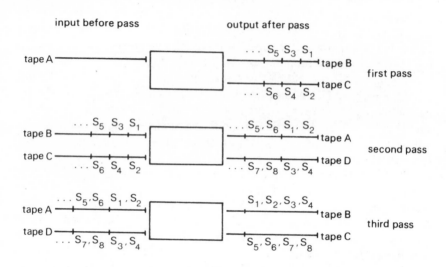

Fig. 5.7. Diagrammatic representation of the first three passes of a balanced two-way merge. S_1, S_2, ... are the subfiles created by internal sorting on the first pass.

The simplest solution is to leave the index unsorted, and use as the search algorithm a simple scan through all the keys until the correct one is found. The average time taken, assuming all records are equally likely to be wanted, will be approximately $\frac{1}{2}nC$. If the index is ordered then the scan can be stopped once the key numbers exceed that being looked for, but the average time is still $\frac{1}{2}nC$, as the only gain is when the required key is missing.

The commonest method of searching an index that is sorted in key order is the **binary search**. The required key is compared with the key of the middle record in the index: the $\frac{1}{2}n$th record if n is even and the $\frac{1}{2}(n+1)$th record if n is odd. If this is the record that is required then the search is over, otherwise a further comparison is made to see if the required key comes earlier or later in the index. If earlier, then the test is repeated on the first half of the index; if later, it is repeated on the second half. Thus the length of the section of the index to be searched is successively halved each time until the correct key is found. The average time for binary searching is of the order of $\log_2 n$, considerably faster than the previous method; but it requires more programming, it requires the index to be sorted, and it requires being able to find the middle record in the index easily.

A binary search example is given below; the file to be searched has 1000 records with key numbers k[1], k[2], ..., k [1000], ordered sequentially:

comparison	result	range of records	midpoint of range
k > k[500]	true	501–1000	750
k > k[750]	false	501–750	625
k > k[625]	true	626–750	688
k > k[688]	false	626–688	657
k > k[657]	false	626–657	641
k > k[641]	false	626–641	633
k > k[633]	false	636–633	629
k > k[629]	true	630–633	631
k > k[631]	false	630–631	630
k > k[630]	true	631	

When there is a hierarchy of primary and secondary indexes, the search time is minimised when the secondary indexes or sets of records have approximately the same number of items. The indexing structure should be chosen with this in mind, because some natural and otherwise convenient forms of indexing may not have this feature: the thumb index of the dictionary is a primary index on the letters of the alphabet, but there are many more English words starting with the letter R than with the letter Z. When such difficulties

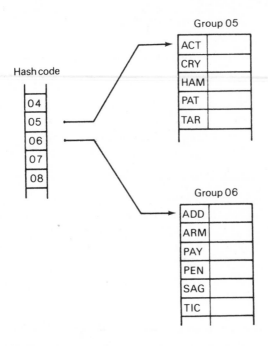

Fig. 5.8. Schematic representation of a hashing process, showing hash codes obtained from three-letter keys by the algorithm described in the text, and some of the records which would be associated with two of them by means of the algorithm. (Only the keys for the records are shown.)

arise, they can be overcome by using the hashing functions which were introduced in the last section.

A hashing function splits a file of records into small, approximately equal sized groups, each then being sorted. If the groups are small enough, each can be contained within one block. A record can then be located found by performing the hash on the required key, simply by giving the block number, usually without any searching. An example of a hashing function which splits a file of records whose keys are 3 alphabetic characters into 100 approximately equal groups is as follows:

Each key may be expressed as an integer by coding each letter $A \to 0$, $B \to 1$, $C \to 2$, ... , $Z \to 25$ and then converting the 3 character key by $c_1 c_2 c_3 \to 26^2.c_1 + 26.c_2 + c_3$ (e.g. $CAT \to 26^2.2 + 26.0 + 19 \to 1371$). This is not really a hashing function at all; each group will contain only one record or none at all, many code numbers will not be used, and the search time will be longer than if we used the original keys. A true hashing is obtained by squaring the number obtained (e.g. $1371^2 = 1879641$) and taking two of the middle digits (e.g. 79). This will give an integer in the range 0 to 99 inclusive, and will split the records into approximately equal groups. Taking the bottom two digits will not work since no square ends in 3 or 7; neither will taking the top two digits, since these will be strongly related to the first letter. Words that are close together in the alphabet can be in different groups, and words that are far apart alphabetically can be in the same group. The latter phenomenon is shown in Fig. 5.8 while the former is demonstrated by the following table:

3 letter word	code	square	group number
HAD	4735	22420225	20
HAG	4738	22448644	48
HAM	4744	22505536	05
HAT	4751	22572001	72
HAY	4756	22619536	19

There are many other techniques for sorting and searching: we have chosen these examples because they are commonly used and because they indicate some of the problems involved. This is an important and interesting area of computing and there is a specific reference in the reading list at the end of the book for those who wish to follow it up.

5.5 Operational Research

Our discussion so far has been concerned with using computers to perform tasks that were previously done manually, as the payroll would have been if computers were not available. Using computers simply enables them to be done faster and more efficiently. But in other areas, such as stock control, the effect of using computers is also that far more tasks can be done than was possible before, and more accurate and up-to-date information can be made available. Because of this a manufacturer may be able to reduce the capital tied up in stock since he does not have to allow for such large error margins. Examples are also to be found in opinion sampling and in particular market research. There has been a great increase during the last two decades. Computers have made it possible to collect and analyse much more data than before within reasonable timescales.

The use of computers may not directly reduce the running costs of an organisation. The direct savings in one area are often used to finance other operations not previously possible. The aim of such new operations within a commercial organisation is to increase profitability. In the past big organisations needed large and powerful computer systems to handle the routine work which was needed to be done within specific time scales. The systems were sometimes expensive to purchase and run and so it was necessary to get the most out of them. Moreover many people in computer installations were enthusiastic to exploit computers in every possible way.

These factors, among others, led to the rapid growth of the field of **operational research**. Like much else in computing the origins of operational research lay in military necessity, and in particular the military science of logistics. Operational research is an applied science and is used to help management to make decisions. It consists of stating problems in mathematical or statistical terms, and evolving techniques to obtain solutions. The techniques are usually a combination of computing, mathematics and statistics. We shall describe a few of the types of problem that can be solved by operational research methods, but we shall not attempt to describe how to solve the problems. There are many books on the mathematics and techniques of the subject, to which those who are interested can refer.

Our first example of operational research is **Critical Path Analysis**. In this technique a given project is split into individual, self-contained steps or activities. The time that each activity is expected to take is specified together with a precedence-ordering, i.e. for each activity there is a list of activities which must be finished before it can commence. The problem is, what is the earliest completion date for the project and what is the 'critical path', in other words which activities are critical to completing the project on time?

The problem can be drawn as a network as illustrated in Fig. 5.9 which details the various activities involved in launching a new product. Each activity is represented by a line, and the number by each line is the time required to complete that activity. The diagram is read from left to right with increasing time, each line being linked with its immediate predecessors in the ordering, e.g. materials must be ordered before they are delivered, and this must occur before any production takes place. In this example it is easy to find the critical path and to see which activities have slack, e.g. the drafting and approval of the publicity material can overrun by thirteen weeks before delaying the project. However, if the project contains several hundreds of

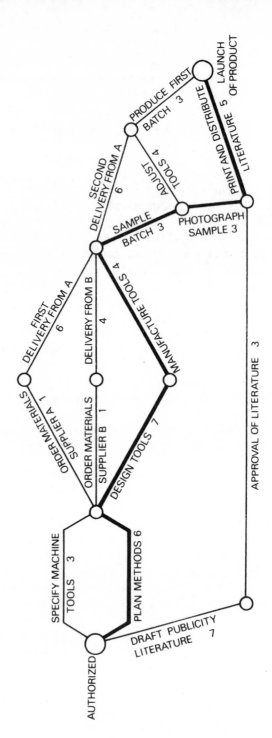

Fig. 5.9. Example of a network for the critical path analysis of the process of introducing a new product. The numbers indicate the time estimates for the various activities, in weeks. The thick line is the critical path; delays in any of the activities along the critical path will delay the launch of the product unless any later activities can make up the time by completion ahead of schedule (though this could change the critical path).

activities, a computer is needed to perform the analysis. This type of problem is so common that many manufacturers provide PERT (Project Evaluation and Review Techniques) packages as part of their software. To use PERT, the user only has to input lists of activities, times for each activity, and list of precedences: the package produces the critical path and other scheduling information as required. Critical Path Analysis can be used in forward planning to make the maximum use of resources and to make more accurate tenders, etc., and can also be used during the course of the project to review its scheduling, e.g. if some unforeseen circumstance has occurred such as a strike or an industrial accident.

Critical Path Analysis can be extended to include extra conditions, e.g. not just the time but also the manpower available for each activity, imposing conditions on the maximum number of men working on the project at any one time. Another extension could be to assign a minimum, likely and maximum time to each activity.

Our next example is **linear programming**. A typical problem for a production manager is that a set of jobs has to be completed, with sufficient resources for each job. Some jobs can be done in different ways by using different amounts and combinations of resources, and some of these ways are better than others, better in the sense of being less costly or more profitable. Some or all of the jobs must be done, but there are constraints in that there are not enough resources, e.g. of manpower or materials, to do every job in the best way. The problem is how to allocate the resources between the jobs so that the objective is achieved at either minimum cost or maximum profit.

A typical example is that a company manufactures three products A, B and C with respective profits 8, 15 and 25 per unit. The minimum weekly production requirements are 10, 15 and 7 units of A, B and C respectively. The time required at each stage of production for each unit is given in the following table:

		manufacturing	assembling	packaging
	A	3	4	1
product	B	3.5	5	1.5
	C	5	8	3

The figures are man-hours for each product at each stage.

The available manpower is 150 man-hours for manufacturing, 200 man-hours for assembly and 60 man-hours for packaging.

The problem can be restated mathematically as follows: if the number of units produced of each product is x_1, x_2 and x_3 respectively, then the manager wants to maximise the profit, i.e. the linear expression

$$8x_1 + 15x_2 + 25x_3$$

subject to several constraints,

e.g. $\qquad\qquad x_1 \geqslant 10,\ x_2 \geqslant 15$ and $x_3 \geqslant 7.$

These are the minimum weekly requirements, and there are some further constraints because of the limited manpower:

$$3x_1 + 3{\cdot}5x_2 + 5x_3 \leqslant 150$$
$$4x_1 + 5x_2 + 8x_3 \leqslant 200$$
$$x_1 + 1{\cdot}5x_2 + 3x_3 \leqslant 60.$$

This can be seen to have solution $x_1 = 16{\cdot}5$, $x_2 = 15$ and $x_3 = 7$, i.e. all the spare manpower after meeting the minimum requirement should be spent on producing product A. Not all problems have such simple solutions.

Mathematically the general linear programming problem can be stated as follows: given a number of variables x_i ($i = 1$ to n) and the two sets of constraints

$$x_i \geqslant b_i\ (i = 1 \text{ to } n)$$

(the b_i are often 0 to stop negative production) and

$$\sum_j a_{ij}x_j \leqslant b_i \quad (i = n{+}1 \text{ to } m),$$

find the values of the x_i satisfying these constraints which minimise the function

$$c_1x_1 + c_2x_2 + \ldots + c_nx_n.$$

(The requirement to maximise profit, i.e. maximise the given function, can be represented by changing the signs of the coefficients c_i.)

When only a few variables are involved the linear programming problem is easy to deal with. In practical cases in industry the number of variables will be much larger, with a corresponding increase in the number of constraints. Computers have the capacity to handle the large amount of data and computations involved and algorithms have been developed to obtain the optimal solution, the best known being the simplex method.

One assumption of linear programming is that the costs and the profits are proportional to the production of each product; the other main assumption is that the factors in the constraints are also proportional to the manufactured quantity of each product. In many cases of practical importance the function to be minimised or maximised, and all or some of the constraints, will not be linear functions of the variables. Computer techniques are important here because only the linear case has been fully analysed by mathematicians. The subject as a whole is called **mathematical programming**. It should be noted that 'programming' in this context does not mean computer programming, although computer programs are often used in solving mathematical programming problems.

Our last example is **simulation**. Many managerial decision problems are too complex to be solved either by computer techniques or by mathematical theory. Difficulties often arise because the problem involves probabilities rather than certainties, e.g. the likely frequency of given events. In such cases the system to be analysed is **simulated,** i.e. a program is written which behaves in a similar way to the simulated system. The simulation may be that of an existing system (e.g. the flow of traffic through a road network) which is undertaken to try to understand how it behaves and how it might be controlled, or it may be a hypothetical system, whose behaviour can be examined without the cost and perhaps the risk found in 'live' experiments. The basis of the simulation may be a theoretical model derived from general principles, such as a simulation of the behaviour of a nuclear reactor or the landing of a space module on the surface of the moon, where known physical laws give a reliable prediction of how the system will behave. There may be no theoretical model because there are no known general laws or principles, as when random events are involved, or in individual human behaviour. In this case simulation is still possible and often more valuable; it can be based on, for example, empirically obtained probability distributions of the occurrence of certain events. Several high-level languages have been developed specifically to help the writing of simulation programs, the best known being SIMULA, SIMSCRIPT and GPSS (General Purpose System Simulator).

An example of a system which is very difficult to analyse mathematically is the following queuing problem. A supermarket manager has several cashiers and a number of check-out points, and also knows the frequency of customers throughout each day. The customers arrive at the check-out counters, and if all the counters are busy the customers queue in a single line and are served on a 'first come first served' basis. The manager wants to know how the system behaves, and if the system is stable, if the queue will grow without limit, are more check-out points needed and if so how many, how should the cashiers be organised into a shift system, what is the maximum time a customer will have to wait, and so on? Without a computer the manager can only trust to keen observation, judgement and luck. Using a simulation based on observed probability distributions of the arrival rates of customers at the check-outs at different times, the manager can experiment with different organisations of the factors within his control, and arrive at an informed and efficient solution.

In this section we have only been able to scratch the surface of operational research, and have omitted many important areas such as the problems of mathematical programming when some or all of the variables must be integers (e.g. one can send half a load of goods to a given destination, but not in half a lorry with half a driver), or the theory of games and economic decision-making, where one's decisions and their effect are influenced by the existence of and decisions made by competitors. Operational research is a fascinating subject for the mathematical theorist, for the computer scientist simply interested in applications of computers, and for the person interested in how to achieve desired ends most effectively.

Chapter 6

The Computer as a Watchdog

In many areas of computing time is crucial, in the discussion of sorting techniques and numerical analysis there was emphasis on the processing time. There is another important time factor, namely the total time taken to collect the data and send it to the computer, plus the time the computer takes to process it, plus the time taken to send back the results. This is the **real-time**, i.e. the elapsed time in hours, minutes and seconds from start to finish of the complete job, rather than the amount of **mill-time**, which is the time that the computer's arithmetic unit spends in processing. These two times are related, but they present different types of problems.

In this chapter we are mainly concerned with real-time computing, which is computing with external time constraints. Not only must the computer perform the necessary calculations within a specific elapsed time, but it must also perform all the associated data transfers within that time.

Real-time computing problems cannot usually be solved by using a more powerful number-crunching machine, since most problems arise in the organisation and efficient use of all the resources controlled by the computer. The input and output of information into and from main store is particularly important, but there are other factors such as the efficient use of resources within the computer, e.g. central processor, main store capacity, and the organisation of programs there. To understand real-time computing one must not only understand how the applications work but also how the computer controls and uses the resources.

6.1 Applications of Process Control

When computers were first used for analysing experimental scientific data, the scientist in the laboratory performed his experiment as usual, taking his readings and writing them down in the laboratory notebook. Instead of then sitting down and analysing his data with pencil and paper or a desk calculator he would transfer the data to punched cards or paper tape, and use a computer to do the analysis. There could have been many reasons for using the computer: to get the results more quickly; to avoid having to do a routine and boring task; to reduce the risks of numerical error; to perform a more detailed or more accurate analysis than would have been feasible by hand. Much laboratory analysis is still done in this way, and much is still done manually because it is easy and does not warrant the use of a computer.

A typical case from the authors' own university is a student laboratory exercise. In the past students would spend time in a laboratory class using a piece of apparatus, and then sit down for the remainder of the practical period to do lengthy but routine calculations. Now, by a combination of getting the results faster and saving their own time, they can use the apparatus, feed in the data to a computer and obtain the results quickly. Using the results already obtained they then have time to plan a further experiment on the same apparatus and carry it out in the same way. This has the double advantage that they have more practice with the equipment, and have the opportunity to exercise judgement in the interpretation of the results. These teaching advantages are paralleled in the research or industrial laboratory: a research worker can be more ambitious in planning his work programme, an industrial scientist engaged in, say, quality control tests of samples, can test more samples in the same time.

In this kind of computing it is not the mill time but the real time that is important, and this makes it different from most of those we have already discussed. The laboratory use of computers has developed beyond this, and at least three stages of development can be distinguished. The first stage was to remove the involvement of humans in the recording of measurements from the experimental process and the converting of these into machine readable form. This was done by designing the apparatus so that the readings could be taken automatically and then directly recorded on some medium suitable for input to the computer. In the past this was commonly paper tape, since paper tape punches are much cheaper and lighter than card punches.

This system is called a **data logging system**, and has a number of advantages. One is that time is saved, and another is that the human errors in reading and transcribing the data are eliminated, though of course the chance of mechanical error can never be completely eliminated. More important is that the experimenter does not have to be present all the time and the data logger is automatic. The problems of running an experiment continuously for forty-eight hours with frequent readings at precisely timed intervals are much reduced. Guaranteed its electrical supply, a data logger can continue to take readings until its supply of paper tape runs out – and a standard reel of tape can hold 120,000 digits or other characters. Further, a data logger records faster than a human because it operates at electromechanical rather than human speed. A teleprinter can be used as a simple, slow speed data logger – relatively expensive, but with the advantage that it simultaneously produces a visible record of what it is punching, so that a human machine minder can look at the data being recorded and perhaps take action if things are going wrong. A slow teleprinter works at ten characters a second: a human would find it difficult to write down correctly a pair of 4-digit numbers every second for half an hour. If faster logging is required, cheaper paper tape punches can be used at typical speeds of seventy-five characters per second but without simultaneous printing. At the start of the 1970s cassette magnetic tapes were beginning to supplant paper tape equipment for data logging, data being recorded on cassettes similar to those produced commercially for music recordings. Cassette data loggers are more expensive than the punches, but can record at much faster rates.

Free from the limitations of human recording, data loggers have enabled new experiments to be devised. But the recorded data, whether on cassette or on paper tape, still has to be read into the computer for processing. The next stage of development was to eliminate the intermediate paper tape or other input medium and instead to send the data directly from the apparatus into the computer. This had two immediate consequences: the recording could now take place at electronic speeds, and there was the possibility of analysing the data and outputting results while the experiment was still in progress. There are two factors which may prevent such analysis. Some kinds of analysis and calculation of results are not possible until all of the data has been collected. Data logging directly into the computer is unnecessary and probably not cost-effective if only this kind of analysis is needed, unless electronic recording speeds are involved or if it is important to minimise the time between obtaining the last data item and doing the calculation. (This is no longer strictly true since in the 1970s the dropping cost of tiny processors, called microprocessors, has meant that using a microcomputer is sometimes the cheapest way of collecting data, even if the required speed of collection is low.) The other factor which is more interesting here is that there may be insufficient time to perform the necessary analysis between the collection of one data item and the next.

This is an example of the kind of problem that can arise in real-time computing. Real-time applications involve writing programs so that the external time constraints are satisfied. The laboratory scientist designing his experiment may be handicapped by real-time constraints. Often his data is coming in at regular intervals, but where the intervals are irregular estimating the processing speed can be very difficult. Since the experiment is within his control, if the computer system cannot meet the time constraint, he can usually get round this either by giving up the simultaneous analysis or by settling for taking fewer readings in a given time. In other real-time applications the choices may be more difficult.

It can be seen that one great advantage of continuous analysis while an experiment is in progress is that the scientist can monitor its activity, think about what is happening, and perhaps gain a clearer insight into the pheno-menon that he is investigating. We have already mentioned the advantage of teleprinter data logging with simultaneous printout so that if things go wrong this can be seen and the experiment stopped. In many cases it may be impos-sible to tell from the raw input data whether things are going wrong, because this will only appear after analysis. With continuous analysis of directly input data this situation may also be covered, thus saving time and perhaps resources.

Fig. 6.1. A typical computer-based laboratory system: an A.E.I. mass spectrometer system installed in the Chemistry Department, Queen Elizabeth College. The processor (a Data General Nova) is in the tall central cabinet, with a small disk unit below it (another Nova can be seen in Fig. 2.5). The mass spectrometer itself is to the right; the specimen to be analysed is loaded into the top cabinet on the right with the front handle; the screen to the left of the processor displays results, including computer spectra in graphical form; the teletype on the extreme left is the control console for the processor. Not shown is a unit to produce permanent printed copies of displayed spectra: the technician is studying such a printed spectrum.

[*Photograph by Tony Kerr, Queen Elizabeth College*]

Reappraisal during the course of an experiment is only one of the things that the scientist can do. Continuous analysis may make it possible for him to design new kinds of experiments, in which he can actively participate in a more sophisticated and sensitive way than would be possible otherwise. Experiments whose result is affected by outside intervention are common – the chemist turning up the heat from a bunsen burner, the physicist reducing the current through a circuit. But modern experimental science often requires more precision than a human can provide or involves more intricate or complex systems than a human can control during an experiment. Continuous computer analysis adds to the scientist's observational techniques and may allow human judgement to be exercised in situations where previously it might have been impossible or disastrous. It must be repeated that this does not mean that such techniques can be usefully employed in every case in every scientific area, but the use of computers has significantly widened the range of possibilities for such experimentation.

The next stage of development of computer involvement in scientific laboratory work is for the computer to control some aspects of the experiment while it is in progress. The scientist need no longer observe the continuous analysis during the experiment, taking action when required: the program has been extended to become a **control program**. When some specified condition arises, the computer itself initiates the required adjustment in the experimental conditions. Simple forms of automatic control have been in existence for some time, in servomechanisms like thermostats, gyroscopic pilots and governors on motors, but a properly programmed computer is capable of more complex control. Progress in this direction has been limited by cost – of the computers themselves, of the monitoring and control links between the computer and the apparatus, and of the effort involved in the necessary programming. The growth of low cost mini-computers and micro-computer communications equipment can be expected to fall because of standardisation and because of increased demand making mass production feasible. The costs of writing accurate and reliable programs for this kind of work cannot be expected to reduce like the hardware. However, the difficulties of writing programs to run under real-time constraints have been eased by the development of several special purpose languages for real-time work, e.g. CORAL 66 and RTL2, and by a better understanding of the problems concerned and the development of techniques to solve them.

It is clear that the monitoring and controlling of equipment in scientific experiments can be applied to industrial machinery. First we shall look at the kind of communications between the equipment and the computer that are necessary. Sometimes when monitoring, the events to be observed are **discrete**; either a given situation does occur or it does not, or a number of distinct occurrences can be counted. For example, a chemical test on a sample will be positive or negative, or a count will be made of the number of gamma rays striking a given target in a nuclear physics experiment. Most events are **continuous** and involve continuous measurement, such as voltages, temperatures, and pressures. Even though what is measured may not be electrical, the output from the measuring device is normally a continuously varying electrical signal. This is more accurate than in a human-monitored experiment where the measurement may be a discrete approximation from a scale or a meter. The distinction between 'discrete' and 'continuous' was made in Chapter 2; here we have an **analogue** signal which is to be input to a **digital** computer, and hence an analogue-to-digital converter is required. Many converters exist, and are usually specific to the kind of analogue signal produced and the kind of digital input the computer requires. There are numerous codes or 'protocols' for carrying information by electrical signals in both analogue and digital form. (Though discussion of these is outside our scope, readers will be familiar with such differences in the related area of radio signals, i.e. amplitude-modulation or frequency-modulation.) By the mid-1970s a number of standards were in existence, some endorsed by bodies such as ISO (International Standardisation Organisation) or CCITT (International Consultative Telegraph and Telephone Committee), and others the result of common practice. There appears to be a trend towards international standardisation.

While analogue-to-digital converters are needed for experimental monitoring, equally so will digital-to-analogue converters be needed for experimental control. Thus, when a temperature is being monitored, some kind of thermocouple-based device will probably be used to provide the signal for the analogue-to-digital converter: whereas when a temperature is being controlled then the signal from a digital-to-analogue converter might be used to change a thermostat setting. Note that the use of a simple servomechanism like a thermostat, to perform the switching on and off of heating or cooling devices needed to maintain a temperature, eliminates the need to use a computer directly for such control.

As we mentioned, computer monitoring and control is not confined to the laboratory. It also occurs in industry, with the difference that what is monitored and/or controlled is a manufacturing process and not an experiment. One of the simplest and earliest applications was in the numerical control of machines, one example being where a complicated shape has to be cut out from a piece of sheet metal. The movement of the cutting head can be accurately controlled by supplying instructions for its movement across the cutting area. The instructions are derived from the coordinates, with respect to some axes and some scale, of a succession of points on the perimeter of the shape. The accuracy with which the shape will be cut depends partly on the precision to which the machine can obey these signals, and also on the separations between the points and on the accuracy to which their positions are specified. Numerically controlled machine tools can be controlled by paper tapes punched with the necessary information. These tapes can be produced manually, but a computer-aided design process can be used to generate the control tapes for the machine tools much faster and more accurately. Here the computer control is indirect, and the computer involvement occurs long before the process goes into production.

In recent years computers have been increasingly used to monitor the behaviour of industrial processes. The techniques are similar to those used in scientific experiments; and the immediate aim, to collect data about progress, is the same. The purpose, though, is different, being in this case to ensure that the process is behaving properly. There are many reasons for using computers.

Fig. 6.2. Part of the main control room at the Central Electricity Generating Board atomic power station 'Hinckley B' (see main text). The computer-driven displays enable any part of the system to be monitored and the size of the control room is reduced by the replacement of many conventional instruments.

[Photograph courtesy of Central Electricity Generating Board, via GEC Process Automation Ltd.]

There is the speed with which an unusual circumstance, i.e. a potential fault, can be detected and reported. Computer monitors do not suffer from human fatigue, and they are able to make checks and reports far more frequently and accurately than humans. It is possible to collect and collate quickly information from several different parts of the process. Recently there has been the additional advantage that the cost of computer control has been decreasing, while all the time wages and salaries have been increasing.

Process automation also extends naturally to control. While some of the most spectacular uses of the automatic computer control of processes have occurred in the realm of space exploration, they have been introduced successfully in many other areas, and their scope is continually widening.

An example of industrial process control, giving some indication of the scope of current developments, is the monitoring and partial control of nuclear power stations, such as Hinkley B. This station has two reactors, each served by its own GEC-Elliott March 2140 computer. Each computer monitors some 6500 points and reports information to the main control room, in particular detected faults or the appearance of undesirable conditions. The monitoring rate for a given point varies between about a quarter of a second and one minute. These figures indicate the complexity of the real-time constraints which have to be satisfied by the monitoring program. There is a further constraint which is often present in industrial applications and is especially acute here: the factor of safety. The possible consequences of unreliable operation of a nuclear reactor need not be stressed. Many units and connections in the computer system are duplicated, and there is also a complete stand-by computer which can take over from either of the others in the case of failure. Each computer contains a separate independent processor with a timing device which interrogates the main processor at regular intervals – a watchdog to watch the watchdog. If a failure of the main processor is detected, an alarm is given, and control is transferred to the standby. While the system is mainly used for monitoring, it is also used for direct control of starting up the turbines.

In almost every area of industry there are actual or potential real-time applications of computers. In an oil refinery the quality and constituents of the crude oil can vary, and maximising the useful yield of refined products can depend on a detailed analysis, calculation, and consequent adjustment of the refining process. Real-time control can allow all this to be carried out automatically. The speed and yield of many chemical processes depend critically on maintaining exactly the right conditions, pointing to yet another situation with scope for computer control. On the organisational side, the flow of work through a factory production line depends on the right components being in the right place at the right time. Computer control can ensure that the flow of parts is maintained at the right level, and that maximum efficiency is attained.

One well-known industrial use of computer control is worth mentioning because it is an extremely good example of the value of real-time processing: the steel rolling mill. In a rolling mill red-hot steel 'billets' are rolled out as required, e.g. into sheets of specified thickness, and then cut into required lengths. This has to be done quickly before the steel cools. Before the advent of computer control, the lengths to be cut had to be determined in advance, before the total available from the billet was accurately known. The offcuts could be resmelted, but this resulted in a lower-grade steel. Nowadays, within the real-time constraints imposed by the cooling time and the speed of the rolling, a process control computer can determine, while the rolling is actually in progress, how much of this thickness of sheet is available. It can then decide from a stored list of required lengths how the sheet should be cut to obtain the maximum usable length from the billet, and cause the cutting mechanism to be adjusted accordingly.

In many of these examples we have referred to the value of the computer in minimising waste, maximising efficiency, etc. These are again problems in mathematical programming, and show that operational research which in Chapter 5 was applied to managerial decisions has also important applications in real-time computing.

6.2 Operating Systems

Over the years, computer hardware has become more complicated and the uses of computer have become more sophisticated. This has led to the development of complex control systems to control the computer system itself, especially on the larger computers which have to deal with a great variety of work or with specialist but complicated applications. The set of programs which make up this control system is known as an **operating system**, and this has become a basic part of the computer in many people's minds. It is sold by the manufacturer as part of the computer, and all user programs are normally run under its control, though for specialised applications a special operating system may be written, or that provided by the manufacturer may be 'tailored' to meet the requirements of the particular application.

In order to appreciate what an operating system does, we shall consider first what the user expects from it. The user will have a number of different tasks which he may want the computer to perform. These may be to modify a program, compile it and then run it, e.g. when he is developing an existing program. The tasks may be to run existing programs, e.g. the weekly payroll program or one to solve differential equations. They may be requests to the computer to provide information such as the amount of a particular item held at a specific warehouse in a stock control system, or to update information, e.g. make a flight reservation on an aeroplane. The user may issue a request to start a process control system. A particular computer installation does not normally have all of the above tasks to do, but may often have several of them. For most of this section we shall consider one of the commonest types of computer installation, where a number of different users submit jobs, which involve running different types of existing programs or developing new ones. At most installations the instructions to the operating system to control the running of the jobs can be punched on cards or paper tape and passed to a computer operator for input to the machine. The user then waits until the job has been run and the operator has returned the output to him. This type of job submission and running is known as **batch processing**. Many installations also allow the user to submit a job by typing commands at a terminal and then, while the job is running, to interact with the program, e.g. to type in data to it. This type of running is known as **multi-access**, because a large number of users can be accessing the computer at the same time. It gives the user more direct involvement with the machine, as when using mini-computers – or as in the early days of computing.

Many computer installations support a mixture of batch and multi-access jobs, with the operating system controlling the mix of the two types of jobs to make best use of the resources. This system may allow ways of running jobs which combine some features of batch and multi-access use. For example, there may be more than one input device and more than one output device being used for batch jobs; and some of these devices can be sited in scattered locations physically distant from the computer, similarly to the case of multi-access terminals. This mode of inputting batch jobs is known as **remote job entry**. It is possible to have remote job entry even when the system does not support multi-access terminals. A multi-access user may be given the option of using his terminal for part of his work, e.g. editing a program, and then sending a command to the operating system to run the rest of the work as a batch job. Such an operating system will often allow the progress of batch jobs to be monitored, so that the user can find out, for example, if the job has started and if so how much mill time it has so far used. On certain systems it is possible to submit a job in batch mode but to have monitoring information output to a multi-access terminal.

There is a specialised form of system which uses terminal accessing, known as **transaction processing**. This is used for applications where the computer system is normally dealing with a large number of short transactions, each one of a limited number of types. An airline flight reservation system is a typical example, in which booking a seat on a specified flight would be one type of short transaction. A transaction processing system normally deals with a data base, which it updates or accesses in real time. Typically, the number of transactions of each type throughout the day is predictable and therefore the operating system can use this prediction to organise the resources more efficiently.

Whatever modes of job submissions and running are allowed the basic functions of the operating system are still the same. The operating system must control the submission of jobs and decide which to run at what time, so as to make best use of the available resources and meet external time constraints. It must allocate resources such as main store and filestore to individual jobs, monitor the use of such resources, and probably calculate the cost – the last for the information of the management of the system, and perhaps also in order to charge the user. It must also be able to protect one program from interference by another during running, to control the input and output of data, and to handle errors in input and output of data and in users' programs.

The batch user submits his job to the computer by giving instructions in a **job control language**. Each operating system has its own job control language, some of which are much easier to learn than others. The example of job control which we give here is for a batch job using a hypothetical job control language which exhibits some of the features of job control languages on current computers.

The example below is of a job to compile and run a FORTRAN program:

```
JOB (JOBNAME=TEST, USER=SMITH, MAINSTORE=60K)
FORTRAN (SOURCE=FORTSOURCE, OBJECT=PROG)
ASSIGN (FILE1, CHANNEL6)
ASSIGN (FILE2, CHANNEL7)
RUN (PROG)
ENDJOB
```

The JOB command tells the operating system about the job to be run, e.g. its identity (in case the user wants to enquire about it later), to whom it belongs (so the system knows who to charge for it), the amount of mainstore the job requires, etc. There are often many more parameters which could be given, such as how urgent the job is, the maximum amount of mill time it should be allowed in running, etc. The operating system chooses 'default' values for any parameters not specified by the user, i.e. standard values which are assumed to apply if the user does not specify otherwise.

The FORTRAN command tells the operating system that the user wants to compile a FORTRAN program. In this example the source program is to be read from a file called FORTSOURCE and the object program which is produced by the compiler is to be output to a file called PROG.

In order to run the program, the user must specify which files to use. The ASSIGN commands specify the names of the files which are to correspond with files in the FORTRAN program known as 'channels' 6 and 7. A program will usually have at least one input and one output file. The RUN command specifies the name of the program to be run, and ENDJOB says that this is the end of the job.

In recent years the facilities available in job control languages have been expanded considerably; in fact, they have become much more like other high-level languages. Many job control languages include macros; the FORTRAN command in our example could be a macro command which expands into a number of job control commands (e.g. to assign all the files required, etc.)

before calling the compiler. The operating system may include standard macros for facilities such as compilers, and the user may be able to add further macros for running his own programs.

Another useful facility is the inclusion of conditional statements. The simplest form is for each program to leave a condition code in the accumulator on exit, and for the job control program to include statements such as

$$\text{IF CONDITION} = 0, \text{ENDJOB}$$

so that, for example, if a preliminary part of the job fails (e.g. it fails to set up a file needed in a later operation), the job is terminated at once instead of proceeding until it can go no further. Again the object is to promote efficiency by eliminating wasteful use of resources; it is often in the user's own interest to exploit such facilities as he will thus avoid being charged for wasted computing.

In some operating systems the job control language has been extended to include other features of high-level languages such as complex conditional statements and the ability to execute loops. In such cases the job control statements may have to go through a compilation process like a program in an ordinary high-level language.

When using the multi-access method of running a job, a job control language is still necessary because the user will still need to specify the programs that he needs to use, such as a text editor to modify the text of his programs. The first command of the language which he will use has to be one to enable him to enter the system at all; the process of entering the system and being recognised by it is called 'logging in' and the command word LOGIN is often used. On or immediately after the LOGIN command, the system will expect the user to identify himself. It will also normally require him to give an additional 'password', known only to him and the computer installation; this is because terminals are often accessible to people who may not be authorised to use the computing facilities.

Once the session has started, the user types in commands similar in form to those used in the batch case. Instead of typing in all the commands for a job and then having them all obeyed in a batch, the system deals with each command immediately it has been typed. The user expects the computer to respond to his request quickly in real time: ideally in only a second or two. If this 'response time' gets very long the result is irritation and frustration unless the user has asked for a lengthy piece of work to be done and expects to wait. On a good multi-access system, each user will have the illusion of instant response, and of having the machine to himself. Response time is dependent on the number of terminals simultaneously active, and therefore a slower response must be expected at peak load periods. (A big multi-access system can have hundreds of simultaneously active terminals.)

Once the user has typed in a command, the system validates it and outputs any error message to the terminal, giving the user the opportunity to correct it straight away. The command could be to call a compiler. If so, the user can then type in his program at the terminal. The compiler may run in a batch-like mode, e.g. storing the statements but not compiling the program until it has been completely input; alternatively, it may check the statements for validity as they are typed in, rejecting or storing them as the case may be, but not obeying them until the necessary command is given. A third alternative is for the compiler to translate each instruction and obey it (if valid) as soon as it is typed in, the instructions being either stored for future use, or discarded. A number of special programming languages have been designed explicitly to be used at multi-access terminals, the best known being BASIC, APL and POP-2. While conventional programming languages like ALGOL and FORTRAN can be adapted for use in this way, for various reasons they are not ideal.

A user program, once compiled, may also employ this mode of working, which is called **interactive** because the user at his terminal interacts with the program. An interactive program needs to be designed and written rather differently from a batch program. For example, a batch program performing numerical integration will have to include internal checks on the speed of convergence, or risk being stopped by the operating system because it is taking too much time before producing useful results. An interactive program could instead be written to output the currently calculated value, perhaps with an estimate of the error, and then to wait for a decision from the user at the terminal on whether to stop, to continue as before, or to continue with some other modification.

In a multi-access session, conditional statements are not needed in the job control language because any condition code is normally output to the terminal, and the user himself can then decide what to do in consequence. At the end of the multi-access session the user 'logs out', using a LOGOUT or similar command, to tell the system that he is no longer using the terminal. He will then receive a response from the system giving details of the amount of resources that he has used during his session.

In a transaction processing system the user at the terminal does not, as in batch or multi-access work, need a job control language because he will only need to ask for one of a set of standard transactions instead of writing and running his own programs. He requests a particular type of transaction, and then simply types in his data.

Whichever mode of operation or job control language is used, an important function of any operating system is to organise the jobs submitted to it so that it can make the best possible use of the resources available. The operating system itself uses resources (store, processor time, etc.) and must ensure that the resources it uses, in seeking the most efficient way to organise the work, do not exceed the savings that it makes. This is not always simple: in fact, the design of a good operating system is a severe test both of programming skills and of the ability to devise suitable algorithms to solve such problems of efficiency. Since the availability and utilisation of resources are naturally expressed in numerical terms, mathematical skills may also be needed. The design of operating systems has therefore attracted the best programmers over the years, and has become an important research area in academic computer science. We cannot go into this area in any depth, but we shall briefly survey in general terms the kinds of problem that arise, in order to give some appreciation of what is involved, and also because anyone who uses computers is greatly aided if he has some idea of what is going on behind the scenes, and is aware of the kinds of demands which the work he is doing is likely to place on the operating system.

In principle, a batch operating system could simply read in a job from the card reader, process it, and then output the result to the line-printer. If it does this, then the CPU of the computer is almost idle during the input and output, and the card reader and lineprinter are idle during the processing. Normally buffering will not help since there is not enough processing in relation to the quantity of input and output. It is now normal to input jobs from the card reader into filestore and maintain a queue of jobs waiting to be run, at the same time as processing jobs already input. Similarly output is written temporarily to filestore, for later output when the lineprinter becomes free. The queue of jobs waiting to be run is not associated with any one particular device. Any card reader or paper tape reader can be used to input jobs to the job queue. The input device may be remote from the computer when using remote job entry. In this case the operating system records where the remote input came from, so that it can output results to the same remote site later.

The job queue is likely to be more complicated than a simple first in, first out queue. The operating system must deal with jobs from a number of different users each with different and perhaps conflicting requirements, and the system must prevent any one program 'hogging' the machine unfairly to the detriment of others. The input routine can interpret the JOB command to decide on the priority of the job. Separate queues may be kept for jobs with different requirements, e.g. different urgencies or resource requirements (different amounts of CPU time, main store, filestore, etc.). A separate queue may be kept for short jobs, i.e. those with an expected processing time of less than a small number of milliseconds. The operating system includes a **job scheduler** which decides which job to run next. When resources become available, e.g. an amount of main store and some magnetic tape drives, the job scheduler looks through the job queue(s) to choose a suitable job to run. There are normally a number of user jobs running at any one time. The scheduler tries to ensure that the mix of jobs currently running makes the best use of resources; if a program is running which involves a lot of input/output it may spend considerable time waiting for data transfers, so this program would be balanced if possible by a number-crunching program running at the same time and using up the mill time. The scheduler may also try to give a faster service to short jobs, thus encouraging programmers to keep their jobs short and so make better use of the resources. A job scheduler may have to deal with a number of other complications, e.g. a job may have to be suspended because it needs to use files which another job has exclusive access to, or a complex job with many job steps may re-enter the job scheduler while it is running so that new resource requirements can be dealt with.

The output queue is normally much simpler than the input queue as there is not such a complicated scheduling requirement. Output is often 'first in, first out', except possibly for a priority output category. However, the output routine must choose the right lineprinter or terminal for the correct output, just as when a job has been submitted from a remote site. Output is normally, but not always, directed to a lineprinter at the same site. Where there is more than one lineprinter at the central site, i.e. with the computer, there may still be some criteria for choosing a particular lineprinter for particular output, e.g. it may be that only one of the lineprinters includes lower case letters in its character set, or one may be loaded with special stationery for printing (say) payslips or cheques.

Multi-access jobs are not queued and scheduled in the same way. When a multi-access user sits at his terminal and logs in, the job is normally allowed to start straight away, though there may be a limit on the number of terminals which can be active at any one time. Scheduling of multi-access jobs causes some special difficulties, since a multi-access program spends a long time waiting for input – a user often takes several seconds to type just one line at a terminal. If the program is using a lot of main store, the operating system will often copy it out to backing store after one line has been processed and copy it back in when the next line has been received. If this is not done then the number of active terminals which can be supported is very limited because of the amount of main store required to support them. This unfortunately causes a large overhead of backing store transfers in a multi-access session. To overcome this, systems are often designed to take the maximum advantage of the possibility of sharing programs, subprograms, utilities or even data between different users; examples are systems in which (say) the BASIC compiler is permanently resident in main store and available to all users, or many transaction processing systems where the most-used routines are similarly always available. In order to reduce inefficiency, some installations insist that programs which use a lot of main store must be run only in batch mode and not in multi-access mode.

A multi-access session uses resources in the same way as in a batch job, and so the job scheduler in an operating system will often deal with both batch and multi-access jobs. Some output from a multi-access session will be output to the user's terminal, but sometimes the amount of output is too great to be output on a slow-speed device, in which case it may be queued for printing at a suitable lineprinter (such as the remote job entry terminal nearest to the multi-access user) in the same way as for batch output.

Most user programs input their data from files, and output their data to files. Even when the data is input from cards or paper tape, the data will normally be 'spooled' to a file first, so that the user program still reads from a file. Similarly output to lineprinters is normally via filestore.

The operating system is responsible for controlling access to files. It therefore provides facilities for creating, deleting and extending files, as well as providing facilities to access them once they are created. The user refers to files by name; he does not normally know (or need to know) where the files are held in filestore. When he needs a new file he specifies its characteristics, e.g. its name, its type (serial, index sequential, source program, object program, etc., where relevant), and (for some types of file) its size.

The operating system normally maintains a central catalogue at the installation which keeps a record of users and lists the files each user owns and the location of those files. As a safety check, an individual volume (such as a disk pack) will also have a record of all files are held on it and details of these files. Since the central catalogue lists files as belonging to users, it is easy to provide a security mechanism enabling a user to keep his files private. He may sometimes want to share his files; and many of the standard systems files such as compilers are available to all users. These are often stored under a dummy user name such as SYSTEM. A user can specify which files may be shared and under what conditions, e.g. he may allow other users to read his files but not to modify or delete them, or he may stop other users from accessing his file when he is in the process of updating it.

If a user wants to access a file, he refers to it by name. The operating system will locate it for him, normally searching the catalogue under his user name, and then under the user name SYSTEM. If the user wants to access files belonging to other users, he specifies the user name as well as the file name. In some operating systems, he may also need the correct password to give him the type of access that he needs, e.g. for reading, writing or, if a program file, executing.

The user specifies the file he wants to use in the job control instructions, in our example with the ASSIGN command. The program is written to be independent of the particular file used, so that the same program can be run using different files at different times. Obviously, a file-listing utility must be able to list any specified file; in fact most user programs also need to be independent of the specific file used, if only because they are likely to use different generations of a file on different runs. The program therefore uses internally some arbitrary name for the file, and uses the ASSIGN command in the job control instructions to specify which actual file is to correspond to this name during the current run. In some high-level languages, e.g. FORTRAN, a number rather than a name is used within the program to refer to the file. The operating system maintains a list of the names or numbers by which the program is referring to its files.

Operating systems normally go further than this in helping the programmer, and allow him to write programs which are independent, not only of the name of the file he is using, but also of its type. For any type of file there are a number of items of information that the user may provide when he wants to read or write a record of data. These include the identity of the file he is reading or writing, the buffer to hold the data, the key of the record (or whether he just wants the next record in the file). Most of these can be specified whatever the type of file. The file access software will find the record required, using the indexes or chains for the file concerned, and transfer the appropriate record for the user. The program can thus be written to be independent of the organisation of the file that it is using (though it must be aware of whether it can ask for records in random as well as sequential order). Even where a user is directly accessing an input or output device rather than a file in filestore, there is likely to be a standard operating system 'interface' (i.e. means of reference) which he can use for this, which makes the device appear to be a file to the program. Again the operating system will handle the differences between the different devices, not expecting the user to be an expert in the details of their characteristics.

So far we have considered the facilities which the operating system provides for the user and which directly affect him. Many functions of an operating system are less visible to the user, e.g. those concerned with control of the hardware and with providing protection between users. Nevertheless these functions do affect the running of jobs, and a programmer will make more effective use of the computer if he has some understanding of them. It is these parts of the operating system that we shall consider next.

The operating system must control the transfer of data between main store and peripheral devices. In the early days of computing this was fairly simple – when an input instruction was obeyed the CPU was held up until the data had been input. In a modern computer, input and output are done by a **peripheral processor** which can operate at the same time as, but independently from, the CPU. This peripheral processor may be very simple with just a few logic circuits, and is sometimes called a **channel**. In this case it is a special purpose device dedicated to its particular task. In some very big systems the peripheral processor is a complete programmable computer which the operating system designer (though not the individual user) can program to be used in a variety of ways.

In either case, when the central processor encounters an input or output instruction, it sends a command to a peripheral processor to perform the necessary operations, and then continues processing. When the data has been input or output, the peripheral processor sends a signal to the central processor, which may be an interrupt signal or a 'flag' signal. An interrupt signal causes the sequence of instructions being obeyed in the CPU to be interrupted and control transferred to a particular instruction. A flag signal does not cause an immediate interrupt; instead a particular code (often a single bit is sufficient) is placed in a given register which is regularly scanned. The interrupt therefore occurs when the signal is picked up during scanning. Either way, the central processor starts obeying the new instruction sequence, normally fairly simple, which interprets the signal and causes any necessary further action to be taken. When this has been done, the interrupted sequence of instructions is normally resumed.

A peripheral processor may handle a number of input or output devices, and one instruction to a peripheral processor may ask for a number of actions, e.g. moving the read/write heads to a particular cylinder on a disk and reading a particular block from it. For some devices, e.g. most multi-access terminals, the peripheral processor may also have to keep checking the devices to see if they have data to send.

When a data transfer to main store is complete, the peripheral processor sends a message with its signal, to say whether the data was transferred correctly and if not, what went wrong.

From the above, it is clear that the action taken by the operating system when the user requests a data transfer is far from simple. The operating system will normally have to keep a queue of outstanding requests for input or output for each device. When the device becomes free, the next transfer is sent. If an error occurred during the transfer, the operating system deciphers it and may try to repeat the transfer if necessary, e.g. it may backspace over a block mis-read from magnetic tape and try to re-read it. A user will normally be informed if this has happened so that he can decide whether to have the reel properly checked before writing important data to it. The system operators will also need be to informed, as operator intervention may be necessary. In a batch job the user may be able to specify in job control instructions what to do in such circumstances, or the decision may be left to the system operators.

In some cases a serious error may have developed on the device and the operating system, having been informed of this automatically or by the operators, may have to take more complex action. For example, if a line-printer fails in the middle of printing a file of data, output may have to be started again, from the beginning of the file, on another lineprinter. Some computer systems have to run for twenty-four hours a day, and if a device containing an important file fails the operating system will have to get access to another copy, possibly by finding an 'archive' copy (i.e. one stored off-line and no longer in normal active use) and reapplying to it any updates done to the file since that copy was stored.

The user is usually unaware of these complications. After he has requested a transfer, his program is often suspended until the transfer together with any necessary correcting action is complete, and the operating system finds other jobs to run in the interim. Sometimes processing can be continued without waiting for the data transfers, at least for a time, as in the case when the user program has been written to include double-buffering techniques, described in Section 5.1.

Another of the resources that the operating system must control is the CPU itself. At any one time an operating system will be engaged in processing a number of activities or processes. A **process** may be a user job, or a system activity such as a spooling process outputting to a lineprinter. The operating system must keep a record of all the processes currently in progress together with details of them.

We considered earlier the job scheduler, which decides which job to start next. Now we must consider which process to activate next. The low-level scheduler (often called the **dispatcher**) is concerned with allocating the CPU to processes (or, in a multi-machine system, the CPUs to processes). For each process the operating system must know its current state, i.e. whether it is ready to run or is waiting for input–output, and the priority of the process compared with others. (Certain systems processes will have very high priority, whereas number-crunching programs are normally run at low priority to use up mill time when no other process requires the mill.) It must also know the values to be set in the registers when the process is resumed.

When there is only one CPU, only one process can be active at any given time. When a process has been running for some time, i.e. a few milliseconds, it is likely to be suspended because a hardware interrupt signal has been received by the CPU, or because it has to wait for some event such as input or output, or because it is time to return control to the operating system. The low-level scheduler, after dealing with the cause of the interrupt, has to decide which process to activate next. Different schedulers have different strategies depending on the type of the work normally handled by the operating system; a common strategy is to choose the process which has been waiting longest at the highest priority. This CPU priority is usually specified by the job scheduler, sometimes in accordance with a parameter on the JOB command of a batch job, and passed to the low-level scheduler when the job is started. Having chosen a process, the low-level scheduler restores the registers to their required values and activates the process, possibly specifying an allowed time interval (if this is not automatic), after which the process will be suspended again and put at the bottom of the queue for that priority so as to give other programs a chance.

An operating system will normally also provide facilities for processes to communicate, e.g. for one process to wait for an event in another so as to share resources with it.

Each process will need some main store to hold programs or data. The operating system must allocate the available store between the processes currently running, and prevent one process from writing into the area of store being used by another process. When a new batch job is entered into the system, the user specifies with the JOB command how much main store is needed (or the operating system will choose a suitable default value), and the job will only be started when a sufficient amount of store is available.

The operating system will allocate a suitable amount of space in an available area of main store. The user would like to see his part of store as starting at address 0 wherever it is actually held in main store. Computers which support multi-programming have special hardware to deal with this. A simple but effective hardware mechanism is to have two extra registers, a **base register** and a **limit register**. The starting address of the user's allocated area of main store is stored in the base register and its highest address in the limit register. Whenever the user addresses a location in store, the contents of the base register are added to the address he specifies and the resultant address is checked to make sure that it is within the user's area by comparing it with the limit register. This means that the user can proceed as if he has the machine to himself, and is also protected from other users.

This method of addressing store requires each user area to be one contiguous area of main store. When a process is finished and its main store is freed, a gap is left in main store. As the next program loaded may require a different amount of main store, the store may become fragmented and this may mean moving running programs around in main store. A more flexible method of allocating main store is to use **paging**, where for each user program a table is kept with an entry for each unit of main store (or **page**) recording its position in main store. Each page is a fixed size (e.g. 1024 bytes) and the address specified by the program is interpreted as a page number and address within the page. The hardware converts the page number into a main store address using the table. Thus the user has the impression that he has a continuous area of store, but the operating system can divide the real main store into equally sized pages and allocate pages as required to the user's processes. A paging system gives one further advantage: a page of the user process need not be in main store at all, as the address could be one in secondary store. In this case, when the user attempts to access a location in a page which is not in main store, an interrupt is caused and the operating system can bring the required page into main store before the instruction is obeyed.

This store strategy has a profound effect on the user program, since the program can apparently directly access more store than is actually available in main store. The terms **virtual storage** or **virtual memory** are used for this technique. It has to be used with care both by the operating system designer and by the individual programmer, so that an excessive amount of time is not wasted in transferring pages to and from main store. The operating system will detect that such excessive transferring is happening and may decide to abandon the program. The programmer will then have to resubmit his job requesting a larger main store quota.

In a system using hardware base and limit registers, the program may be larger than the amount of main store it has been allocated. In this case, it must be divided into logical parts (normally called **segments** or **overlays**) and individual segments moved into main store when required, overlaying segments which are already in store. In the payroll example, the part of the program which sorts the input could be one segment and the part of the program which processes the sorted file with the semi-permanent file could be another. Once the sort is complete, the main processing segment can overlay the sorting segment which is no longer required. For a large, complicated program, considerable effort may be needed to make the overlaying as efficient as possible.

Even when using paging hardware, the concept of segments may still be useful, for instance if logically connected parts can be put into the same segment and the paging strategy of the operating system can be influenced by this, e.g. bringing in several pages of a segment (or perhaps the entire segment) when a user accesses a page which is not in main store. To make the best use of a computer anyone writing a program of substantial size should be aware of the sort of store strategy used by the operating system concerned.

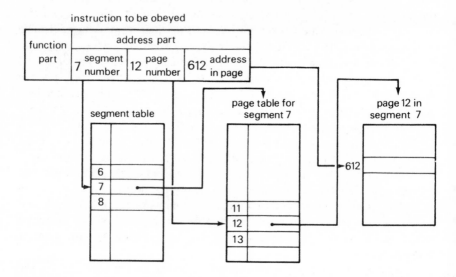

Fig. 6.3. Diagrammatic representation of the means of addressing store locations on a machine using segments and pages. The address part of an instruction is divided into three fields identifying the segment number, page number within the segment, and address within the page of the required store location. The control unit refers to the user's segment table to obtain the page table for the required segment, to the page table for that segment to find the required page, and can then access the required location. To speed this process the current segment and/or page tables may be held in fast store associated with the CPU.

So far we have considered how the operating system allocates store to individual processes. In some cases, it is desirable to share store between processes, as when a compiler or editor or library routine is in use by more than one program at a time. This is particularly true in the case of multi-access and transaction processing systems where there is often a large number of users sharing one program. The way that such sharing is organised depends on the hardware used. On most machines in the 1960s, the only method of sharing between user programs was to make their store areas overlap: normally only a section of the operating system itself could access all the store, and this ran in a privileged mode. When segmenting (or paging) hardware is used, the address associated with a particular user segment (or page) can point to the same area of real store.

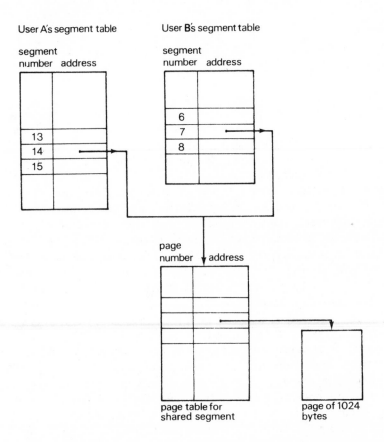

Fig. 6.4. Diagrammatic representation of a situation in which two users are sharing the same segment. Segment 14 of user A and segment 7 of user B both refer to the same page table.

The protection between users in the past has tended to be an 'all or nothing' approach; either a user could not access another user's store area at all, or sharing was arranged as described above and he could access it in any way he wanted. In a segmented machine there are opportunities for far better protection schemes. Each user can have a segment table with an entry for each segment he can access. When a segment is shared between users, there can be an entry for it in the segment table of each user who is sharing it. The entry for a segment in a segment table can include an access key saying how that user can access that segment. This allows several users to share a segment, but for some of them to have only limited access to it, e.g. several users might be allowed to execute code in a particular segment (such as one containing a compiler) but only one user might be allowed to write to the segment (to load the program into store) or delete the segment. This also allows certain segments to be marked as 'execute only' or 'read only' so a program cannot corrupt its code (this is especially important when the code is being shared).

On some machines an even more flexible protection mechanism is available; for example on ICL 2900 series machines there is a protection level associated with each segment, and the access rights are associated with these levels making it possible to prevent code in a less protected level reading from and/or writing to a segment at a more protected level. This allows the user to develop his programs in parts, and to protect the parts that are working from those still under development. It also allows most of the operating system to be run as part of the user process (rather than a special supervisor process being entered when the user program calls on the operating system for some facility), since the segments of the operating system are safe from corruption by the user programs, being in a more protected level and held in areas to which the user has not been given write access.

When segments have the same access permissions for all users, it would be wasteful to have entries in each user's segment table. This is the case, for example, for most of the segments of the operating system itself. Because of this there is one special segment table, shared by all users, which contains entries about such segments.

We have not tried to give a comprehensive account of operating systems, but only of some of the important features which the user should understand if he wants to use a computer efficiently. No two computers are the same, and in complex applications the user should (if he has a choice) spend as much care in selecting the right computer with its associated operating system as in choosing the right programming language. We have seen how operating systems have to cope with the demands of different modes of operating – batch, real time, interactive and multi-access. Programs can be run interactively on a dedicated machine without multi-access but this is usually only done on mini-computers. Interactive and batch programs call for different techniques and attitudes from both the user and the writer (who need not be the same person). Experience suggests that interactive programs are more attractive to most people, especially when they are well written, and interactive processing is certainly more flexible in its application than batch processing. Nevertheless batch processing will remain with us, for big number-crunching and data processing jobs especially, since few users would want to sit at a terminal for hours on end while magnetic tapes are loaded, read, rewound, and written, or while the processor is bound up for long periods in a massive calculation which does not need intervention. Nevertheless many believe that much of the future of computing lies in the interactive mode of operation based on man-machine interaction. In the next section we shall look at a

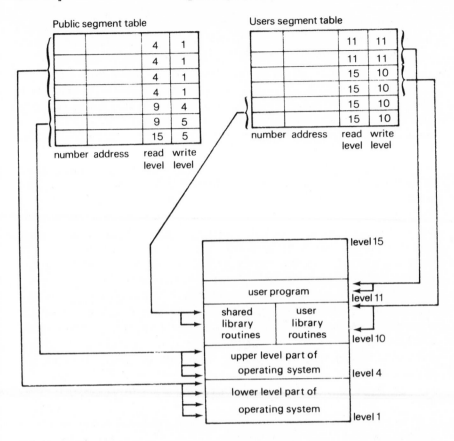

Fig. 6.5. Schematic representation of the way in which a single user has different levels of protection. The low-level part of the operating system can only be changed by itself, because all of its segments have write access from level 1 only; it can only be read by parts of the operating system at levels 4 and below. It is thus protected from casual interference or exploitation. Only one part of the operating system can be read by the user program, and no part can be changed by it.

transaction processing application of the kind which may well become increasingly important in our daily lives, something which we shall discuss in Chapter 8. Interactive working also happens to be a very enjoyable way of using computers, as will appear again in Chapter 7.

6.3 Airline Reservation System

We close this chapter with a short description of a typical transaction processing application: the airline booking system. Transaction processing systems are characterised by involving a large number of modifications to the data base being made at frequent intervals. We shall describe what is required from the system and some of the problems involved, but again we shall not describe how they are solved. The reader will see that many of the facilities of operating systems mentioned in the last section are needed, together with refinements that were not mentioned.

The system consists of a central computer with a large number of terminals, some of which are in different cities and hence at considerable distances from the computer. These terminals are alphanumeric visual display units with keyboards, designed so that they can be used by operators without computer training. This is a multi-access system where there are a large number of active terminals at any one time.

A customer will arrive at an airline agent's desk and inquire about flights to a specific destination. He will pick a particular flight and the agent types a request via the terminal to find how many seats of each type are available on this flight, this information then being displayed visually. Next the customer picks a seat and the agent transmits the booking to the computer. As mentioned in the last section, the agent does not have to learn any job control or programming language, but merely specifies one of a number of standard transactions and then inputs the data particular to the transaction.

There are several difficulties which are specific to this type of application. The information supplied to the agent must be up-to-date (e.g. it must not show the seat is free when it was sold one minute earlier via another agent) and hence the system must update information on bookings as soon as it is received. The data base must therefore be carefully designed, since there is a great deal of accessing and updating. It is often held on disks or drums with fixed heads, so that the only delay in accessing is due to the rotation rather than head movement.

Between the time of the agent making the enquiry and the customer making his booking the system must not book the seat to another customer via another agent. The file must be protected during this period, so the operating system reserves or locks the flight record for the agent during the period of the transaction. This is an important and non-trivial feature which must be handled by the operating system and not involve action on the part of the user.

The programs and the indexes to the data base are usually held permanently in main store and shared between the users. The information needed for each individual user will be a small amount of data and hence the scheduler in the operating system is relatively simple. The scheduler in a transaction processing system usually allows a certain number of simultaneous transactions of each type. The pattern of bookings during the day is predictable, and hence the system 'housekeeping' (i.e. checking files, etc.) will be done outside the normal peak periods. The scheduler will change the balance between different types of transactions during the day, and in periods of low transaction activity batch or multi-access work will be allowed at low priority.

Such a system will be capable of more than booking seats. If a given flight is full, then the potential passenger can be placed on a wait list, so that if seats become available the passenger is automatically notified. This is a common feature, since a certain percentage of seats will be cancelled. This percentage is reasonably predictable but depends on the route and the time of year; because of it, most airlines overbook seats by a certain amount. Thus the system must cope with cancellations and confirmations of bookings; and also must cope with double bookings for the same passenger (a surprisingly common event, often due to a seat being booked once by a businessman and then again by his secretary for safety). These factors mean that files must also be indexed by passenger names, the records holding their addresses, etc. Most bookings and cancellations are done by telephone and this raises an interesting difficulty of a kind which we shall discuss in the next chapter. This is that very possibly certain passenger names will be misspelt, e.g. a booking could be recorded in the name BOOKER and the cancellation in the name BROOKER. The search procedure in the file of passenger names must therefore allow for misspelling. One way to minimise double booking is to search for the passenger's name on a flight whenever a booking is made, and query any duplication of names.

Yet more factors are involved. The system must know which terminal a request comes from, so that responses can be sent to the right terminal, and must also know something about where each terminal is situated, because for example local times at different terminals may vary. During bookings the system should keep note of special passenger requirements, e.g. for a vegetarian meal, or for baby foods, or for help with feeding bottles, or for invalid chairs; and a list of passengers with these details can be produced at the airport ready for checking-in, so that passengers can be ticked off the list as they arrive at the check-in counter. Not only are seats cancelled before check-in; some passengers who fail to arrive at the airport have not cancelled. This again is partly allowed for in overbooking, so there will often be some spare seats. There are also some passengers who arrive at the airport without booking, hoping for such last-minute vacancies. Again, a flight might be cancelled at the last moment and the passengers have to be transferred to other flights. All of these problems can be eased by including a computer terminal at the airport check-in counter. A bonus provided by such a terminal is that a check can be made of passengers and luggage. The system can then calculate the weight and the distribution of the load on the aircraft, and can keep them updated until just before take-off, and hence can also calculate how much cargo can be carried on the flight.

It is obvious that the system must be reliable, and numerous measures are taken to ensure this. All files may be held in duplicate and are simultaneously updated. When a booking is made on a flight by an agent, the central computer responds with more details of the flight and repeats the passenger's name and relevant information. The agent then confirms that this is correct and the files are not updated until this confirmation is received. Hence there will be no unfortunate effects if the information is corrupted between the terminal and the computer. Even this may not provide enough protection because there is always the possibility, however small, of computer failure; and so airline reservation systems, like nuclear power station systems discussed earlier, have a second computer as standby. All peripheral equipment such as disk drives and the communications equipment handling the terminals can be switched to this standby in case of need, thus maintaining an uninterrupted service.

There are several other transaction processing systems such as in banking and stock control, but the main features are the same as in the airline reservation system. This sort of system may seem to be only suitable for large-scale applications because of the cost and complexity of the system, but the growth of mini-computers is starting to make it feasible for smaller applications.

Chapter 7

The Computer as an Entertainment

The first computer which either of the authors saw was at the Festival of Britain Exhibition in 1951, and was an English Electric DEUCE. It was not calculating planetary orbits, or working out income tax, but was taking on all-comers at the game of Nim. The capabilities of a computer are often more effectively demonstrated by using a special program than by showing the machine performing one of its routine tasks. From the earliest days, either for such demonstrations or for their own amusement, people have written computer programs for playing games, for printing calendars, for making pictures of cartoon characters, or for playing tunes. Computer programming tends to be addictive, and computers are very versatile: it is not surprising that over the years many programmers have continued to write programs when seeking relaxation, and have found enjoyment in using computers for what might be regarded as frivolous purposes.

In this chapter we shall not be concerned with entertainment solely in the escapist sense. In recent years there have been an increasing number of attempts to exploit computer techniques for serious artistic purposes. Also some of the technical problems of using computers in this way are of interest in themselves. Most important, some of the actual or potential methods involved have applications in other realms of computer use, sometimes several years after these methods were devised.

7.1 Games and Artificial Intelligence

The most obvious form of computer entertainment is game-playing, where the programmer attempts to turn the computer into a player as good as or better than a human. Games vary greatly in type – chess, poker and Monopoly are examples of popular games which are very different in form. For the purposes of writing a computer program the obvious physical differences, such as that one game is played with pieces on a board while another is played with cards, are not important. There are other and more fundamental characteristics which are of greater relevance when a game is being analysed.

One is the number of players involved – chess is a two-person game, for example, whereas poker can be played by several players. Another characteristic is the nature and extent of the information available to the players. In some games (e.g. draughts or chess) all the players have complete information about the state of the game. In other games some information may not be available to any of the players, as in a game with an element of chance where the future path of the game will depend on the throw of dice or the turn of a card. In some games different players have different information, typically in a card game with concealed hands where each player knows the cards in his own hand but not those of his opponents. Poker is a card game with both kinds of incomplete information.

A further important feature is the number of possible states of the game. A 'finite-state' game is one in which the number of possible different situations is finite; since a digital computer is also a finite-state device we shall only consider games of this type. All the games we have mentioned so far are finite-state. Billiards is an example of a non-finite-state game, as the position of the balls at any time can only be described approximately.

One important result from the mathematical theory of games is that a finite-state game with complete information always has an algorithm for its solution. This means that it is theoretically possible for either player at any stage of the game to determine which of the possibilities of win, lose or draw are still open to him, and to adopt an appropriate strategy. Since this includes the starting position, the result will be predetermined if both players know the algorithm and make no mistakes.

Our first example is Nim, which is a two-person, finite-state game with complete information. There are a number of variants, but the essence of the game is that there are a number of piles of counters. Each player in turn removes some counters, the rules being that he may take from only one pile at each turn and that he must take at least one counter but may take more; he may take a whole pile if he wishes. A player wins the game if he forces his opponent to take the last counter. Since the number of counters reduces at each turn a draw is impossible – one player or the other must win.

Nim is a game where an algorithm exists and is known, and if both players use the algorithm correctly the winner is determined by the number of piles at the start of the game and the number of counters in each pile. If there are three piles with two counters in each, the first player can force a win by taking the whole of one pile, leaving two piles of two counters. Whether his opponent now takes one counter or both counters in another pile, the first player can then leave him with only one. On the other hand, if the three piles start with one, two and three counters respectively, then it is the second player who can force a win regardless of the first player's opening move. The reader unfamiliar with the algorithm should be able to work out the details and discover the algorithm for himself. An even better-known example of a game with a known algorithm is 'noughts-and-crosses', where the result will always be a draw if both players play correctly.

Making the computer play games like these correctly is simply a matter of coding the algorithm correctly, as with any other algorithm. This does not mean that the computer will be unbeatable; a 'fair' Nim program will give its human opponent the choice of going first or second with a given starting position, so that a human who plays correctly will win. Nevertheless, even in these simple cases the coding can be of interest. Like many other teachers of programming the authors have often set students the problem of writing a program to play noughts-and-crosses correctly. Valuable lessons can be drawn from the wide variations in storage requirements and execution times of different attempts, and can be used to emphasise the importance of intelligent analysis and organisation of any problem to be programmed.

A relevant question at this stage is, why do people bother to play finite-state, complete information games at all, if their result is predetermined? Chess is a game of this type, yet it is widely played. The answer is that, while it has been proved that an algorithm must exist for every such game, what the actual algorithm is may not be known in a given instance. Even when the algorithm is known, one or both of the players may not know it. The algorithm may be so complicated and difficult to remember that in practice no individual can be expected to know it perfectly, and possibly even a computer will not have the capacity to store it. Chess is an example of a game where *nobody* knows what the algorithm for its solution is; it is not even known if the first player has an advantage, although experience suggests that this is likely. This is why international grandmasters and even world champions do not automatically win every game that they play, why books on chess abound, and why the game is as popular and as intellectually demanding as ever after thousands of years. Although the theory of games shows that an algorithm must logically exist, it has so far provided no general rules for finding out what it is in any particular case. As far as chess is concerned, it is quite possible that no algorithm will ever be found; all that can be said with any confidence is that any algorithm for it is likely to be extremely complex, although even this is not absolutely certain as a simple but subtle algorithm may conceivably exist.

When dealing with games with no known algorithmic solution, whether finite-state or not, the computer scientist can adopt various approaches. One might be to set the computer to find the required algorithm, but there are two difficulties with this. One is that there is no known algorithm for finding algorithms. The 'sledgehammer' technique of exhaustively searching all of the possibilities is out of the question in most games, certainly in those of any interest. This is because of the 'combinatorial explosion', where the number of possible combinations of positions and moves multiplies so rapidly that the time required to enumerate them, even at electronic speeds, can escalate to thousands of years. It has been estimated that there are approximately 10^{46} different arrangements of pieces on the chess board, or 'positions' as they are called, many admittedly highly improbable, and that there are approximately 10^{23} 'good' games of not more than fifty moves by each player. This partly explains why the various openings (where there is only one starting position) and end game situations (where the number of pieces and possible moves is relatively small) have been extensively analysed, whereas no such analysis in depth exists for the middle game. Even master players can rarely see more than two or three moves ahead in complex situations.

The second difficulty in such an approach is that even if an algorithm-finding algorithm were known, it would be of no use for games with no algorithmic solution. Therefore an alternative is needed. We shall discuss briefly two simple alternative approaches, the *learning* approach and the *evaluation* approach.

In the learning approach at its most basic, the computer simply starts with the rules of the game. It then begins to play a sequence of games against human opponents. Usually in such programs the computer moves at random, but the program also includes means of storing information about winning moves and positions, and/or losing moves and positions, which it encounters. Thus as the sequence of games progresses the program gathers an increasing store of knowledge about the game, and when its turn comes to move, can look for winning moves and try to avoid losing moves. Typically the machine will be very easy to beat at first, but will gradually become more and more 'clever'.

It is an interesting exercise to write a learning program for a game with a known algorithm, like noughts-and-crosses, and see how long the machine takes to 'learn' how to avoid losing. More entertaining are programs for games without a known algorithm, since the human opponent has less of a built-in advantage. Such a game is Tac-Tix, which has simple rules and takes less storage and programming than chess. This is a game with affinities to Nim which was devised by Piet Hein. The counters are arranged in an $m \times n$ rectangular array. Each player in turn takes at least one counter, and may take any number of counters in adjacent positions in any one row or column of the array. As in Nim, the object is to force one's opponent to take the last

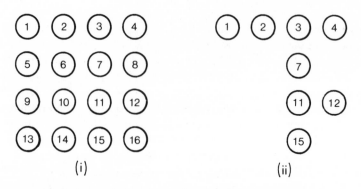

Fig. 7.1. The game of Tac-Tix (see main text): (i) shows the starting position for a 4 × 4 game; (ii) shows the position later in a game, when the next player can enforce a win.
(by taking pieces 3 and 7)

counter. No general algorithm is known for this game, though it has been analysed for small values of m and n and must have an algorithm as it is a finite-state, complete information game. A program written by one of the authors for an 8K 18-bit mini-computer, and using a 6×6 array, is very easy to beat to begin with, but even within the limited store available becomes very difficult to beat after relatively few games.

The main drawback of learning programs is a consequence of the combinatorial explosion: the number of different winning and losing moves to be recorded will expand rapidly for all but trivial games. For games like chess they would quickly fill all the available main and secondary store. Even if unlimited backing store devices were available, the time taken at each move to check all of the winning and losing possibilities would similarly increase and soon become impractical. A chess-playing computer programmed on this principle would not get far in any chess tournament because of the time limit rules.

This problem occurred in the Tac-Tix learning program just mentioned. In an early version of the program a board position was stored as a binary bit pattern in two consecutive locations, thus allowing a maximum of 4096 positions to be stored without allowing space in store for the program. This was clearly impractical, since with only two counters left on the board there are still $36 \times 35 = 1260$ different possible positions. However, there are only two essentially different types of position, one where the two counters are adjacent and the other where they are not. Similar arguments apply when there are more counters. A lot of interesting work, using concepts from graph theory, was needed to find ways of describing the logically different positions with a minimum number of parameters. This increased the number of actual positions that could be stored, and also improved the search times. Nevertheless the 'think time' when the program is experienced and is playing a good game is noticeably longer than when it is beginning to learn. This is less remarkable to its human opponent than in a corresponding noughts-and-crosses learning program for the same machine, because in that case the human player is used to the algorithm and expects an experienced player to play quickly, not slowly!

There are some other interesting features of the Tac-Tix program. The program's memory of winning and losing positions can be output or input at any time so that a human player can choose how experienced a program he wants to have as an opponent. To enable the program to gain experience without human aid, it is so written that it can simulate an opponent and hence play against itself. The program generates a sequence of random numbers; when it is faced with several possible moves, one is picked at random.

Such learning programs suffer from the limitation that while information is collected about winning and losing, it is only used to check possible moves. On the other hand, a human will soon begin to make inferences from the data that he has collected, and make inductive hypotheses about how best to play.

Consciously or subconsciously he will be searching for an algorithm, or at least some guiding rules. Computers have no subconscious, nor relevant motivations such as intellectual curiosity or the desire to win.

A computer program can only be made to simulate certain aspects of a human's conscious behaviour, and even here there are difficulties. An important area of computer activity is the field of Artificial Intelligence, which tries to analyse how humans learn and how they make decisions, and to simulate these processes by machines. One problem is to get a machine to develop, by inference or inductive reasoning from a collection of observed data, some model or set of hypotheses which can account for this data and which can be used to predict future observations. Prediction is something that the human brain appears to accomplish with relative ease, and humans are good at spotting short cuts to problems and then formulating principles about these short cuts. These aspects have proved difficult to simulate. Learning programs for games are important research tools in artificial intelligence.

In games like chess, where the combinatorial explosion is an impossible barrier to the use of simple learning programs, a more practical approach is to use evaluation. Evaluative games-playing programs require more knowledge and analysis of the game by the programmer than merely knowing the formal rules, but they stop short of the complete analysis implied by programming a complete algorithmic solution.

The simplest evaluation technique occurs in games with a large element of chance, such as card games like poker and pontoon. Here the computer can be programmed to evaluate a position by calculating the probabilities of a given hand being able to win, of it being improved by the exchange or addition of a card, etc. In such games no algorithm can guarantee success, but the program can be made to play a good steady game. In games where one player can improve his chances by exploiting knowledge of an opponent's style of play, the programmer can help to foil his program's human opponents by building a certain amount of unpredictability into the computer's play. Enabling the program to learn opponents' habits of play is a different problem and clearly much more complicated.

Evaluative techniques can also be used in contexts where chance is not a factor. The effectiveness of such methods clearly depends critically on the programmer's understanding of the game and the effectiveness of the evaluation. A lot of work has gone into developing programs to play chess, both for the game's own sake and because of its value in studying the problems of artificial intelligence. Chess and computer experts are divided over whether a computer program will ever become as good as the best human players, though the standard of one program in 1970 would rank it about 500th among British players and there are regular matches between American and Russian programs.

It has been found that evaluation alone is not particularly successful in chess programs and a more suitable method has been to combine learning and evaluation into an evaluative technique which includes the possibility of learning, by adjusting some of the parameters in the light of experience. We shall not give a detailed description of any particular program but just give a few features to give a flavour of them. First, each position is evaluated by a function, which incorporates four main features of the position: the amount of material (i.e. number and value of pieces), the mobility of the pieces, the area that the pieces control, and the amount of defence around the King.

The conventional way of evaluating material is to assign a value to each piece, e.g. Pawn = 1, Knight = 3, Bishop = 3, Rook = 5 and Queen = 9. This is over-simple, as the values of pieces can depend on the state of the game. For instance, a King becomes more valuable in the end game, and two Knights are less valuable than a Rook when the only other pieces are Kings, since mate cannot be forced with two Knights and a King against a King. Because of this and other factors the evaluation alters at different times of the game, one suggestion being that in the middle game a Knight = 5 and a Rook = 4. The evaluation function itself should not be linear, since one must allow for interaction between pieces, for example two adjacent Bishops on squares of different colours are very powerful. The function is usually a polynomial and its terms and coefficients are normally changed not after each game but move by move.

During a game the program must make moves, and the approach used in simpler games, of analysing every possible position in depth, is impossible. The usual technique is to select the best seven moves from the current position, 'best' being determined by the evaluation function. From each of these seven best positions the program then selects the best seven moves again, giving forty-nine possible positions. A position will be discarded unless the evaluated score is higher than the score for the previous position, and hence the actual number of positions will probably be less than forty-nine. This is continued to four or five levels, i.e. between two and three moves by each player, which is approximately the depth of a human player's analysis.

It has been found that different routines are needed for the three phases of the game, the opening, the middle game and the end game, and that possibly several standard openings should be stored in the program. Again this is just reflecting the way that a human normally plays. One must not expect too much from such programs: very few human players discover new principles of strategy and therefore one should not require a program to do this.

One would like to see the same amount of effort spent in developing programs to play Japanese chess, which more closely resembles warfare. After some pieces have crossed a line on the board they may be promoted with extra movement. The pieces are more like mercenaries, in that if a player captures one of his opponent's pieces he can then introduce it on his side later in the game. These features make Japanese chess more interesting than the usual form and also bring it closer to the war and business games which we shall mention later.

We now turn to an alternative form of participation in games by a computer, where the computer acts as a referee and/or controller of the environment of the game, in which the actual players are one or more humans interacting with the program. In a one-person game the player attempts to achieve some goal within certain constraints (time taken, number of moves, etc.) or to achieve the best score he can, according to the scoring rules of the game, by using his skill and judgement. Generally these games are easy to play without the aid of a computer, and the programming is relatively simple without needing any special techniques.

Some games have been invented where the power or other facilities of the computer is essential. One of the best known of these is Space War, which is a two-person game, using a graphic display unit and a number of keys. Each player has a space craft which he controls by keys, his objective being to destroy the opponent's vessel before his own is destroyed. Each player is able to move his craft in any direction and to spin the vessel, and he is also provided with a limited number of missiles to fire at his opponent. The map of space fills the display screen, and shows the positions of the two vessels and the paths of the missiles. Since the missiles travel at finite speed each vessel has an opportunity to avoid a missile after it has been fired. The vessels can fire while moving and can fire and spin simultaneously. The fascination of the game, which is very popular with night operators at computer installations, is in the nature of the space. In some versions, when a missile reaches one edge of the display screen it reappears on the opposite side, and hence a vessel can shoot itself unless it moves after firing – this is equivalent to playing on the surface of a torus. Some versions also include a sun with a gravity field: vessels can orbit the sun but must make sure that they are not captured by gravity and fall into the sun. The gravity field also has the effect of distorting the paths of the missiles, which no longer travel in straight lines. Space war is a game which has been designed to use particular computer devices and the computer has some number-crunching to do when calculating the courses of the vessels and the missiles.

There is one important warning that we must give: the average reader must not expect to be able to write or run games-playing programs to any great extent. He is unlikely to obtain funds for the amount of machine resources that are used, and computer installations will certainly not allow free use of its resources for such purposes! While commercial versions may come about (see the next chapter) they are not likely to form a cheap means of entertainment.

In games with two or more players the computer can also act as a referee, a simple example being Kriegspiel where the referee is an integral part of the game. This is a variant of chess in which each player knows only the position of his own pieces. When one player attempts a move, the referee must tell him if the move is possible and, if he has captured a piece, what he has captured. The referee also warns the opponent if the move has placed his King in check.

Kriegspiel is not particularly difficult to program but provides light relief from writing chess-playing programs and also serves to validate and test the efficiency of the chosen representation of the various pieces and positions on the board in a chess-playing program. Playing Kriegspiel on a computer suffers from the disadvantage that 'kibbitzing' is restricted; in most games this would be desirable but Kriegspiel is an exception.

While the use of computers in this refereeing and controlling capacity may seem to have only recreational value, in its way it is as much of serious value as are game-playing programs, but this time not in the area of artificial intelligence. This is because games which are not solely based on chance involve the player making decisions using available information. Hence similar techniques can be used to simulate other situations where human participants also have to make decisions. The monitoring computer can calculate the consequences of the decisions, and possibly some kind of evaluation of their effectiveness.

This has been exploited in two main areas: war games and business games. Both are familiar to most people in the form of board games, e.g. Diplomacy, Monopoly etc., but using a computer enables the games to become more realistic and be of more practical use. In a typical war game, two players or teams are provided with resources of manpower, equipment and perhaps productive capacity, which are initially deployed in a specified way. Each player is also given some information (usually incomplete and/or partially inaccurate) about the corresponding resources of the enemy. The computer then simulates the progress of the conflict, handling the decisions made by either side, updating information where appropriate, and inserting external factors, such as weather conditions in a battle area. Four main uses of such games can be distinguished: developing skills in military decision-making, analysing past war situations, evaluating various strategies or tactics in a planned or possible future situation, and giving assistance to the military and political decision makers in an actual war situation.

Developing the skills of commanders and staff officers without the costs and risks of letting them learn on the job is the most obvious use of the war game technique (though there is the question of whether people will react differently when faced with an actual war situation rather than a simulation). In this teaching use, a real war situation will be simplified so that the instructor can concentrate on the particular aspect that he wants to stress. The effects of background knowledge of the real situation being simulated, which might influence the players' decisions and hence lessen the teaching value of the game, can be eliminated by making the context wholly fictional. It is interesting that when war games are depersonalised in this way (e.g. by making the conflict between Country A and Country B with different characteristics from real countries, rather than, say, East versus West), after a time the players seem to become emotionally involved in the outcome even to the extent of appearing to develop feelings of hatred towards the human players on the

other side. Such games can also be used by psychologists and other behav-
ioural scientists to study the ways that humans act in such situations, or how
they reach decisions.

Simulation and analysis of past battles is interesting academically as well as
being of obvious practical value in a military context. For example, they can
help historians trying to reconstruct the detailed course of a particular battle
or campaign. Simulation of possible future situations is of concern to commanders planning assaults or required to design defensive systems against
potential attacks. Future wars are likely to be fought on the basis of campaigns
mapped out in advance by computer simulation, as was the Israeli campaign
during the Six-Day War. Similarly, commanders in the field will probably be
aided in their decision-making by computer forecasts of developments –
though by this stage the activity is only a 'game' in the narrow technical
sense.

Business games are similar in structure and motivation, except that the field
of conflict is economic rather than military. The division between the two is
not clear since economic warfare is often used in conflicts. When business
games are performed on a large scale, the simulation may include macro-
economic or political factors such as world monetary conditions, governmental taxation or investment policy. The participants in a business game can
have a variety of aims: a simple clear-cut victory, mere survival or a modest
profit. Only in the most predatory commercial contexts is it the aim to drive all
one's opponents into bankruptcy as in the board game Monopoly. A business
game may have no definite finish, similar to a war game which may end in a
temporary armistice. A complex game can have many players or teams of
players, possibly representing competing manufacturers, producers of raw
materials and components, trades unions, governments and banks, and can be
used for economic planning.

Although the applications in this section may have become rather sombre
the reader should remember that the techniques for them originated from
using computers for entertainment. Playing games is an enjoyable way of
becoming familiar with various aspects of computers and one major computer manufacturer holds a yearly business games contest for teams from
various schools.

7.2   People and Manors

Playing games is only one kind of entertainment; there are also the arts, which
we shall come to later, and hobbies of many kinds. A good deal of ingenuity
would be needed to devise some reasonable use of computers for some
hobbies, such as home brewing. In others, some potential application of computers may be more obvious: there must be many computers which have been
used surreptitiously to assist with football pools. Such potential applications
are interesting but relatively straightforward. Instead we shall look at an

application relating to a subject which many people enjoy as a hobby but which also can be pursued as a serious study both in its own right and because of important applications.

This is the reconstruction of aspects of family and parish history. As a hobby, people find enjoyment in it by tracing their ancestors and reconstructing their personal pedigree, but it is also a serious subject of historical study, and in addition can provide information on the genetic structure of human populations which is of great relevance to many aspects of medical genetics, and is also one component of population studies.

The problem of family reconstruction is more than simply genealogy, since one is not trying to find just the ancestors, e.g. parents, grandparents, etc., of one person, but all the descendants of all the population of a particular parish or group of parishes. Ideally all the parish registers would be fed into a computer and complete pedigrees would be output. This does not work for several important reasons. The difficulties can easily be seen if we look at family reconstruction in the field of population studies.

If one is going to study the changes in a population, it is not enough just to count the birth, marriage and death rates. An increase in the number of baptisms in a parish does not necessarily mean that fertility is higher, or that the population is increasing. Even before the industrial revolution, society was more mobile than most people imagine. Comparatively few people stayed in the place where they were born and left children there, which makes it difficult to study the whole population. If one looked only at those who were static in a parish, they would be uncharacteristic; they cannot be used as a sample of the whole population.

The first difficulty is that of incomplete information, in that for some of the population some data will be missing. There can be several reasons, the obvious ones being that a person moved from one parish to another, or emigrated, or that the records themselves are missing, e.g. registers have been destroyed or a birth was never registered. There are also more technical reasons: for instance, there is usually a delay between birth and baptism, so that those who die soon after birth may not be registered, which will distort mortality figures.

The second difficulty is that of inaccurate information, which occurs much frequently than is usually imagined. In the 1851 census of Colyton in Devon, 20% of those who claimed to have been born in the parish could not be found in the Church of England registers. After allowing for those who were Nonconformist or were baptized in neighbouring parishes, there were still several who were missing or gave a different birthplace in subsequent censuses. When a person gives two different birthplaces, which one is right? Nor should information given in registers be taken as correct, as many transcription errors can occur when entries are copied from slips into the register.

These twin difficulties of incomplete information and inaccurate information arise in many areas and need special techniques to overcome them. For example, family reconstruction has been studied by many people; it consists of starting with a large file of records obtained from parish registers and trying to link them together to form family groups. The description that we shall give is based on the work of Dr E. A. Wrigley of Cambridge University.

Anyone who has tried family reconstruction manually is aware of the considerable amount of cross referencing between records and the complex decision-making processes involved. The advantage of using a computer is that the manipulation and comparison of records occurs at electronic speeds, casual errors are virtually eliminated, and its speed allows many alternative solutions to be evaluated and the best selected. Algorithms have been designed including quite complicated decision-making and eliminating the bias and inconsistency which often occurs in manual reconstruction.

There may be many possible links between the records. For instance, in a baptism entry it may be that only the father of the child is named in the register, and if there are two or more families present in the parish with adults of that name a decision must be made between the possible links. This is another instance of incomplete information, the usual result being an increase in the number of possible links. An algorithm must not depend on either complete or accurate information. The requirements of an algorithm are that every possible link must be considered, that there should be a decision procedure if there is more than one possible link, and that this decision process must not just use the records immediately involved but must also consider the effect of these links on all the records in the file which are relevant to the decision.

There are five types of links that can be made: baptism–marriage; marriage-marriage; marriage-burial; baptism–burial and baptism of child–marriage of parents. The first step is to find all possible links and it is likely that there will be ambiguities or inconsistencies between these. Decisions have to be made as to which links to keep and which to delete; nevertheless, it is essential to form all the possible links at an early stage so that the maximum information is available later without any extra searching. In some cases extra records have to be created, e.g. if a parents' marriage corresponding to the baptism of a child cannot be found then a dummy record of the marriage is created and a link formed with it. There are rules which reduce the number of links. For instance a link is excluded which would imply a marriage where the bride or groom was under 12 years of age. When occupations are stated in both records involved in a possible link then no link is made if the occupations are incompatible, e.g. a labourer in one record and a vicar in the other. Rules such as these are not always easy to apply since the year of baptism and year of birth may differ.

The formation of the possible links is not as simple as might first appear. They are normally formed in a specific order (e.g. baptism–marriage of parents links are formed first) and after some types of links are formed, there may be some revision of them before forming any others. It is found that men and women have to be treated differently during the revision of linking, because of the practice of a married woman adopting her husband's surname. Tests which are suitable for male records may not be suitable for female records. For example, if a male baptism record is linked to a marriage record and this marriage record is linked to a burial record, but the baptism record and burial record are not linked, then one of the links must go. This would not be true with comparable female records since no baptism–burial links of this type could have been made. Decisions may have to be made about one type of link before another can be formed. For instance there must be evidence that the previous partner has died before the date of the new marriage of the spouse (divorce was extremely rare before the nineteenth century). Some links can be much stronger than others: for example it was customary in English parish registers that when a woman died while her husband was still living both of their names would be recorded in the burials entry, but if the husband died while his wife was still alive only his name would be recorded.

Having linked the records together, the ambiguities must now be resolved. The strategy chosen will depend on the purpose of the reconstruction, i.e. whether it is important to avoid errors at all cost, which means that only a small number of accurate family groups will be produced, or whether as much reconstruction as possible should be achieved, in which case there will be errors and one needs to have a measure of how many.

The strategy normally takes the form of adopting a scoring system for each link and then choosing the strongest links. The scoring can be based on different fields in each record and will represent agreement or disagreement between the records. This sort of strategy is unique to computer reconstruction since it is impossible to do manually. (Notice that there is a similarity between this part of the program and the evaluation of positions in a game-playing program.) Before we leave family reconstruction we should mention that it is also possible to include other information, e.g. census records, wills, etc., to help find a solution, but not very much has been done in this direction.

The strategy for choosing links to delete must allow for the possibility of inaccurate information; some forms of inaccurate information can affect forming the links at the start of the program. One of the main causes of inaccuracy is the variation in spelling of names, a problem which also occurred in the airline reservation problem in the last chapter. One of the authors has found many variations in the spelling of his surname, including Feathern (in 1652), Fayththorne (1579), Fayrethorne (1553) and even Phyrthorn (1557).

The misspelling problem has received considerable attention since it occurs in many areas, including regional medical records. The misspellings arise either from errors in writing or because of different character representations for phonetic sounds. The examples above are mainly of the second variety. For a number of years the normal procedure was to use the Soundex Code, which codes names into four digit numbers. In its original form the initial letter of the name was retained and then the next three consonants were coded into digits, ignoring vowels. The code grouped together consonants which are similar phonetically. This has shown to be unsatisfactory even with modern spelling. Any method of coding is liable to two kinds of error. First, it may group together names which are genuinely different, e.g. BROWN and BARON. This increases the number of possible links and can be serious unless the records contain fields with additional information (as in the airline reservation system, where this problem is negligible since there will also be an address with the name). Secondly, the method may fail to group together genuine variants in spelling, and this is more serious.

To reduce the errors, especially due to mispronounced first letters, e.g. BOLES and VOWLES, variations on the Soundex Code have been used, one of which is as follows:

The consonants of the name are assigned digits according to the following code and rules:

Code	Letters
1	B, F, P, V
2	C, G, J, K, Q, S, X, Z
3	D, T
4	L
5	M, N
6	R
uncoded	A, E, I, O, U, W, H, Y

Rules (a) The code for any name consists of four digits; if a name does not have sufficient coded consonants, zeros are added to complete the code. If there are more than four coded consonants then the code is truncated.

(b) If two or more consonants which have the same coded number come together, they are coded as only one letter.

(c) Consonants having the same code number but separated by one or more vowels are coded individually.

(d) W and H do not separate consonants. If two consonants having the same code are separated by a W or H, then they are coded as one consonant.

This is easy to program, and all names are usually coded like this at an early stage. Besides trying to overcome misspellings the coding also reduces the size of the name field in each record, as only four digits are needed each of which is in the range 0 to 6 inclusive; hence the name needs only 12 bits. If the name was left in its original form at least 60 bits would be required and even then some long names would have to be truncated. When handling files consisting of thousands of records there is a substantial saving in space. Errors will still occur whatever form of coding is used – two of the variants in our 'Fairthorne' example will code to 1365 and the other two to 1636. This would be serious if we were examining records of people in the sixteenth and seventeenth centuries, but by the late eighteenth century these two variants represented completely disjoint branches of the family, and hence should have been separate. This is common, misspellings occurring more frequently the older the registers are.

One way to avoid the grouping problems which arise from a code is to have an alphabetically sorted dictionary of names together with the standard spelling for each entry. In family reconstruction it is usually impractical to search the dictionary for every name in the file, though this method is used by the Church of Latter Day Saints at Salt Lake City to index, file and print copies of parish records where no reconstruction is attempted. A better way of solving the grouping problem is to use a code to group the names, choosing the code to reduce the chance of grouping different names together erroneously. This will leave several variants of a name outside its main group, but they will tend to be isolated rather than in other large groups. All the small groups are then examined separately and the dictionary of standard spellings searched to find the correct spelling. Although the dictionary search is still used, this will only be for a small proportion of the records in the file and the advantage of small name fields is retained.

We now turn to another problem where there is again incomplete information, only part of a wide range of problems solved by Professor D. G. Kendall of Cambridge University. This problem consists of reconstructing the map of the manor of Whixley in Yorkshire, from incomplete scraps of information, there being no surviving large-scale map of the manor that dates from before the Enclosure Acts of 1836. The arable land in the manor occurred in named field-shaped parcels called **flatts**, which are the basic records, each flatt being divided into parallel strips called selions. Each strip was cultivated by a particular person either as an owner or as a tenant. The description of a selion in manorial surveys consisted of an owner, the area of the selion, its orientation, and the named flatt in which it lay. This information will allocate selions to flatts but will not enable the flatts to be located in the manor; however, the flatts are also described in some surveys. A typical description would be that in flatt Y the selions run from the south (where they abut on flatt A) towards the north (where they abut on flatt B). Hence Y has A and B as neighbours to the south and the north but there is no information as to which flatts are to the east and west of it. The problem can be more complicated, since the shape of the flatts may be irregular. There are two other features which counterbalance this disadvantage. Some of the flatt-names have survived to the present day as the names of fields or from early enclosure maps, which enables some of the flatts to be located; also some of the abuttals in the survey will be with roads, footpaths or streams and again some of these can be identified on modern maps and so are fixed points.

The main early source of information about Whixley is a Cartulary containing deeds and a survey of all the flatts and selions in about 1415. This problem seems to be similar to that of family reconstruction; there linking was to take place between different records referring to the same person, here the linking is to take place between abutting flatts. In both cases there is incomplete information, but here there is unlikely to be inaccurate information, since there is a single primary source document. By using techniques similar to those that he had used in several archaeological problems, Professor Kendall produced a rough map of the manor.

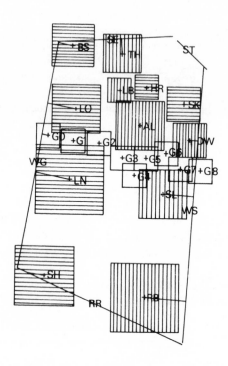

Fig. 7.2. Diagram based on a computer map of mid-south Whixley. The selions have been fitted into each flatt (see main text). The chain of 9 links, G0, G1, ... , G8 is a lost way, linked to the two north–south roads WG and WS. This diagram is included by kind permission of Professor D. G. Kendall, and of the Royal Society, in whose *Proceedings* Professor Kendall's paper, with the original computer map, appeared. This paper also includes an aerial photograph which can be compared with this map: the full reference is given in the reading list.

The survey consisted of two sections and it was originally thought that these sections referred to North Whixley and South Whixley. When the preliminary map was produced this was found not to be the case, since there were flatts from both sections in the north part of the manor, though the program did group all thirteen flatts from the second section of the survey together in one area. Looking again at the survey it was noticed that there were differences in the tenants of flatts in the two sections even where there were tenants belonging to the same family. The pedigree of one of these families was known from a Visitation in 1584/5 showing that the tenants were father and son. This suggested that the second section was a later addition to the survey. Up to this stage Kendall had been using a typescript copy of the survey, but at this point he remembered that there was a marked change in handwriting towards the end of the survey. He wrote to the Archivist of the Yorkshire Archaeological Society suggesting at what point the writing should change, and this was confirmed. Computer techniques thus may not produce a perfect map, this one certainly was not, but with intelligent use they can draw attention to significant features of the problem.

Kendall then realised that the Whixley problem needed a custom-built program. The idea behind the program was to treat each flatt as if it were a star with a gravitational field. Abutting flatts were to attract one another, the unlinked flatts which either do not abut or are not known to abut behave neutrally to one another, and the flatts and roads whose positions are known are fixed at their true positions. A random starting position for the flatts is chosen, and then the 'gravitational forces' are allowed to pull the flatts into their final position. One major difficulty arose, in that the system tends to collapse despite the fixed points. To stop this effect, i.e. to prevent two flatts from occupying the same space, short-range repulsive forces were introduced between all pairs of flatts and between flatts and roads. There was still a difficulty, in moving flatts past others if they were badly positioned to start with, but this was solved by running the program iteratively with the repulsive forces alternately suppressed and turned on. After obtaining a stable map, the selions were inserted into the flatts with their proper widths, and at least one now vanished road was located as a chain of small linked flatts.

This application may seem rather specialised, but the techniques can be applied to a wide range of problems. For instance, in archaeology, relative dating of graves from material found in them is a one-dimensional map problem, here trying to arrange the grave in a linear order but allowing two graves to have the same date. A reference to Kendall's more detailed account of this and related problems is given in the reading list.

While we have come quite a long way from 'entertainment' in the narrow sense, this has served to illustrate how computers can come to be used in unexpected and stimulating ways. Some warning is essential: programs will not be able to produce perfect maps or family trees, and often they will not even be very good ones. Results obtained this way need not be 'right', although many people still have the idea that anything produced by a computer must be perfect. The map-producing program can be misleading in that it always outputs a map, right or wrong. If run again from a different starting position, it will probably output a different map. Any programs like this must be run more than once using different random starting positions, to try to produce at the end maps which are as different-looking as possible. There is always the possibility that, though the programs are designed to work with incomplete information, there may be so little that a solution cannot be found. The results must be treated with reserve, but can suggest features or indications which the specialist can then use.

7.3   Computers and the Arts

Finally in this chapter, we turn our attention to computer arts. Again it is wrong to categorise all computer art activity as mere entertainment, although lineprinter depictions of nudes, or of Snoopy, certainly come into this category, as do computer renderings of nursery rhymes such as *Pop goes the Weasel*. Most computer art started in unpretentious ways such as these, but nowadays computer techniques can be exploited as a means of serious artistic expression. The commonest involvement of computers with art is in using the computer and its associated equipment as a means of realising the artist's imaginative creations. There have also been attempts to give a computer aesthetic judgement and the ability to perform its own creative activity, problems which have affinities with the attempts to provide the power of inductive reasoning to learning programs. They have so far had limited success, as the appraisal of art depends on human feelings and emotions, which are more difficult to analyse than logical reasoning. It is likely that for a long time to come most computer art will depend on human interaction, either in programming or during running.

In the graphic arts the artist may envisage the final creation in its entirety, using the computer only as a means of executing the production of the work more accurately and perhaps more quickly than he could by more conventional means. It is easiest to envisage this in the case of a black-and-white line drawing produced on an incremental plotter. A computer is very good at (and relatively easy to program for) producing with great accuracy repetitive output with, say, small but systematic variations on each repetition. A graphic artist may consider the computer to be a better means of realising such pictures than doing so manually and laboriously with less accuracy. Though the artist is not physically responsible for producing his creation, what has happened is that the imagination has been freed from some physical limitations of hand and eye. The artist still has to program the computer to produce his creation, and this requires certain skills, though different ones from those needed to use pencil or brush.

Of the variations possible on this theme of computer-as-artistic-instrument, we shall mention only two. One is that the computer can control a wide range of different devices and has the potential for developing new graphic art forms. A computer is a dynamic device, operating in time as well as space. Most graphic art forms are static, the major exceptions being film and mobile sculpture. The computer offers to the creative artist easier and more complete control in the time dimension, and also the power to amalgamate graphic art with other art forms, particularly music.

Another variation is the utilisation of the memory capability of the computer, its capacity for rapid and total recall. There is a potential for the graphic artist to use a computer as an intelligent sketch book, in which images and ideas can be stored, recalled, combined and manipulated. The computer can be used not merely for storage and retrieval but to take an image and generate variations upon it in predetermined ways. The artist-operator could interact with the program, holding particular variations for further development, storing those which might be of value. Techniques like these can be used in making cartoons, where pictures of characters and background can be held, and the computer used to combine and animate the cartoon by producing intermediate frames. The resultant frames can be output on a graphic display and photographed using a standard camera.

Music is one art form which can be combined with the visual arts, but applications of computer techniques to music by itself have received just as much attention. In some ways music is more natural for computer methods. It exists dynamically in time; electronic techniques for the production of music are already established, both for high-fidelity recording and for amplified instruments such as guitars and organs; and the mathematical foundations of music have long been known and are well understood.

The roots of computer music lie in the provision within most machines of an output loudspeaker, capable of producing notes of various pitches. This provides the operators with an audible indication that the machine is functioning, and more especially provides different audible signals for different types of computation; if various error conditions arise then the operators can identify them from the pitch of the note. Programmers and engineers on early machines were not slow to entertain themselves by writing programs to play tunes on the loudspeaker – either special-purpose, to play particular tunes, or general-purpose, to accept input and produce the tune as output.

Thus in the early stages the computer was just an instrument, and a very elaborate and expensive one. The main artistic interest in computer music is, rather, on the creative side: a program either does the actual composition or is an aid to the human composer. In either case the computer may also help to execute the composed work, although no serious computer musician would be satisfied with the normal machine's loudspeaker, any more than an artist would be satisfied with a lineprinter as his only means of expression.

Since music has its own written language, pure computer composition in the conventional sense does not absolutely need a special output device, though producing the final composition in normal stave notation involves a great deal of work. The mathematics of music being so well developed, many of the formal conventional rules – of harmony, counterpoint, tempo, etc. – can be programmed with relative ease. The problem lies in the aesthetics. Nevertheless programs have been written which are capable of generating compositions, an early success being the *Iliac Suite for String Quartet*, written by a University of Illinois computer in the mid-1950s.

The main impact of computer techniques upon music has been less in this area than in the field of electronic music. At first sight this may seem natural enough, but a computer is not essential for electronic music and it is worth while considering briefly some of the reasons why some composers have become interested in that technique at all, before looking at the particular involvement of computers. The most obvious appeal of electronic music is the range of new sounds which it opens up, but of more relevance in this context is the factor of *control*. A conventional musical work is produced for the listener by a combination of three processes: composition, interpretation, and actual performance. In some cases these may overlap (as in an improvisation) but for the purposes of this discussion we can take them as separate. An in- strumental soloist will perform his own interpretation of (usually) another's composition; in the case of an orchestral work much of the interpretation will be done by the conductor rather than the performers.

The problem for the composer is therefore that he normally must rely on others to interpret and perform his works as he would wish. However metic- ulous he is in his scoring and however carefully his directions are obeyed, there will still be variations of phrasing, intonation, etc. One of the attractions of electronic music is that it allows the composition, interpretation and per- formance to be rolled into one if this is what the composer wishes; in the simplest case, the composition consists of a high-fidelity sound recording which also produces directly the performance, without the intervention of interpreters or performers.

Nevertheless there are problems with producing electronic music. In the early days it was done by direct manipulation of recordings. Sounds were produced by musical instruments, voices, sonic oscillators or by banging sauce- pan lids together; these were recorded and then these recordings manipulated. Possible manipulations include re-recording faster or slower, backwards, patching together snippets, superimposition, etc. This was usually done by the composer operating tape recording decks and tape splicers, physically mani- pulating lengths of magnetic tape until the desired result was achieved. The trouble with such techniques is that they are cumbersome, tedious, error- prone, and even then do not give the composer complete control over his material, because the devices being operated are essentially analogue devices, capable of limited accuracy. There are other difficulties in that (say) doubling the speed of a tape increases the pitch by an octave, whereas the composer may wish to increase speed without altering the pitch.

This is where the digital computer can become usefully involved. The characteristics of a sound can be stored digitally and (though at that point an approximation) is thereafter under total control. Suitably designed sub- programs can disentangle the various characteristics of the sound which the composer may wish to manipulate – pitch, volume, duration, etc. – and handle them in any required way. The techniques of digitally storing characteristics of sounds so that they can be (to the human ear) faithfully reproduced form an interesting problem in analogue-to-digital conversion with a good deal of mathematical content.

The existence of a well-developed musical electronics technology as well as a digital electronic computer technology has meant that a good deal of progress has been made in this direction and composers can already buy complete computer systems with the basic hardware and software that they need. One advanced system is the computerised SYNTHI developed by Electronic Music Studios (London) Ltd, the firm founded by one of the pioneers in the field, Dr Peter Zinovieff. The 'instrumental' part of the system is the SYNTHI 100 electronic music studio which is able to synthesise an extremely wide range of sounds using waveform generators and the like. Many control devices for filtering, modulation, etc., are provided, as well as an internal sequencer which is effectively a small memory in which a sound sequence can be stored and reproduced at will, at any speed and direction. The SYNTHI 100 can be played 'live' with the aid of two 5-octave keyboards instead of or as well as setting up the sequencer.

The computerised SYNTHI takes this complex of devices and places it under the control of a computer system, based on the PDP–8, a popular low-cost mini-computer manufactured by the Digital Equipment Corporation. It allows the composer to write his 'score' as a program, which is compiled and run in the usual way, the execution run controlling the SYNTHI 100 during the performance. The software, developed by Dr Zinovieff and Peter Grogono, consists of a package called MUSYS, based upon a high-level programming language explicitly designed for easy creation of electronic music scores. The MUSYS package consists of a compiler for the language, and a text editor which the composer can use to modify and correct his program, plus two further run-time programs. The output from the compiler is a set of coded data which is used at run time to control the SYNTHI 100; one run-time program takes this from the computer's disk backing store and prepares the commands for the various parts of the SYNTHI 100 system, while the other actually executes the performance by sending the required data to the correct devices within SYNTHI 100 at the right time. The SYNTHI has some capacity for random generation or variation of signals, but essentially it is a device for human rather than machine composition. Since producing this system EMS have been working upon more advanced facilities using digital rather than analogue oscillators. Among the composers who have worked with Dr Zinovieff on his systems have been Hans Werner Henze and Harrison Birtwhistle, and one of Harrison Birtwhistle's works which resulted from this collaboration has been issued as a commercially available recording; details are given at the end of the reading list.

Another major area of artistic creation is literature. In this case there are no major technical problems of producing suitable output, since computers deal routinely with textual matter and are provided with printing devices. Nevertheless the difficulties are greater than with music or the graphic arts, since there is also the problem of semantics. Computers have been programmed to produce verses of the 'moon in June' variety, by providing a vocabulary, rhyming rules where required, information about stress and scansion, etc.

Fig. 7.3. A computerised SYNTHI 100 music studio (see main text). The Synthi 100 itself is on the left nearest the camera with the instrumental double keyboard in front; the computer system is behind this keyboard, two small magnetic tape drives being visible with the actual processor (a PDP 8) immediately below in the rack.

Providing rules for dealing with the *meaning* of words is quite a different matter, There are really two approaches: to try to produce 'abstract' text, stringing together words according to rules of grammar and sound but ignoring meanings, working on a similar principle to 'monkeys and typewriters' in that something meaningful should eventually appear. The other approach is to limit the realm of discourse so severely that everything generated is bound to have some meaning, or appear to have some meaning. On a crude level the so-called 'buzzword generators' come into this category, where a 'meaningful' sentence can be produced from (say) three sets of clauses, by combining any phrase from the first set, with any from the second and any from the third. One of the more successful attempts to limit the realm of discourse was the computer generation of a script for a 'shoot-out' scene in a Western, involving a robber and a sheriff. The number of possible actions at any stage was strictly limited (sheriff draws gun, robber throws chair, robber jumps on table, etc.); whichever one was chosen helped to determine the range of possible actions at the next stage (e.g., this not being a comedy Western, neither man can fire his gun until he has drawn it).

Though it is certainly entertaining, it hardly qualifies as literature. The main impact of computers in a literary context has been scholastic rather than artistic: the production of concordances, attempts to establish the authorship of texts by statistical tests, etc. These are problems in data handling rather than computer art. An interesting area of scholastic research which does have artistic implications is semantics.

One hope of progress in the problems of semantics lies in developments in computer translation. We have seen how computer languages have been developed, of increasing sophistication, which have to be translated into machine terms. This might lead one to suppose that computer translation of human languages is a natural consequence. This is far from the case. Computer languages have a limited realm of discourse and a strict and unambiguous syntax, and their translation mainly takes account only of syntax, not semantics. This is not the case with natural languages – computer languages exist partly because natural languages are not suitable for programming. Nevertheless a considerable amount of work has been done on analysing natural languages and their semantics, together with many good attempts at translation from one language to another, e.g. from Russian and Chinese into English. Translations have been mainly restricted to technical publications, etc., where the realm of discourse is limited and style is relatively unimportant; translations of literary works are obviously more difficult. If these can be done successfully then the possibility of generating computer literature could be seriously considered – but at present this seems as unlikely as a computer being able to translate Linear A.

Computer techniques have been tried in other art forms (e.g. choreography) but enough has been described to give a general outline of the area. Art is a means of expression by humans; computer techniques in art have tended to exploit the audio and visual output devices of computers as a means of expression. It is not surprising that so far the problems of computer art have tended to overshadow the achievements, and its potentialities are not quite as clear as in other areas. As techniques of man-machine communication develop and become better understood, so may computer techniques of artistic expression.

Chapter 8

The Computer as a Social Force

In earlier chapters we have shown how computers can be used in many kinds of applications. We have far from exhausted the possibilities, but have given examples of the more frequent or interesting types of use. We considered how some mathematical problems may be solved using computers, but showed that many applications are not basically mathematical even though they may use mathematics at some stage. Computer techniques can be applied to a wide range of problems, provided solutions can be found which can be represented systematically in a discrete codified form.

In this final chapter we are concerned with the implications of computers for people in general, both as individuals and as members of human society. There are many social implications of computers, because most human activities involve some sort of processing of information which is amenable to computer methods.

We have looked at both scientific and at commercial applications. The commercial applications bear more directly on everyday life, and consequently have received more public attention, both informed and uninformed. We shall therefore consider the impact of these first. Later we shall show that scientific applications also have important social implications, as do applications which cannot be strictly classed as belonging to either group.

8.1 A Cashless Society?

The most obvious impact of computers in everyday life is in the handling of money. The shift from manual to computer accounting has been apparent to everyone as more and more bills, statements and payslips are computer printed, machine-readable digits appear on cheques, and so on. Trends such as the increased use of cheques and credit transfers would probably have occurred anyway, but computers have made them easier to handle and have probably given an extra impetus to such trends.

However, the rapid expansion in the use of credit cards could not have occurred without computers to handle the necessary accounting. Some years ago, most credit cards were issued by two American companies and were confined mainly to businessmen. Now the use of credit cards has mushroomed, and they are available to virtually anyone with a bank account and to some without one. One of the signs of the times has been the proliferation in High Street windows of the multi-coloured stickers announcing the acceptance of a variety of credit cards. From being mainly confined to restaurants catering for the out-of-town businessman trade, and to furniture and consumer goods stores already used to taking most of their receipts in cheques rather than cash, they began to spread to off-licences, hardware stores, bookshops, and so on. Now the stickers have appeared in the windows of several major chain stores (including some branches of Woolworth's, once regarded as the major bastion of small cash sales) and it is likely that it is only a matter of time before they spread even more widely, with only small businesses such as tobacco kiosks exempt.

Yet even such a revolution need not touch everyone. Those who have always conducted all their transactions in cash have been able to continue in this way without having to be aware of the existence of computers. British traders have not yet followed some of their American counterparts and become suspicious of cash customers on the grounds that if they are not using a credit card they cannot be credit-worthy.

Computers are now becoming involved in everyday cash transactions as well as in the after-sales accounting. Cash registers remained essentially unaltered for many years, but have recently developed to include more electronics so that some, for example, can work out the change to be given to the customer. A further development has been to extend the electronic logic in the cash registers to allow them to be used as computer terminals, and for all the cash registers in a department store to be connected to a central computer. On each sale, details are transmitted to the computer and recorded there, allowing up-to-date information to be available about sales of various types of goods or by particular assistants in any department of the store. The customer is unaware that the cash register is connected to a computer, but the management has an important tool with which to monitor sales in the store. At some wholesale-type establishments, a computer terminal is used to check whether items are in stock and, if so, to reserve them for the customer.

This use of computers in stores and shops is still in its early stages but can be expected to develop further in the future. However, small businesses are not likely to find such on-line sales recording worthwhile unless packages based on mini- or microcomputers become cheap enough to be cost-effective.

Banks, on the other hand, are already using computers for much of their work and many branches already have terminals linked to central computers. These terminals can provide the bank staff with facilities such as being able to query customers' accounts, e.g. obtain the details of an overdraft during the previous six months while preparing to see the customer. In practice, most routine queries from customers concern the current state of their accounts, and these can be answered from lineprinter listings which are produced nightly and sent to the appropriate branches. This is cheaper than using the on-line terminal and frees it for more specialised queries.

Banks are becoming an increasingly important part of today's society as they act as clearing houses for money transactions not involving cash. The increasing use of credit cards is taking us nearer to the 'cashless society'. The theory of a cashless society is to replace the notes, coins and cheque books that we normally carry, by credit cards – perhaps just one state-issued card per person. On making a purchase the customer hands over his card, which is read by the sales terminal while the amount of the transaction is fed into it. The terminal transmits this information to a financial computer network, which checks that the customer has enough money in his account, or a sufficient credit limit. If so, the customer's account can be immediately debited and the shop's account credited by the appropriate amount, the account files recording the date and location of the transaction. An individual could also initiate payments for services or settlements of private debts by presenting his card at a suitable terminal and entering instructions for the payments to be made to the accounts of the payees. It is suggested that the need for cash would thus disappear.

In practice there are many circumstances where it is more sensible to use cash (or tokens) rather than credit cards. (Tokens are normally like coins and are handled very like cash, but are not general means of exchange.) The use of credit cards for transactions involving small amounts of money would involve unacceptable overheads to the system. One obvious instance is the use of coin-in-the-slot machines – the connection to a computer of every chocolate and sweet machine on railway platforms would not be cost-effective.

Any transactions which do not take place at fixed locations are also more simply done using cash rather than credit cards. It is unlikely to be sensible to connect every bus to a computer network via a telecommunications link. Also, life would surely be the poorer without street markets or even ice cream vans. The importance of cash is currently recognised by banks, who provide twenty-four hour cash dispensing machines which a customer can use with a special card or voucher. For such reasons it seems unlikely that a cashless society in the literal sense will come about, though the importance of cash may well continue to decline.

8.2 Central Databanks

In discussing the use of credit cards instead of cash we introduced the idea of central records of all financial transactions made by any particular individual. This is only one set of information which may be recorded centrally about a person. Other information may be kept by various government departments, e.g. inland revenue, health, social security, or by private companies such as the credit agencies, which exist to assess the credit-worthiness of potential customers of clients, e.g. finance houses, credit card organisations, or firms offering hire purchase arrangements.

Once such files exist (and many credit agencies use them already) there is the possibility of their being misused. Instances have come to light of individuals being unreasonably blacklisted, and therefore unable to obtain credit. The victim is often unaware that a file on him exists or that he has been investigated. Even when he knows of the file it has usually proved impossible either to find out what is in the file or, when it is suspected that the file is wrong, to have it changed. Of course these activities can go on without computers, but computers make them much easier. Often such a system is not programmed to make or record any assessment of the relative value and reliability of the information. There is the story of the man who suddenly found his credit withdrawn, his cards rejected and so on. On investigation it turned out that he had been placed on a black list because he too frequently involved himself in litigation and hence was deemed a bad risk. It happened that his job required him on occasion to take out civil actions and to appear in court. Like many computer 'jokes', at the time it was not amusing for the individual concerned. A further danger arises when information is copied from one file to another, something which computers make very easy to do. *Incorrect* information can also be copied, and may find its way into many files before the error can be corrected. There are firms whose trade consists solely in compiling and selling files to other companies. What is worse, the incorrect information may be used in and affect the results of other operations, these results may then be copied and used, and at any stage only the result may be transmitted, without the incorrect information on which it is based. The repercussions of an error may then be impossible to trace, and the consequences of an incorrect credit rating, though quickly corrected in one file, could still lurk in other files and affect the victim of the error, possibly for years.

Databanks of private information can clearly be deliberately misused, from selling goods to an individual by exploiting his known weaknesses, to outright blackmail. Many people are worried about the growth of private files of personal information and the uses to which these are put. Computer professionals, concerned about this, have proposed codes of ethics for personnel in computer installations along the lines of the Hippocratic oath for doctors. Much of the pioneering work on this was done in Britain, and the British Computer Society has adopted such a code for its members. This lead is now being followed in America and elsewhere. Legislation has been drafted in a number of countries, including Britain, for the licensing and control of databanks, and some, as in Sweden, has been passed into law.

A code of ethics is probably even more important for government-held information. The government has far more information about an individual than private companies. There are some perfectly legitimate uses of government files, e.g. a complete financial record could be used to make tax-dodging more difficult, and could also be used to detect anyone dropping below the poverty line and make it easier to initiate rescue action by the social services. It could also be used for far more questionable purposes. If we had a nearly cashless society where most transactions required the use of credit cards, individuals could have their activities traced or kept under surveillance in considerable detail. One argument is that only those with something to hide would have anything to fear, but this would only be true in a utopian society. Some critics fear a paternalistic type of state, raising ideological questions about what constitutes individual freedom and how much initiative might be stifled by psychological dependence on the structure of society. Moreover, once such a system is set up it is open to accidental or deliberate abuse which its originators did not intend: an individual could be harassed by having his card withdrawn or being limited to only certain transactions at particular locations.

An extension of this situation would be for a government to set up a complete network enabling the files held separately by various departments, such as inland revenue or car taxation, to be merged into one central databank forming extensive personal files, or dossiers, on individuals. The question of privacy of information held in such databanks has been widely discussed and written about, but so far little has actually been done about it. Some consider that bringing together the different sets of information about a person would be a threat to privacy, and that if the information needed for different purposes is kept totally separate, it is more difficult to build up a composite picture of any one individual.

Among the issues which have been widely discussed are: who and under what circumstances should have access to information? Should information collected for one purpose be used for another without the permission of the person concerned? Should an individual have the right to know what is on file about him and the right to demand alterations if it is inaccurate? Even this last issue, which appears to many to be a basic human right, is not wholly clear-cut, for unrestricted right of free access could cost a great deal of money and computer time, destroying the efficiency which is the point of the operation. In some circumstances it might be in a person's own interest to withhold information from him, particularly in the case of medical records. Also, how can an individual be certain that there is not some additional secret file about him, easy to attach to the main file by those in the know, but concealed from everyone else? Some of these matters have technical as well as ethical aspects, such as how to ensure that only authorised persons can access files, whether a system can be designed which is secure from illicit tinkering, and whether a technical auditor or ombudsman could detect the existence of concealed files. To their credit, many computer professionals have in recent years given a great deal of attention to such matters, often in their own time. It remains an area of growing importance, and of great interest in its own right quite apart from the ethical implications.

Mention of secret files brings us to the aspect of government computer activity which perhaps causes most concern, namely that of the police and security forces. Obviously some information held by these forces cannot be made readily accessible: it would severely handicap their fight against espionage, subversion and crime if their files were relatively open, or if those files could not contain suspicions as well as verified facts. A lawbreaker would often be helped by knowing what the police knew or suspected about him, and in some cases the mere fact of knowing that a file existed at all would be adequate warning. For efficient operation such information could not all be kept by manual methods or in people's heads. On the other hand, the most law-abiding citizen tends to feel uneasy at the thought that there might be a file on him, and naturally wishes to know if one exists and what it contains. The disclosures in 1975 about the FBI and CIA files show the dangers of allowing such files to proliferate without some form of constraint. A person is also bound to become cynical when told that he can cut off the 'date of birth' item on his computer-produced driving licence, only to find that the same information appears, only thinly disguised, in the driver number which he has to quote on all correspondence. Nevertheless he will not only wish the police to be efficient, but be personally grateful if a computer system helps to trace his stolen car more quickly.

The problems of privacy have no easy solution. The number and size of central databanks will inevitably increase, and, as is seen above it is important to control both the way they develop and the uses to which they are put. This can *only* be done sensibly while the systems are being designed, by making sure that the systems analysts are fully aware of the consequences of their designs.

8.3   Computer Aided Learning

The use of computers in society is not confined to handling data about people or money. There are many other tasks that can be helped by using computers, though usually there are disadvantages as well as advantages in their use.

A good example is the use of computers in an educational context. We shall not be concerned with the educational value of using computers to analyse or simulate situations, of using them in the classroom to perform or check calculations, or even of studying computers and computing. Though these are important, they are little different in principle or practice from conventional studies or from using other products of educational technology: such uses can supplement but never supplant ordinary teaching. We are concerned here with computer-aided learning (CAL) in the full sense, where the pupil uses the computer interactively and the program adjusts its behaviour and that of the system it controls in response to the inputs made by the pupil.

There are two basic situations in CAL, though they are often mixed together. One is where the program offers various options and facilities to the pupil, who chooses between them and guides himself through the process. The other situation is where the program in effect has control, sets out to teach the pupil something and, by presenting information and asking questions, decides whether the pupil is showing sufficient understanding at a given stage. If so the program goes on, if not, it repeats the item or presents it in a different way. Often the term CAL is reserved for the first of these and CAI, computer-aided instruction, for the latter, but as the two can be intermingled we shall use the one term for both. A combination of the two is probably best, since the most effective educational situation occurs when there is a partnership between teacher and pupil, together sharing decisions about how to proceed. CAL can vary its behaviour either in response to explicit demands or as a result of assessing the pupil's requirements from the pupil's inputs. Whereas most educational aids mainly or entirely present information, the pupil's role being purely passive, a teaching program can, like a human teacher, demand active participation from the pupil, and adjust the subject matter and presentation.

A properly programmed computer can therefore react to the pupil much as the teacher does in the classroom in a way which (say) educational television cannot. Of course it takes considerable work to write the program properly and allow for all the possible responses and queries. The success of CAL depends on the care taken at this stage. Once the program has been written and proved to work in a particular teaching situation, it has the advantage of other audio-visual aids, such as television video-tape, that it can be copied and used at will and indefinitely, at least until it needs to be brought up-to-date. (A program should be easier to modify than a television programme or a film.) In a number of subjects there are fewer good, knowledgeable teachers than ideally there should be, so there is an obvious advantage in having one capable of being endlessly duplicated to teach thousands of pupils. This factor has contributed to the success of educational television. Teachers on film or video-tape have other advantages: they can be used whenever the pupil is able to use the equipment; and they do not get tired, make mistakes, or give an insufficient amount of attention to particular pupils because of large classes. CAL shares these advantages too.

A computer program (assuming that it is properly written) gets its fact right and does not exhibit human failings. More important, from each pupil's point of view it can give what seems to be individual attention, and can adjust the speed of learning to the capabilities of the pupil concerned. Since terminals can be placed anywhere which has a telephone connection, this individual attention need not be at school but can for example be in the home (if the pupil lives in a remote location) or in a hospital (if the pupil is unable to attend school because of illness or disability).

CAL thus combines the advantages of audio-visual aids with many of the advantages of the individual tutor. The main problem in CAL is in the design of the program, because this requires experienced teachers who can anticipate all of the responses of a pupil (it is very difficult to predict all likely wrong answers). CAL will become much more widely used once there are enough experienced teachers involved in writing programs for it, and the cost of the equipment is sufficiently low.

It does have some disadvantages. One fear often expressed is that replacing the human teacher by a machine will cause psychological harm, as will learning wholly alone rather than as a member of a group. Many teachers believe that a pupil learns more in an interacting group than he does from an individual tutor or in a teacher–class situation. One of the main lessons a child must learn is how to communicate with other people, and so CAL can never completely replace the human teacher.

Other advantages of a human teacher are that he can achieve rapport with his pupil or class, that he can sense, and probably encourage, a 'take-off point' in understanding which a computer program could not, and that he can inspire as well as simply instruct. Even when a human teacher is present, he is unlikely to be able to exploit this if a computer is doing most of the teaching. Moreover there would be a marked psychological effect in schools resulting from the changed role of the human teacher if most of the teaching (even if only routine instruction) were done by computer. The teacher's role could be more rewarding, with much of the existing drudgery, such as marking exercises, removed: but on the other hand there is a danger that the teacher, in his own eyes and in those of his pupils, might be reduced to little more than a machine-minder and hand-holder. Whether or not CAL ultimately replaces human teachers, either in general or in particular subjects where there are teacher shortages, a substantial shift towards CAL will clearly have a major effect both on the pattern of the school day and on the possibilities for further and adult education. It could prove invaluable in private study, where there is no human teacher to replace, and one can envisage the development of an extension of correspondence courses, albeit at present an expensive extension.

Another potential disadvantage of the widespread adoption of CAL is that every pupil could, in effect, have the *same* teacher. This could stifle innovation, since experimenting with new approaches would need a great deal more preparation and effort than now; but if a human teacher remains in ultimate charge he could always resort to conventional methods to try out something new. The teacher would also be needed to prevent unconventional responses by pupils always being stifled. A more alarming possibility takes us back to the 'police state' situation: if all CAL programs were produced under state supervision, there would be a potential for much tighter control over what is taught. One needs only to envisage a situation where all teaching of history and philosophy was performed by programs written by the educational branch of the political police.

8.4 Computers in Everyday Life

In this section we shall show how computers can enrich everyday human life. Many people spend most of their lives either at home or at their place of work; indeed for some the two are the same, notably in the case of housewives. Hence the greatest impact of computers on most people is potentially at home and at work. In recent years we have seen a substantial change in the pattern of home life, with the emergence of television as the most important medium for entertainment. The question arises as to whether computers can have a similar effect, both at home and at work.

At work, the answer is clearly that in some areas they already have had a considerable effect. This is most obvious in the case of clerical and administrative activities, and it has also begun to occur in industrial contexts through the use of process control. Since the Industrial Revolution, mechanisation has provided means for freeing human beings from many kinds of arduous and dangerous physical drudgery. But there are many kinds of work still done by humans which are potentially or actually suitable for computer applications. Humans still do many jobs of a relatively automatic nature which have never been mechanised, either because the degree of control or judgement required cannot be achieved by purely mechanical means, or because machinery able to perform the same functions is too expensive. In addition, many machines which perform physical tasks still require human operators for their control.

Many such kinds of human work can be made redundant by the techniques of automation, especially with the coming of cheap, mass-produced processors, and by designing plant and whole factories to take advantage of them rather than merely adapting what exists. Ideally this leaves human beings free to do the creative work, the planning and design, the decision-making and trouble-shooting of a non-routine kind. There will always be a residue of jobs which for technical or economic reasons resist automation, or which for psychological or related reasons have to be done by humans. Nevertheless, if a significant part of what is possible does occur, there will certainly be major changes in the patterns of employment.

One consequence of widespread automation could be a big reduction in the standard working week, with a corresponding increase in leisure time. Education would also become increasingly important, as more skill and knowledge would become necessary for many kinds of work. As there would be a demand for more facilities and opportunities for leisure and entertainment, the job opportunities in those fields would probably increase.

Computers can not only help to create leisure, but also aid or affect it in many ways, both direct and indirect. It does this to a considerable extent already, a direct example being the booking of seats for theatres and sporting events. A sign of the way that computers are beginning to enter everyday activities was the installation by a number of Football League clubs in the mid-1970s of tailor-made booking systems based on computers. One of the pioneers, Chelsea Football Club, installed in 1975 a system based on a GEC 2050 mini-computer, with magnetic disks and cassette tapes. This is not a transaction processing system in the usual sense as there is only one terminal, and hence the operating system is much simpler. It has many of the characteristics of commercial computing, including fail-safe mechanisms such as son–father–grandfather files.

The terminal consists of a video display, a keyboard and a printer, and is situated in the booking office. A customer wanting to book seats for a future match chooses a particular block of the stand. The operator then types the details of the match and the block on the keyboard, and a seating plan for this block is displayed on the screen showing which seats are sold, reserved and free for that match. The customer is then able to choose which seats he wants, their numbers are typed on the keyboard, the transaction recorded on cassette, the seating plan updated and the tickets printed automatically – the whole process can take less than a minute. Unlike some other users of such systems, Chelsea Football Club like their customers to be able to see the video display. They have found that some are interested and that it overcomes many of the common prejudices against computers.

A way in which a computer application can affect leisure indirectly is through weather forecasting. Many outdoor leisure activities are affected by the weather – cricket, skiing holidays, picnics, etc. – and in some cases detailed meteorological knowledge is required as in sailing or flying. There is a need for accurate information about existing weather conditions as well as accurate weather forecasting; many people have attempted to do this by various methods for thousands of years, with variable degrees of success. While it is unlikely that computers will make forecasting infallible, they may be used to help in analysing weather patterns and hence improve the accuracy of forecasts. Of course information about weather is not just needed to help with leisure; there is a more serious side, e.g. the provision of information to shipping, and the use of satellites in tracking the path developments of hurricanes.

A considerable amount of effort has been spent in this field, with weather ships and land stations in various parts of the world all recording the weather. There are also satellites which record weather information in the form of visual and infra-red pictures. The satellites transmit the pictures to receiving stations on the ground and also act as relay stations in the transmission of data from one place to another. A large amount of information is generated and needs to be brought together to form a comprehensive picture. The obvious way of doing this is by using computers – but although it is obvious it is not simple.

The data being input from a satellite must be corrected to compensate for the different camera angles from the satellite to the ground and clouds above. There are also corrections to remove transmission errors, similar to the computer 'sharpening' of pictures from space probes. All of this involves a large amount of number-crunching which has to be done quickly, so quickly that it is often done by special hardware. Once the information has been corrected and recorded, various sets of information can be extracted from it and sent to interested users, i.e. weather charts sent to meteorological offices which include surface temperatures, wind charts, cloud analysis, etc. The computer is also used to monitor the orbit of the satellite and control it by sending signals to correct the orbit if required. Such a system is extremely complex and contains

Fig. 8.1(a) Computer terminal in the box office at Chelsea Football Club (see main text). When a customer enquires about a match the box office clerk can use the keyboard on the right to display a block of seats in one of the stands on the display screen, showing seats sold, available, reserved, etc. When the customer has chosen his seat the clerk uses the keyboard again and the system prints the required ticket (the printer is the rectangular box on the counter beneath the display screen), and records the sale of the ticket and that the seat is no longer available for the match concerned. The "customer" in the picture is Kenny Swain, one of the Chelsea team.

[Photograph by Mick Mears, Chelsea Football Club

Fig. 8.1(b) A specimen ticket printed "while you wait" by the computer system described in (a).

many features which we have not described, e.g. standby machines in case of failures. This application is typical in that although it is primarily intended for one area, the scientific, it affects indirectly many others.

The increased leisure generated by the widespread use of computers will obviously have a substantial effect on home life. The trend from the situation where working members of the family spend most of their weekday time away from home to one where all of the family is at home most of the time could be accelerated as a result of network developments. One possibility is the use of a nationwide communications network based on the telephone system. Besides the existing telephone network such a system could carry communications to and between computers and could also be connected to sound and television 'broadcasting' channels. It is suggested that this would allow people to do much of their work at home through the network; even the monitoring of an automatic factory could be done this way. As well as incorporating all the existing functions of the telephone, postal and broadcasting services, such a network has a wide range of potential uses. For example, a customer could contact a shop, see the goods displayed on a screen, order and pay for them; a viewer could access a film library and retrieve and view a particular film instead of waiting for it to appear on television; a student could access CAL programs; for conferences, the system could link individuals together simultaneously via the screen and by voice.

This is not all speculation, as some of it is already happening. Telephone links are already used for computer networks and computer terminals can be placed in people's homes, e.g. allowing a programmer to use a multi-access system from there. Work is in progress on systems for providing more general information in the home. In the mid-1970s three such systems were being developed in Britain: Ceefax (BBC), Oracle (IBA) and Viewdata (Post Office): All three systems are information services providing on-line access via adapted domestic television receivers. Viewdata uses a telephone line while the other two systems broadcast the information. The controls are the standard television controls together with a hand-held keypad or some equivalent means to select the information to be displayed on the screen.

The BBC and IBA systems are relatively small and are designed for instant updating of information and for allowing a large number of accesses to a particular piece of information at the same time, similar to the telephone service providing up-to-date weather or road reports. The aim of Viewdata is different. In its experimental form it consists of a central computer provided with a very large database held on disks, split up into 'pages'. A user accesses a particular page via a sequence of indexes which are displayed on the screen; he selects the number of the next index that he wants and may go through eight levels before reaching the required information. (The relationship to file indexing discussed in Chapter 5 is clear.) If the user wants to access the information frequently he can note the page number and thereafter bypass the index by just giving that number. Each page is displayed as a sequence

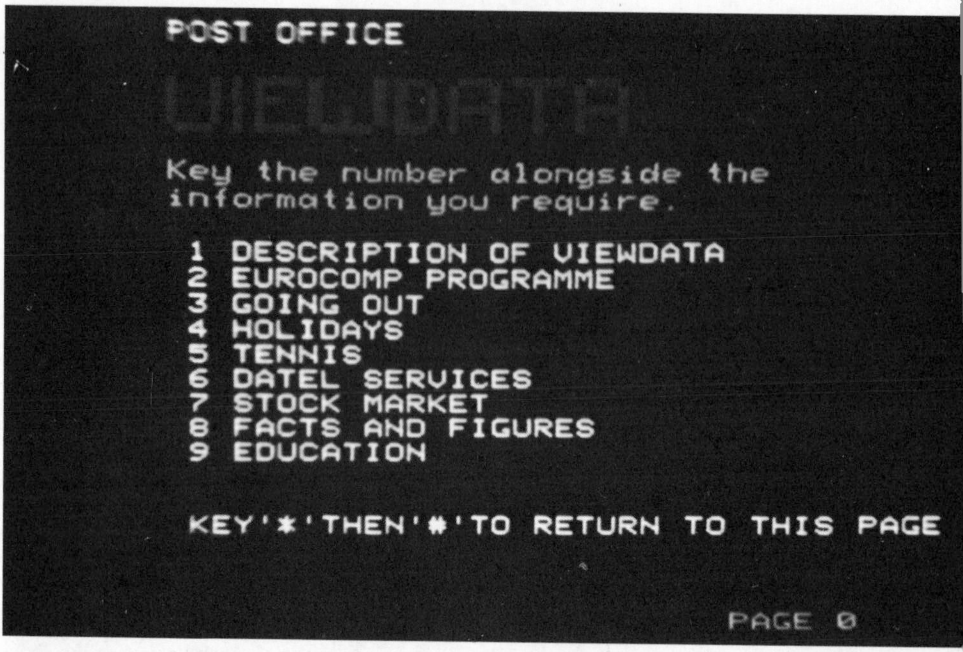

POST OFFICE

VIEWDATA

Key the number alongside the
information you require.

```
1  DESCRIPTION OF VIEWDATA
2  EUROCOMP PROGRAMME
3  GOING OUT
4  HOLIDAYS
5  TENNIS
6  DATEL SERVICES
7  STOCK MARKET
8  FACTS AND FIGURES
9  EDUCATION
```

KEY'*'THEN'#'TO RETURN TO THIS PAGE

PAGE 0

Frame (a)

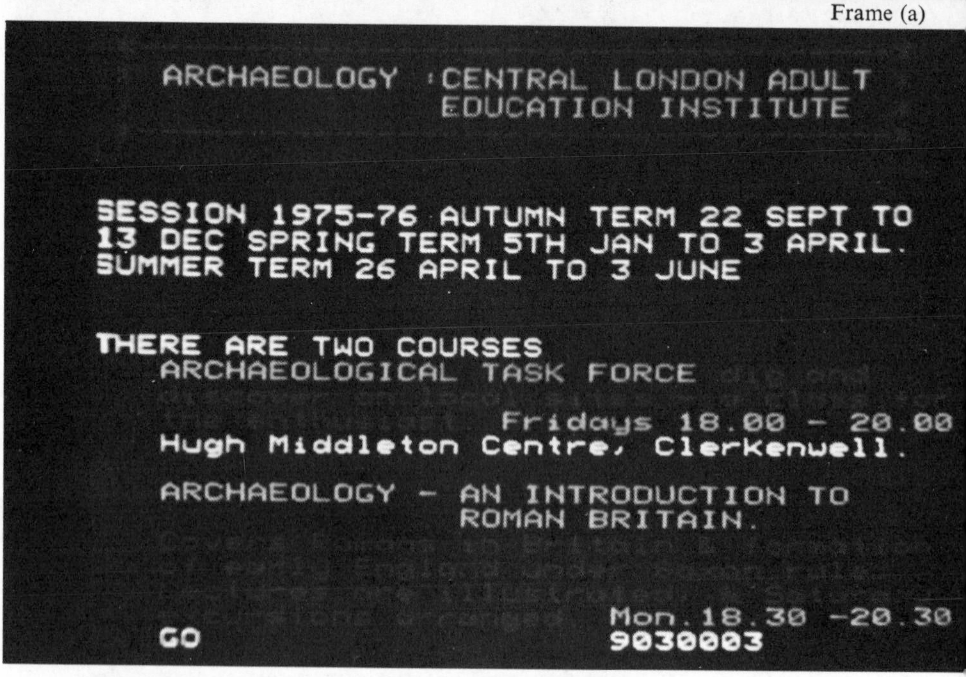

ARCHAEOLOGY :CENTRAL LONDON ADULT
EDUCATION INSTITUTE

SESSION 1975-76 AUTUMN TERM 22 SEPT TO
13 DEC SPRING TERM 5TH JAN TO 3 APRIL.
SUMMER TERM 26 APRIL TO 3 JUNE

THERE ARE TWO COURSES
ARCHAEOLOGICAL TASK FORCE

                    Fridays 18.00 - 20.00
Hugh Middleton Centre, Clerkenwell.

ARCHAEOLOGY - AN INTRODUCTION TO
ROMAN BRITAIN.

                    Mon.18.30 -20.30
GO   9030003

Frame (b)

Fig. 8.2. Two frames from the experimental Post Office Viewdata service (see main text).
Frame (a) shows the information facilities available and the code numbers to be keyed by
the user for each. Frame (b) shows a later display obtained by keying 9 (education) after
frame (a) and then similarly keying options to give further education courses in archaeology. The frames are in colour, hence the variations in intensity in these reproductions.
[*Photographs courtesy of Post Office Telecommunications*]

of 'frames', each of up to 960 characters (the capacity of the TV screen) containing the required information together with prompts to help the user continue.

The kinds of information being made available include news, tourist guides, education (e.g. lists of evening classes), stock market reports, recipes, etc. Of special interest is the provision of interactive facilities. A user can send a message to another user through the system, for example if he sees an advertisement that interests him he can send a message to the advertiser asking for further information not held in the database. He can also select standard messages to send to other domestic users, on the lines of 'happy birthday', 'please telephone your office', etc. Each user has an identifying number, used for accounting purposes and as protection from misuse, but which also enables him to receive messages from anyone who knows the number. The recipient of a message may refuse to accept it, so enabling the individual to have some privacy. It is planned to extend this message facility to allow the user to send his own messages instead of just selecting given ones, by providing a larger keypad than than that in the pilot scheme which is basically just numeric. As well as for sending messages the keypad can be used to play simple interactive games with the computer. A further leisure facility is the provision of quizzes; these are not interactive in the pilot version but could easily be made so. At the time of writing the Post Office is conducting market trials and intends to introduce a full public service in 1978. The system is designed for the residential market, and the Post Office, BBC and IBA are cooperating in standardising their equipment.

Such systems could obviously have a great effect on people's daily lives, especially if developed to provide computing facilities associated with work for the home user. There would be noticeable social effects. Commuting to work would decrease, which would offset the extra load on transport facilities which the additional leisure time would generate. It could also help to develop more community life in dormitory suburbs – though in turn this may be affected by the even greater leisure facilities available at home, as television has already done.

Not all of these prospects are necessarily welcome to everyone, but the full exploitation of computers could provide the potential for people to fulfil themselves to a greater extent than now.

8.5 Conclusion

We have emphasised in this chapter our basic philosophy, namely that using computers is on the whole a good thing rather than a bad thing provided you know what you are doing and understand the consequences. It may seem in many applications that computers can do nothing but good – for example, computer-based medical records can ensure that a patient's medical history can be available in seconds, something which can often be vital during emergency treatment. But once the records are on a computer file then they are open to misuse, so even here the blessing is not unmixed.

Ultimately it will be the human designers and controllers of computer systems who determine if they are used for good or for ill. Everyone has some part to play in making these decisions. People in positions of authority and influence have a duty to learn the capabilities of computers and to use them responsibly, guided by considerations other than just those of efficiency and economics. Ordinary citizens can play their part by demanding safeguards, protesting against abuses, and bringing public pressure to bear on those in authority. But most of all responsibility lies with computer professionals, to see that the public are informed both of the real potential for good of computer techniques, and of possible dangers. They must construct technical safeguards, ensure they are built into the systems they design, and see they are used. As we have said, many of today's computer professionals have taken the lead in setting down codes of ethics, and this effort must not be wasted.

Introducing computer methods into any realm of human activity has its attendant dangers, and it is either dishonest or irresponsible to pretend that all will be for the best in a computerised world. This does *not* mean that one should reject computer methods; as is shown by the variety of applications we have discussed, computers are already of great benefit to mankind and can become much more so.

The next few decades offer exciting prospects, and many challenges. Using computers will become as commonplace as using roads, or electric light. If computers are used responsibly, the world will be a better place.

Reading List

The following is a selection of books and articles known to the authors which are suitable for further reading or for more detailed information on points discussed in the main text. It is not a complete bibliography.

General

HOLLINGDALE, S. H. and TOOTILL, G. C., *Electronic Computers*, 2nd edition (revised) Penguin Books, 1975
An introduction for the general reader.

RALSTON, A., *Introduction to Programming and Computer Science*, McGraw-Hill, 1972
A good introduction for someone who wishes to take computer science as a serious academic subject.

Chapter 1

MORRISON, P. and MORRISON, E. (Eds), *Charles Babbage and his Calculating Engines*, Dover, 1961
A collection of papers by Babbage and others, including Lady Lovelace's translation and notes for Menabrea's description of Babbage's Analytical Engine.

MOSELEY, M., *Irascible Genius, A Life of Charles Babbage, Inventor*, Hutchinson, 1964
A lively biography of Babbage with many personal details.

GOLDSTINE, HERMAN H., *The Computer from Pascal to von Neumann*, Princeton University Press, 1972
The author was a leading member of the ENIAC and EDVAC teams, and the central part of the book is the story of those projects from the point of view of a participant, together with the contribution to the development of computing made by von Neumann, with whom the author closely collaborated. The book also has a long historical introduction.

RANDELL, B. (Ed.), *The Origins of Digital Computers – Selected Papers*, Springer–Verlag, 1973
A carefully chosen collection of published papers of importance in the early history of digital computers, with linking survey notes by Professor Randell. A surprising feature is the large number of papers which are readable and have not dated. There is a large and detailed bibliography.

Chapter 3

Communications of the Association for Computing Machinery, 25th anniversary issue, July 1972, **Vol. 15**, No. 7
Contains many interesting articles including Ancient Babylonian Algorithms (D. E. Knuth), History of Programming (Jean E. Sammet) and one by R. E. Sprague which reveals how flow diagrams were invented (in a hotel bedroom).

GOTTFRIED, B. S., *Programming with BASIC*, McGraw-Hill Schaum Outline Series, 1975
A good introduction to programming using a simple useful language designed for interactive use.

MEEK, B. L., *Algol By Problems*, McGraw-Hill, 1971
An introduction to ALGOL 60 through a set of programming exercises, chosen so as not to depend on mathematical knowledge. Especially suitable for those with little programming experience.

McCRACKEN, Daniel D., *A Guide to Fortran IV Programming* (*2nd Ed.*), John Wiley, 1972
A popular guide to the most common scientific programming language.

Chapter 4

ACTON, F. S., *Numerical Methods that Work*, Harper & Row, 1970
Contains much practical advice and common sense suitable for anyone contemplating numerical computing.

McCALLA, T. R., *Introduction to Numerical Methods and Fortran Programming*, John Wiley, 1967
Includes the method of least squares, and has more technical details than the book by Acton.

Chapter 5

WATERS, S. J., *Introduction to Systems Design*, National Computing Centre, 1973
A good and critical introduction to business computing.

KNUTH, Donald E., *The Art of Computer Programming: Vol. 3, Sorting and Searching*, Addison-Wesley, 1973
One of a projected series of seven volumes, three of which have so far appeared, intended for specialists in computer science. This volume contains a wealth of information and good advice on sorting and searching, together with mathematical analysis of the different methods. Most programmers would benefit from this volume.

WAGNER, Harvey M., *Principles of Operations Research*, Prentice Hall, 1972
A comprehensive book with emphasis on a mathematical approach. The material has been carefully organised so that it can be followed by readers with different backgrounds.

Chapter 6

LISTER, A. M., *Fundamentals of Operating Systems*, Macmillan, 1975
A good technical introduction to operating systems with emphasis on their structure. Oriented towards scientific rather than small commercial operating systems.

BRIGNELL, J. E. and RHODES, G. M., *Laboratory On-line Computing*, Intertext Books, 1975
An up-to-date discussion of the principles and practice of the use of computers for the monitoring and control of scientific experiments.

MARTIN, J., *Design of Real-Time Computer Systems*, Prentice Hall, 1967
Concerned with real-time commercial systems with their special problems and dangers. It is suitable both for analysts interested in detailed aspects of systems implementation, and for the general reader.

Chapter 7

LEVY, D. N. L., *Computer Chess – A Case Study on the CDC 6600*, p. 151–65 in Machine Intelligence 6, Meltzer, B. and Michie, D. (Eds), Edinburgh U.P., 1971
A short historical review of computer chess together with a well annotated game.

GOOD, I. J., *A Five-year Plan for Automatic Chess*, p. 89–118 in Machine Intelligence 2, Dale, E. and Michie, D. (Eds), Edinburgh U.P., 1967
A stimulating paper with a large number of ideas.

KENDALL, D. G., F.R.S., 'The Recovery of Structure from Fragmentary Information', *Philosophical Transactions of Royal Society of London*, **279** (1291) p. 547–82, (1975). (Obtainable as a separate pamphlet.)
Besides giving a fascinating account of the reconstruction of the manorial

map of Whixley, Professor Kendall also gives a review of seriation (arranging items into a meaningful sequence solely on the basis of comparisons between them) with applications in archaeology.

WRIGLEY, E. A. (Ed.), *Identifying People in the Past*, Edward Arnold, 1973
A collection of papers which includes one by Drs Wrigley and Schofield on nominal record linkage by computer and the logic of family reconstruction, and a survey of relevant literature by Dr I. Winchester. The book contains a select bibliography.

DORAN, J. E. and HODSON, F. R., *Mathematics and Computers in Archaeology*, Edinburgh University Press, 1975
Designed for those interested in archaeology, giving several applications including data analysis, seriation, simulation and databanks. Suitable as both a reference and a course text book.

Chapter 8

WARNER, M. and STONE, M., *The Databank Society*, Allen and Unwin, 1970
A discussion of the social impact of computers with particular emphasis on the privacy issue.

AVEBURY, Lord, COVERSON, R., HUMPHRIES, J., and MEEK, B. L. (Eds.), *Computers and the Year 2000*, National Computing Centre 1972
A discussion of the potential social, economic and political effects of computers up to the beginning of the twenty-first century, with particular emphasis on how and where political and administrative decisions can be made to influence these developments.

MARTIN, J., and NORMAN, A., *The Computerised Society*, Prentice Hall, 1970; also available as a Pelican (Penguin Books)
The social implications of 'the computer revolution'.

Gramophone record

Harrison Birtwhistle: *Chronometer* (Argo ZRG790, issued 1975)
A composition resulting from the collaboration of the composer with Dr Peter Zinovieff (see Chapter 7). The original sound sources are clocks and watches; the electronic transformations were made using computer techniques developed by Dr Zinovieff. The piece is interestingly coupled with a conventionally scored orchestral work based on the theme of time, *The Triumph of Time*, which is played by the BBC Symphony Orchestra conducted by Pierre Boulez.

Index

abacus 13
access (to files): *see* random access, sequential access; *see also* hashing
access (to records) 117
accumulation of numerical errors 79–80, 90, 93–4, 96, 99, 100
accumulator 49–50, 51–2, 53, 61, 68, 70
accuracy of computation 10, 11, 12, 46–7, 51
adder circuit 51 (fig)
address (of word in computer store) 47–8; modification of 53–4, 69; alphabetic mnemonics for 61; labelling 67
address field (of instruction word) 49, 54
aesthetic judgement and computers 176
Aiken, Howard 21, 22, 31
airline reservation, computer methods for 24, 115, 140, 141, 155–8, 172
algebraic equations: Babylonian methods for solution 12; *see also* polynomial functions, roots of equations, simultaneous linear equations
ALGOL *60* (programming language) 71–3, 74, 75, 144
ALGOL *68* (programming language) 75
algorithm 59, 62, 78, 98–9; for solution of simultaneous linear equations 60, 94–8; representation by flow diagram 62; choice of 63–5, 91, 98–9; for calculation of square root 64; expression of in high-level language 73, 74, 75; and iterative methods 78; and numerical error 78–81; for roots of equations 81–6; for numerical integration 86–91; for solution of differential equations 91–4; for sorting 117–23; for searching 124–6; for linear programming 130; for playing games
. 160, 161, 163–4; for family reconstruction 170
allocation: of disk space 112–13; of resources (by operating system) 141–2, 145–6
alphanumeric display 56, 156
AMD (microcomputer component manufacturer) 28 (photo)
analogue computer, definition of 11
analogue-to-digital conversion 136–7; of sounds 178
Analytical Engine (of Babbage) 16, 20, 77; comparison with modern computer 19; description of by Menabrea 19; resemblance to ASCC 21
AND gate 50–1
APL (programming language) 75, 144
approximation 10, 11; to functions by polynomials 15; to real numbers 47, 79; method for square root 64; method of in algorithms 78–80; to roots of equations 81–6; to definite integral values 86–91
archaeology, computer applications in 175
archive file, archive information 41, 149
arithmetic and logic unit 30, 52; *see also* arithmetic unit
arithmetic unit 19, 24, 30, 52; *see also* mill
artificial intelligence 164; *see also* learning programs
arts, computer applications in 176–82
ASCC (Automatic Sequence Controlled Computer) 21, 22, 23, 27, 31

assembler 65–71; definition of 67; directive to 69
assembly language 67–70, 71; comparison of with high-level language 73
Atlas (computer) 24
auxiliary register 51–2, 61

Babbage, Charles 13–20, 22, 31, 77
Babylonian arithmetic 12
backing store 31, 36, 41, 42, 43, 55, 102, 123; use of by operating system 146; *see also* secondary store
balanced sort, 123–4
banking, computer applications in 158, 184–5
base register 151
BASIC (programming language) 75, 144, 146
batch processing 141, 142, 143, 144, 145, 148, 150, 154, 156
batch total (method of checking) 108
binary arithmetic 41–7, 51–2
binary digit (bit) 36, 41–54, 65, 67, 69, 163, 172
binary search 124–5
Birtwhistle, Harrison 179
bit: *see* binary digit
block: of information 43, 105–6, 111–15, 126; of store 48
block index 113–14
bootstrap 54
British Computer Society 186
bubble sort 120–1, 122
buffering 105–6, 145, 149
business games 167, 168
byte 43, 44, 48, 50, 52, 151

CAL (computer aided learning) 188–90
calculators: electronic, mechanical, electro-mechanical 13
call (of procedure) 72–3
card: *see* mark-sensed card, pre-scored card, punched card
card punch 25 (photo), 42 (photo)
card reader 25 (photo), 42 (photo), 55, 110, 145
cash register 13, 184
cashless society 183–5; and privacy 186–7
cassette tape: *see* magnetic tape
cathode ray tube, use of: in Williams tube memory 31–2; in alphanumeric displays and graphical displays, 56
CCITT 137
CDC (Control Data Corporation) 77; CDC 7600 computer 77
Ceefax (TV information service) 195
central processor: *see* processor
chain (of free file space) 116, 148
channel (for input-output) 148
character (of textual information) 54, 68, 72; storage of as byte 44
check digit 109
Chelsea Football Club (computerised ticket system) 191–2, 193–4 (photos)
chess (problems of playing by computer) 159, 161–2, 163, 164–5
Church, Richard 21
COBOL (programming language) 75
combinatorial explosion, problems created by 161, 163

commercial uses of computers 55, 75, 101–31; social implications of 183–5
communication with remote computers 24; see also remote job entry, terminal
compiler 73–4, 75, 142, 143–4, 146, 152, 154
computer: derivation of term 10, definition 10, 11, 30
computer aided learning: see CAL
concordances, production by computer 181
conditional jump: machine instruction 52, 53; statement in job control language 143, 144
continuous: events (monitoring of) 136; lines (on graphs) 56; and see real number
Control Data Corporation: see CDC
control instructions 52
control of machines by computers 11, 57, 135–6; see also process control
control program 136
control register 48; and use of index registers 53
control unit 30, 48, 152
convergence (of iterative processes) 78–9, 80, 82–3, 90–1, 99
CORAL 66 (programming language) 76, 136
core store: see magnetic core storage
counting: and exact arithmetic 10, 11; early methods of 12; unsuitability of floating point numbers for 47
CPU (central processing unit): see processor
creative activity (possibility of by computers) 176
credit agencies 185–6
credit cards 183–5
crime (use of computers against) 187–8
critical path analysis 127–9; example of (diagram) 128
cyclic storage 32, 33, 34, 40, 41, 43
cylinder (of magnetic disk) 111, 112, 113–15, 116
cylinder index 113–14

data 54, 62, 65, 77, 96; processing of large quantities of 55, 101–31, 154; from laboratory experiments 132–5; handling of by operating system 142, 146–7, 148–9
databanks 185–8
data base 102, 109, 141, 155–6, 197
Data General (computer manufacturer) 38, 135
data logging 133, 134
data preparation 55; problems of 106–10; see also verification
DEC (Digital Equipment Corporation) 27, 179; see also PDP-8, PDP-11
decimal to binary conversion 65–6; subroutine for 70
declaration 69
delay line 31, 32, 33
DEUCE (computer) 33, 159
device 30
dialect (of programming language) 74
Difference Engine (of Babbage) 15–16, 19; realisation of by Scheutz 16, 17–18 (photos)
differencing (of tabular values) 14
differential equations (numerical solution of) 91–4
digital computer: definition of 11; accuracy of, 11
digital signals 136–7
digital-to-analogue converter 137
diode 50
direct access 115
direct data entry 108, 110
directive (to assembler) 69
discrete: arithmetic 10; signals for graphical output 56; events (monitoring of) 136

disk: see magnetic disk
disk pack see exchangeable disk pack
dispatcher 150
double buffering: see buffering
drum: see magnetic drum
duplex file 115

Eckert, John 21, 23
EDSAC computer 23, 71
education (computer applications in) 188–90
EDVAC computer 23
efficiency: comparison of between high-level and assembly language 73; of numerical algorithms 99; of data handling 101, 104, 117; improvement in by use of buffering 105–6; in use of disks 111–12; importance of in real-time computing 132, 140; in relation to operating system 141, 143, 144–5, 146, 154; in use of overlays 152
electron beam memory 32
electronic digital computer (explanation of term) 11
electronic music (use of computer techniques in) 177–9, 180 (photo)
Electronic Music Studios (London) Ltd 179, 180
electronics: importance of for computing 11, 21, 22, 23; circuits used in computers 50, 51
Elliott: 903 computer 26 (photo); see also GEC
ENIAC (first electronic calculating machine) 21–2, 34
equations: see polynomial functions, roots of algebraic equations, simultaneous linear equations
error: in mathematical tables 14–15; in programming 62, 69, 78; in data (guarding against in programs) 62–3, (possible consequences of) 94, 96–8 (see also data preparation); detection of in programs 73–4; in iterative processes 79–81, 94; in files 104, 111; in direct input documents 110; handling of by operating system 142, 148; see also accumulation of numerical errors, ill-conditioning, instability, parity error, rounding error, semantic error, syntax error, transcription error, truncation error
error analysis 81, 86, 98, 99
ethics (code of for computer professionals) 186, 187, 198
evaluation method (in games-playing programs) 162, 164–5
exact numerical work 10, 11
exchange sort 120–1
exchangeable: storage generally 37, 39, 41; disk packs 40, 41, 42 (photo), 111, 112
external sorting 117, 123, 124
family reconstruction by computer 169–73; limitations of 175
family life (effects of computers on) 195, 197
'father and son' files 104–5, 191
ferrite core 32, 34, 35; see also magnetic core storage
field (of computer word) 49; see also address field, function field, index field
file 102, 103–4, 172; 'father and son' 104–5; on magnetic disk 112–16; sorting of 116–23; merging of files 123; searching of 123–6; handling by operating system 142, 143, 146, 147, 148, 149, 151; in databank (on individual person) 185–8
filestore 110–16; control of by operating system 141–2, 145, 147, 148
finite-state game 160
flag signal: see interrupt

floating point 77, 79, 80; representation of real numbers 46–7; functions in computers 52; *see also* real number arithmetic

flow chart, flow diagram 62; for solution of simultaneous linear equations 63, 97; for extraction of square root 64; for decimal to binary conversion 66; for obtaining roots of equations 85; for numerical integration 89

format checking 108–9

FORTRAN (programming language) 74, 75, 142, 144, 147

function field (of instruction word) 49, 54

games and computers 159–68

gate: *see* AND gate, NOT gate, OR gate

Gaussian elimination (method for solution of simultaneous linear equations) 95–7

GEC (General Electric Company) 139; GEC 2050 computer 191

generations (of computers) 27

Gill, Stanley 71

Gödel, Kurt, Gödel's Theorem 21

government: support for computer development by 16, 20, 23; use of computers by 185, 186–8

GPSS 131

graphic arts (computer applications in) 176–7

graphical display, graphical display unit 56, 166; artistic applications of 177

graphical output (from computers) 56, 135

Grogono, Peter 179

half-adder circuit 51 (fig)

hardware: definition of 58; special items of (for subroutines) 71, (for paging) 151

hashing 115–16, 125–6

Hein, Piet 162

Henze, Hans Werner 179

high-level (programming) language 71–6; for simulation 130; and job control language 142–3; and files 147

history of computing 11–29

Hollerith, Herman 20

home, effect of computers on the 190–1, 194–7

human language: translation of by computer 181; relation to programming language 181

hybrid computer 11

hysteresis 34–5

IBM (International Business Machines) 20, 23; support of for development of ASCC 23; dominant position of 23; IBM 650 computer 25 (photo), 33, 34; disk drive 40 (photo); IBM 370/168 computer 42 (photo); development of FORTRAN by 74; development of PL/I by 75

ICL (International Computers Limited): ICL 2903 computer 108; ICL 2900 series computers 154

identifier 67

IFIP (International Federation for Information Processing) 74, 75

Iliac Suite (musical composition by computer) 177

ill-conditioning 96–8

incomplete information, computer techniques for 169–75; limitations of 175

incremental plotter 56; application of in graphic arts 176

index (of file) 112, 113–14, 116, 123–5, 148, 156–7

index field (of instruction word) 53–4

index register 53–4, 68, 69, 70

index sequential file 113, 115

industrial applications of computers 136

initial instructions, initial program loader 55

initial value problem 91

input, input device 19, 24, 30, 54–55, 56–7; control of by operating system 141–2, 148, 149; and peripheral processor 148–9

input-output, input-output device 30, 43, 47; magnetic tape considered as 39; multi-access terminal as 56; and use of buffering 105–6; control of by operating system 141–2, 148–9; and peripheral processor 148–9

insertion sorting 118–19, 120

instability (of differential equations) 94

instruction, machine (of computer) 19, 44, 62, 65; stored in machine memory 19, 22 (*see also* stored program); repetition of a sequence of 21 (*see also* loop); coded representation of 22; decoding of 30; computer form of 47–54; input of 54, 65; for input-output 55–6, 65, 72, 74; mnemonic forms for 61, 67

integer arithmetic 10; in binary 44–5, 51–2

integer, conversion of from decimal to binary, 65–6

integrated circuits, 27, 28, 36

integration: *see* numerical integration

Intel (microprocessor manufacturer) 28 (photo)

interactive computing 75, 144, 154–5; use of in CAL 188–9; use of by Viewdata 197

interblock gap 111

internal sorting 117–23

International Business Machines Corporation: *see* IBM

International Computers Limited: *see* ICL

International Federation for Information Processing: *see* IFIP

International Standardisation Organisation: *see* ISO

interrupt (of computer process) 148–9, 150, 151

ISO (International Standardisation Organisation) 137

iterative process 77–8; finite type of 78, 80, 89, 95; infinite type of 78, 89; convergence of 78–9; error in 79–81; for finding roots of equations 81–6; for numerical integration 86–91; double 89; for solution of differential equations 92–4, (problems in use of) 93; for solution of simultaneous linear equations 95–8

Jacquard loom 16, 20

Japanese chess 165

job control language 142–3, 144, 148, 156

job priority, job queue, job scheduler 145–6, 150, 156

Jordan form of Gaussian elimination method 95–6

jump, jump instruction 70, 72; *see also* conditional jump, unconditional jump

K (as in 4K, 8K etc.) 48

Kendall, D. G. 173–5

key, key number (of record in file) 112–21, 123–6; key sorting 117

keyboard: as input device 55 (*see also* direct data entry); as part of multi-access terminal 56, 156; use of with graphical display 56; special form of needed for APL 75; use of for verification 107–8

key-to-disk, key-to-tape (methods of data preparation) 55, 108

Kimball tags 109–10

Kriegspiel 166–7

label (in programming language) 67, 69, 72

laboratory experiments, computer use in conjunction with 132–6; (photo of system) 135

language: *see* human language, programming language
learning, computer aided: *see* CAL
learning programs 162, 165, 176
leisure, implications of computer developments for 191–7
LEO computer 23
level: of storage 33–4; of protection 154–5
light pen 56
limit register 151
line printer 24, 42 (photo), 56, 65, 102, 145, 176; under control of operating system 146, 147, 148
linear programming 129–30
link (between subroutine and program) 70, 73
link (in family reconstruction) 170–1
link-editing 75
link method (for free file space) 116
list sorting 117
literal (assembly language mnemonic) 69
literature, computer applications in 179–81
logarithms 11, 12–13
logging in, logging out (to multi-access system) 143, 144, 146
loop (of computer instructions) 53–4, 77–8, 143
Lovelace, Augusta Ada, Countess of 19–20, 21
low-level (programming) language 71
low-level scheduler 150

machine code 67, 71, 73
macro 70, 71, 142–3
magnetic core storage 26, 34–6, 41, 43, 47
magnetic disk (storage) 36, 39–41, 42, 102, 104, 105, 108, 111–12, 156, 191; diagram of 39; photo of 40
magnetic drum (storage) 25, 32–4, 36, 37, 41, 111, 112, 156; diagram of 33
magnetic ink 56, 109
magnetic tape (storage) 36–9, 41, 42, 47, 102, 104, 105, 108, 111, 112, 123, 154, 191; diagram of 37; photo of 38; parity errors on 44; cassette form of used for data logging 134; control of by operating system 145, 148
main store 24, 43, 102, 117, 123, 124, 132, 156, 163; definition of 31; core store as 36; addressing of 48, 49; functions for transfer to and from 52; address modification in relation to 53–4; allocation of by operating system 141–2, 145, 146, 150–2; data transfer to and from under control of operating system 148–9; paging techniques for 151–2
map (of free file space) 116
map reconstruction by computer 173–5; limitations of 175
March 2140 computer 139
mark-sensed card 110
market research 127
mathematical programming 130, 140
mathematical tables: need for 12–13; Babylonian use of 12; Babbage's idea for automatic computation of 14–15; for ballistics, ENIAC developed for production of 21
Mauchly, John 21, 23
measurement: and approximate arithmetic 10; early methods of 12; of continuous signals 136
memory (of computer): *see* store
Menabrea, Luigi 19
merging (of files) 123, 124
microcomputer, microprocessor 134, 184
military uses for computers and computation 13, 21–2, 127, 167–8
mill 30; of Analytical Engine 16, 19, 77; *see also* arithmetic unit
mill time 132, 133, 141, 142, 150

minicomputer 27 (photo), 38 (photo), 44, 49, 135 (photo), 136, 141, 154, 158, 184, 191
misspelling, problems of 156, 171–3
module (of store) 48
Moseley, Mabeth 14
Motorola (microcomputer manufacturer) 28 (photo)
Muller, J. H. 15
multi-access 24, 55, 75, 108, 115, 141, 143, 144, 146, 152, 154, 156
multi-file volume 111
multipass compilation 73
multiprogramming 24, 150–1
multi-reel file 111
music, computer applications in 177–9, 180 (photo); composition of (by computer) 177, (aided by computer methods) 178–80
MUSYS (computer aided composition system) 179

negative integer, binary representation of 44
network, communications 195
Newton-Raphson method (for finding roots of equations) 81–6, 89–90
Nim (game played on computer) 159, 160–1, 162
Nova computer 38 (photo), 135 (photo)
nuclear power station, use of computers in 138 (photo), 139, 158
number-crunching 77, 132, 150, 154, 166, 193
numerical analysis, numerical analyst 78, 81, 99, 100
numerical control (of machines) 137
numerical integration 86–91

object code 73, 142
OCP (order code processor): *see* processor
off-line: preparation of data etc. 55; storage 31, 39, 41, 149
on-line 55, 184
operating system 140–55, 156
operator (of computer system), role of 53, 141, 148
operational research 126–31, 140
optical character recognition 56, 109, 110
optical mark reader 110
OR gate 50–1
Oracle (TV information system) 195
order code processor: *see* processor
output, output device 19, 24, 30, 54, 55–7, 103; control of by operating system 141, 148–9; and peripheral processor 148–9
overflow (in numerical computation) 45, 49, 51, 52, 68
overflow area (of disk storage) 114–15
overlay 151

packing density (of disk file) 113, 115
paging 24, 151–3
paper tape, paper tape equipment 16, 20, 55, 56, 65, 107, 132, 141, 145, 146; use of in ASCC 21, 22; advantages and disadvantages of 55; part of program for input from 67–9; use of for data logging 133–4; use of for numerical control of machines 137
parallel (transfer of information) 47
parish registers in family reconstruction by computer 169
parity, parity checking 44, 109
passwords, use of by operating system 143, 147
payroll (example of commercial application) 101, 103–7, 108–9, 110, 113, 126, 140, 151
PDP-8 computer 27 (photo), 179, 180 (photo)
PDP-11 computer 27 (photo)
Pegasus computer 33
peripheral: device 30, 42; processor 148–9

PERT (critical path analysis program) 129
pivoting (in simultaneous linear equations algorithm) 96
PL/I (programming language) 75
police, use of computers by 187–8, 190
polynomial functions: relation of to mathematical tables 14; calculation of by Difference Engine 15; calculation of roots of 81, 98; and Simpson's Rule 86; as evaluation functions in games-playing programs 165
POP-2 (programming language) 144
Post Office Viewdata system 193, 195–6
predictor-corrector methods (for numerical solution of differential equations) 94
pre-scored cards 110
priority (of jobs) 145, 150
privacy, computers and individual 186–8
procedure 70–1; example of in ALGOL 60 (square root) 72; see also subroutine
process (within an operating system) 149–50, 152, 154
process control 75–6, 137–40; social implications of 191
processor 28, 30, 31, 132, 145, 152; and instructions for 47–54, 148; time, use and control of by operating system 144–5, 149–50 (see also mill time); allocation of by low-level scheduler 150; multiple processors 54, 139, 150; see also peripheral processor
program 58; stages in development of 58–9, 73–4; ability to cope with any data as desirable attribute of 62–3, 99; input of 65, 66–7; use of procedures within 72–3; importance of testing of 73–4; machine independence of 74; with time constraints 134, 136; for control of experiments 136; control of by operating system 140, 142–8, 152, 154–5; different attributes of depending on whether batch or interactive 144, 154; use of overlays in 151–2; use of in transaction processing 156; for CAL 188–9
program library 99, 152; anticipated by Babbage 19
programmer 55, 58; activities of 58–9; risk of errors by when using machine code 61–2; value to of flow diagrams 62; need for care by in choice of algorithm 64–5, 117, 120; use by of high-level language 73–4, 76; problems for of numerical error 79, 81, 84, 94, 96; advice to 98–100; problems for in commercial computing 102, 103; operating systems and 145, 147–8
programming: principles worked out by Lady Lovelace 19; definition of 58; principles of 58–9; difficulty of at machine level 61–2; difficulty of eased by assemblers 67; pitfalls in 98–100; distinction between 'mathematical programming' and 130; with real-time constraints 136; of operating systems 144–5
programming language 67, 71–6, 156; for real-time computing 136; for interactive computing 144; choice of 154; human language contrasted with 181; see also assembly language, high-level language
protection (of running programs against interference) 24, 142, 148, 151, 154–5
punched cards 55, 56, 65, 107, 132, 141, 146; origination of idea of in automatic loom 16, 20; use of in Analytical Engine 16; invention of in modern form 20; use of in ASCC 21; use of in ENIAC 22; advantages and disadvantages of 55

random access: storage 32, 34, 112; to files 111, 112, 113, 115

range check 108
rational numbers (exactness of) 10
real number arithmetic 10, 45–7; in ALGOL 60 program 73; error in 79
real-time computing 76, 132–40, 141, 154
record (subdivision of file) 103–5, 108, 110–26, 148; arrangement of in blocks 111; insertion and deletion of 112, 113–15
register (of computer) 48, 54; control of by operating system 150; see also accumulator, auxiliary register, base register, control register, index register, limit register, sequence control register
remote job entry 141, 145
representation of quantities, exact or approximate 10, 11
response time (of multi-access system) 143
ring counter 21, 31
roots of equations 81–6, 98
rounding error 79–80, 90, 93, 96
RTL2 (programming language) 136
Runge-Kutta formulae (for numerical solution of differential equations) 91–4

scheduler: see job scheduler, low-level scheduler
Scheutz, George and Edvard 16–18
searching (of file) 104, 112, 116–17, 118, 123–6
secondary storage 24, 151, 163; definition of 31; see also backing store
security (of computer systems) 101, 103, 105, 115, 139, 147, 157–8, 187
segmented hardware, segmented machine 153–4
segmented program 151–2
selection sorting 119–20
semantic error 73–4, 99
semantics, problem of (application of computers in literary field) 179, 181
semiconductor store: replacement for core store 36
sequence control register 48; modification of by control instructions 52, 53
sequential: access 112, 113, 115, 116; storage 37, 39, 41, 43, 111
serial access: see sequential access
Shell's sorting method 121–2
Simpson's Rule (for numerical integration) 86–91, 92, 93
simulation 129–30, 167–8
simultaneous linear equations: solution of two (program for) 59–61, (improvement to program for) 62, (flow diagram for) 63, (ALGOL 60 program for) 71–2; solution of general case 94–8, (flow diagram for) 97
slide rule 11, 13
social implications of computing 183–98
software 129; definition of 58
software house 58, 73
sorting (of file) 104, 116–23
Soundex code (for names) 171–3
source code 73, 142
source documents (for data preparation) 107, 108, 109
Space War (computer game) 166
speech recognition, speech synthesis 56
square root, extraction of: by hand 12; unsuitability of manual method for computers 63–4; flow diagram for 64; ALGOL 60 procedure for 72; features of number-crunching exhibited by 77; as example of iterative process 78, 82
Star 100 computer 77
steel mill (use of computers in) 139–40
stock control (commercial application of computers) 102, 110, 126–7, 140, 158

208 Index

store 30, 31–41, 47; of Analytical Engine 19; use of to hold either instructions or data 23; *see also* backing store, main store, off-line storage
stored program (concept of): invented by von Neumann 22; first instances of use of in computers 23; importance of 23
subprogram: *see* subroutine
subroutine 65, 70–1, 72, 99; *see also* procedure
syntax error 73–4, 99
SYNTHI (electronic music system) 179, 180 (photo)
systems analysis, systems analyst 102, 103, 116, 188

tables: *see* mathematical tables, index
Tac-Tix (game played on computer) 162
tape: *see* magnetic tape, paper tape
teleprinter, teletype, teletypewriter 56, 135; as data logging device 133, 134
terminal (in multi-access system) 56, 115, 141, 143, 144, 146, 154; similarity of to typewriter 24; use of for data entry 108; use of in transaction processing 156–7; development of cash register into 184; use of in financial computer network 185; use of in CAL 189; ticket-issuing version of 191–2, 193 (photo)
test data, use of 59, 73–4, 100
textual information: encodable in numerical form 10; digital representation of 11; *see also* character
theory of computation 20–1
theory of games 160–1
time-sharing 24; *see also* multi-access
track: of magnetic drum 33; of magnetic disk 40–1, 111, 112, 113–15
track index 113–14
transaction processing 141, 144, 146, 152, 155–8, 191

transcription error 107–8
transistors 26, 27
translation (of human language by computer) 181
truncation error 79, 80, 90
Turing, Alan 21
twos complement (representation of negative numbers) 45, 46

unconditional jump (machine instruction) 52
UNIVAC computer 23
user (of computer system): 55, 65, 74, 115, 129, 156; *see also* operating system *passim*; *see also* programmer

VDU (visual display unit) 42, 108
verification 107–8
Viewdata 193, 195–6
virtual memory, virtual storage 151
visual display unit: *see* VDU
visual information: encoding of in numerical form 10; digital representation of 11
von Neumann, John 22, 24, 29
war games 167–8
weather forecasting, computer methods in 193–4

Whixley manor (computer reconstruction of map of) 173–5; map 174
whole number: *see* integer
Williams, F. C. 31
Williams tube 31–2
Wrigley, E. A. 170
word (of computer storage) 33, 43, 44, 45, 46, 47–8, 49, 50, 54, 65, 67
work, impact of computing upon patterns of 191

Zinovieff, Peter 179
Zuse, Konrad 21, 23